RENEWALS 458-4574

DATE DUE

Music, Ireland and the Seventeenth Century

IRISH MUSICAL STUDIES
General editors: Gerard Gillen and Harry White

Irish Musical Studies

10: MUSIC, IRELAND AND THE SEVENTEENTH CENTURY

Edited by
Barra Boydell & Kerry Houston

FOUR COURTS PRESS

Published by
FOUR COURTS PRESS LTD
7 Malpas Street, Dublin 8, Ireland
email: info@fourcourtspress.ie
http://www.fourcourtspress.ie
and in North America by
FOUR COURTS PRESS
c/o ISBS, 920 N.E. 58th Avenue, Suite 300, Portland, OR 97213.

ISBN 978–1–84682–140–0

Published in association with
The Society for Musicology in Ireland
Aontas Ceoleolaíochta na hÉireann

Typeset by Carrigboy Typesetting Services.
Printed by Athenaeum Press, Gateshead, England.

Contents

Contributors

MARTIN ADAMS is a senior lecturer in music and a fellow of Trinity College Dublin. His research interests lie in English music of the seventeenth century (mainly Purcell) and the late-nineteenth/early-twentieth centuries. His book *Henry Purcell: the origins and development of his musical style* (Cambridge, 1995) is the only extensive and detailed study of this composer's compositional practice.

BARRA BOYDELL is a professor of musicology at NUI Maynooth. He has published widely on the history of music in Ireland, his books including *Music and paintings at the National Gallery of Ireland* (1985), *Music at Christ Church before 1800: documents and selected anthems* (1998), and *A history of music at Christ Church cathedral* (2004). He is general editor with Harry White of the *Encyclopaedia of music in Ireland* (forthcoming: UCD Press).

JOHN CUNNINGHAM is a graduate of UCD and a research associate of the University of Leeds where he completed his PhD on 'Music for the Privy Chamber: studies in the consort music of William Lawes (1602–45)'. He is writing a monograph on William Lawes and, with Peter Holman, is editing a volume of Matthew Locke's consort music for *Musica Britannica*.

MÁIRE EGAN-BUFFET is an associate professor of music and recipient in 2003 of a President's Research Fellowship at UCD. Recent publications include *Manuscript sources of French music theory: Paris, Bibliothèque Nationale, Arsenal, MS 3042* (2005) and 'Le *cantus firmus* dans le *Traicté de musique* (1583) d'Adrian Le Roy d'après deux sources manuscrites: B.N. MS.FR.19100 (1634) et Bibl. de L'Arsenal MS 3042 (1670–1680)' (2007).

CHRISTOPHER D.S. FIELD is a former senior lecturer and dean of the faculty of music at the University of Edinburgh. Co-editor of the consort music of Alfonso Ferrabosco the younger for *Musica Britannica* (2003), he is currently preparing with Dr Benjamin Wardhaugh an edition of John Birchensha's writings for the series *Music theory in Britain, 1500–1700*.

RAYMOND GILLESPIE is a professor of history at NUI Maynooth, his principal research interest being in social and cultural change in early modern Ireland. His extensive publications include *Devoted people: belief and religion in early modern Ireland* (Manchester, 1997) and *Reading Ireland: print reading and social change in early modern Ireland* (Manchester, 2005). His most recent book is *Early Belfast: the origins and growth of an Ulster town to 1750* (Belfast, 2007).

7

KERRY HOUSTON is head of the Department of Academic Studies at the DIT Conservatory of Music and Drama, assistant keeper of the music at St Patrick's cathedral and director of chapel music at Trinity College Dublin. He is contributing chapters to a new history of St Patrick's cathedral (forthcoming: Four Courts Press) and is a subject editor for sacred music in the *Encyclopaedia of music in Ireland*.

DENISE NEARY obtained an MA in historical musicology with first class honours from NUI Maynooth. She then studied for a PhD at the University of Cambridge, researching English cathedral music in the eighteenth and early nineteenth centuries. She was senior lecturer in music at Canterbury Christ Church University and is currently lecturer in academic studies at the Royal Irish Academy of Music.

ANDREW ROBINSON completed his MA in renaissance music at QUB and teaches viola da gamba in the DIT Conservatory of Music and Drama and the Royal Irish Academy of Music. He has published on William and Henry Lawes, edited consort music by William Cranford from the part-books in Marsh's library and transcribed traditional music for Allen Feldman and Eamon O'Doherty, *The northern fiddler* (Belfast, 1979).

ADRIAN SCAHILL is a lecturer in ethnomusicology (Irish traditional music) at NUI Maynooth, a performer specializing in Irish traditional music, and subject editor for Irish traditional music in the *Encyclopaedia of music in Ireland*. He completed his PhD entitled 'The knotted chord: harmonic accompaniment in printed and recorded sources of Irish traditional music' at UCD in 2005.

Acknowledgments

The preparation of this volume would not have been possible without the encouragement and support of many people and institutions. Above all the editors would like to record their debt of thanks to the individual contributors both for their forbearance in response to editorial queries and suggestions, and for their patience throughout the sometimes protracted processes of editing and publishing this volume. The general editors of *Irish Musical Studies,* Harry White and Gerard Gillen, welcomed the proposal to publish this volume and the editors gratefully acknowledge their encouragement and support. The editors would also like to thank Michael Adams, Martin Fanning and the staff at Four Courts Press, Darren Magee for typesetting musical examples, Philip Graydon for compiling the index and both the music department at the National University of Ireland Maynooth and the DIT Conservatory of Music and Drama for facilitating the editors in the preparation of this volume.

Particular thanks are due to the following institutions and organisations for permission to reproduce copyright material: the Musikhistorisk Museum, Copenhagen (photograph by Ole Woldbye) for the image in chapter 4; the Keeper of Armagh Public Library for the image in chapter 6; the Board of Trinity College Dublin for the images in chapter 9; the Bodleian Library, University of Oxford and ProQuest/Early English Books Online for the image in chapter 11 (Bodleian Library, G.Pamph 2226 (3), p.1); and Durham Cathedral for the cover illustration. Chapter 5 first appeared as an article in the *Records of Early English Drama Newsletter* and is reprinted here in revised form by kind permission of the editors.

Funding provided by the Dublin Institute of Technology under the Faculty of Applied Arts Research Support Scheme and by the National University of Ireland Publications Scheme is most gratefully acknowledged by the editors, as is the support of the Society for Musicology in Ireland.

EDITORIAL PROCEDURES

The spelling, capitalization and punctuation of original quotations including those from contemporary printed sources have been silently modernized and abbreviations expanded. Where relevant, dates have been adjusted to conform to modern practice (the new year falling on 1 January not 25 March).

Abbreviations

CSPD	*Calendar of state papers (domestic)* (London, 1856–1972)
DHR	*Dublin Historical Record*
EF	*Ethnomusicology Forum*
EM	*Early Music*
EMIR	*Encyclopaedia of Music in Ireland*
GSJ	*Galpin Society Journal*
IMS 2	*Irish Musical Studies, 2: Music and the church,* ed. Gerard Gillen & Harry White (Dublin, 1993)
IMS 3	*Irish Musical Studies, 3: Music and Irish cultural history,* ed. Gerard Gillen & Harry White (Dublin, 1995)
IMS 4	*Irish Musical Studies, 4: The Maynooth international musicological conference 1995 selected proceedings: part I,* ed. Patrick Devine & Harry White (Dublin, 1996)
IMS 5	*Irish Musical Studies, 5: The Maynooth international musicological conference 1995 selected proceedings part II,* ed. Patrick Devine & Harry White (Dublin, 1996)
IMS 6	*Irish Musical Studies, 6: A historical anthology of Irish church music,* ed. Gerard Gillen & Andrew Johnstone (Dublin, 2001)
JAF	*Journal of American Folklore*
JRMA	*Journal of the Royal Musical Association*
ML	*Music & Letters*
MS(S)	Manuscript(s)
MT	*Musical Times*
NG	*The New Grove dictionary of music and musicians,* ed. Stanley Sadie, 20 vols (London, 1980)
NG II	*The New Grove dictionary of music and musicians.* Second edition, ed. Stanley Sadie & John Tyrell, 29 vols (London, 2001)
NHI	*A new history of Ireland,* ed. T.W. Moody et. al, 9 vols (Oxford, 1976–2005)
NLI	National Library of Ireland
NMI	National Museum of Ireland
NUI	National University of Ireland
ODNB	*Oxford Dictionary of National Biography*, ed. H.C.G. Matthew & Brian Harrison, 60 vols (Oxford, 2004)
OED	*Oxford English Dictionary*
QUB	Queen's University Belfast
RECM	Andrew Ashbee (ed.), *Records of English court music*, 9 vols (Snodland, 1986–91 [vols. 1–4]; Aldershot, 1991–6 [vols. 5–9])
REED	*Records of Early English Drama*
RISM	Répertoire International des Sources Musicales
RMA	Royal Musical Association
RS	Royal Society, London
SIMG	*Sammelbände der Internationalen Musik-Gesellschaft*
TCD	Trinity College, Dublin

UCC	University College Cork (NUI Cork)
UCD	University College Dublin (NUI Dublin)
UL	University of Limerick

LIBRARY SIGLA

B-Br	Brussels, Bibliothèque Royale Albert Ier
D-W	Wolfenbüttel, Herzog-August-Bibliothek
GB-Cmc	Cambridge, Magdalene College, Pepys Library
GB-Cu	Cambridge, University Library
GB-DRc	Durham Cathedral Library
GB-EL	Ely, Cathedral Library (in GB-Cu)
GB-Lbl	London, British Library
GB-Lpro	London, Public Record Office
GB-Ob	Oxford, Bodleian Library
GB-Och	Oxford, Christ Church Library
GB-Y	York Minster Library
IRL-Da	Dublin, Royal Irish Academy Library
IRL-Dcc	Christ Church Cathedral Library
IRL-Dm	Dublin, Archbishop Marsh's Library
IRL-Dpc	Dublin, St Patrick's Cathedral Library
IRL-Drcb	Dublin, Representative Church Body Library
IRL-Dtc	Dublin, Trinity College Library
IRL-Dtm	Dublin, Irish Traditional Music Archive
IRL-Mrjp	NUI Maynooth, Russell and John Paul II Libraries
IRL(N)-Ar	Armagh, Public Library (Robinson Library)
IRL(N)-Bpro	Belfast, Public Record Office of Northern Ireland
J-Tn	Tokyo, Nanki Ongaku Bunko

BIBLIOGRAPHICAL SOURCES CITED IN TWO OR MORE CHAPTERS

Ashbee & Holman, *Jenkins*	Andrew Ashbee & Peter Holman (eds), *John Jenkins and his time: studies in English consort music* (Oxford, 1996)
Bacon, *Sylva sylvarum*	Francis Bacon, *Sylva sylvarum* (London, 1627)
Billinge & Shaljean, 'Dalway'	Michael Billinge & Bonnie Shaljean, 'The Dalway or Fitzgerald harp (1621)', *EM*, 25 (1987), 175–87
Boydell, 'Dublin city'	Barra Boydell, 'Dublin city musicians in the late middle ages and Renaissance to 1660', *DHR* 34 (1981), 42–53
Boydell, 'Earl of Cork'	Barra Boydell, 'The earl of Cork's musicians: a study in the patronage of music in early seventeenth-century Anglo-Irish society', *REED Newsletter*, 18:2 (1993), 1–15
Boydell, 'Iconography'	Barra Boydell, 'The iconography of the Irish harp as a national symbol' in *IMS* 5, pp 131–45

Boydell, 'Music before 1700'   Brian Boydell, 'Music before 1700', in *NHI*, 4 (Oxford, 1986), 542–67

Boydell, *History of music*   Barra Boydell, *A history of music at Christ Church cathedral, Dublin* (Woodbridge, 2004)

Boydell, *Music at Christ Church*   Barra Boydell, *Music at Christ Church before 1800: documents and selected anthems* (Dublin, 1999)

Boydell, *Musical calendar*   Brian Boydell, *A Dublin musical calendar, 1700–1765* (Blackrock, 1988)

Campbell, 'An account'   J.L. Campbell, 'An account of some Irish harpers as given by Echlin O'Kean, harper, anno 1779', *Éigse*, 6:2 (1950), 146–8

Carolan, 'O'Sullivan Beare'   Nicholas Carolan, 'Philip O'Sullivan Beare on Irish music', *Irish Folk Music Studies: Éigse Cheol Tíre*, 5–6 (1986–2001), 47–60

Charteris, *Catalogue*   Richard Charteris, *A catalogue of printed books on music, printed music, and music manuscripts in Archbishop Marsh's library, Dublin* (Clanbrickan, 1982)

Diary of John Evelyn   *The diary of John Evelyn*, ed. E.S. de Beer, 6 vols (Oxford, 1955)

Diary of Samuel Pepys   *The diary of Samuel Pepys*, ed. Robert Latham & William Matthews, 11 vols (London, 1970–83)

Donnelly, 'A Cork musician'   Séan Donnelly, 'A Cork musician at the early Stuart court: Daniel Duff O'Cahill (*c*.1580–*c*.1660), "The Queen's harper"', *Journal of the Cork Historical and Archaeological Society*, 110 (2000), 1–26

Donnelly, 'An Irish harper and composer'   Seán Donnelly, 'An Irish harper and composer, Cormac Mac Dermott (?–1618)', *Ceol*, 8 (Dec 1986), 40–50

Donnelly, 'An Irish harper in the royal musick'   Seán Donnelly, 'An Irish harper in the royal musick', *Ceol*, 6:2 (April 1984), 34–6

Donnelly, 'Warpipes', i–iv   Seán Donnelly, 'The warpipes in Ireland (i)', *Ceol*, 5:1 (July 1981), 19–24; (ii), 5:2 (March 1982), 55–9; (iii), 6:1 (April 1983), 19–23; (iv), 6:2 (April 1984), 54–7

Donnelly, *Early history*   Seán Donnelly, *The early history of piping in Ireland* (Dublin, 2001)

Donnelly, 'The Irish harp'   Seán Donnelly, 'The Irish harp in England, 1590–1690', *Ceol*, 7:1–2 (Dec 1984), 54–62

Fleischmann, *Sources*   Aloys Fleischmann (ed.), *Sources of Irish traditional music, c.1600–1855*, 2 vols (New York, 1998)

Fletcher, *Drama, performance*   Alan J. Fletcher, *Drama, performance and polity in pre-Cromwellian Ireland* (Cork, 2000)

Fletcher, *Sources*   Alan J. Fletcher, *Drama and the performing arts in pre-Cromwellian Ireland: sources and documents from the earliest times until c.1642* (Woodbridge, 2001)

Flood, *History*   W.H. Grattan Flood, *A history of Irish music* (3rd ed. Dublin, 1913; repr. Shannon, 1970)

Grindle, *Cathedral music*   H.W. Grindle, *Irish cathedral music* (Belfast, 1989)

Grosart, *Lismore* (1)   *The Lismore papers (series 1): autobiographical notes, remembrances and diaries of Sir Richard Boyle, first*

	and 'great' earl of Cork, ed. Alexander B. Grosart, 5 vols (London: 1886)
Grosart, *Lismore* (2)	*The Lismore papers (series 2): selections from the private and public (or state) correspondence of Sir Richard Boyle, first and 'great' earl of Cork*, ed. Alexander B. Grosart, 5 vols (London: 1887–8)
Herissone, *Music theory*	Rebecca Herissone, *Music theory in seventeenth-century England*, (Oxford, 2000)
Holman, 'Harp'	Peter Holman, 'The harp in Stuart England', *EM*, 15 (1987), 188–203
Holman, *Four and twenty fiddlers*	Peter Holman, *Four and twenty fiddlers: the violin at the English court, 1540–1690* (Oxford, 1993)
Houston, 'Music manuscripts'	Kerry Houston, 'The eighteenth-century music manuscripts at Saint Patrick's cathedral, Dublin: sources, lineage, and relationship to other collections', 3 vols, (PhD, TCD, 2003)
Hulse, 'Musical patronage'	Lynn Hulse, 'The musical patronage of Robert Cecil, first earl of Salisbury (1563–1612)', *JRMA*, 116 (1991), 24–40
MacLysaght, *Irish life*	Edward MacLysaght, *Irish life in the seventeenth century* (Shannon, 1969)
Ó Buachalla, 'Lillibulero'	Breandán Ó Buachalla, 'Lillibulero: the new Irish song', *Familia*, 2:7 (1991), 47–59
O'Sullivan, *Carolan*	Donal O'Sullivan, *Carolan: the life, times and music of an Irish harper* (2 vols, London, 1958; 2nd rev. ed. Cork, 2001)
Rainbow, 'Bathe'	Bernarr Rainbow, 'Bathe and his Introductions to Musicke', *MT*, 123 (1982), 243–7
Rimmer, *Irish harp*	Joan Rimmer, *The Irish harp* (3rd ed. Cork, 1984)
Shaw, *Succession of organists*	Watkins Shaw, *The succession of organists of the Chapel Royal and the cathedrals of England and Wales from c.1538: also of the organists of the collegiate churches of Westminster and Windsor, certain academic choral foundations, and the cathedrals of Armagh and Dublin* (Oxford, 1991)
Simpson, *Compendium*	Christopher Simpson, *A compendium of practical musick* (London, 1667)
Spink, *Restoration*	Ian Spink, *Restoration cathedral music, 1660–1714* (Oxford, 1995)
Ua Suilleabháin & Donnelly, 'Music has ended'	Seán Ua Suilleabháin & Seán Donnelly, '"Music has ended": the death of a harper', *Celtica*, 22 (1991), 165–75
Wetenhall, *Of gifts and offices*	Edward Wetenhall, *Of gifts and offices in the publick worship of God* (Dublin, 1678)

Introduction: the seventeenth century and the history of music in Ireland

BARRA BOYDELL & KERRY HOUSTON

The seventeenth century was a pivotal era in Irish cultural and political history. The foundations of the modern era were being laid in Europe as the scientific revolution began to challenge a view of the world based on the unquestioned acceptance of religion and of Classical authorities. But it was also a century marked by conflict as the European political landscape was redefined by the political and religious fault lines generated by exploration, expansion and trade, and by the after-effects of the Reformation. Within Ireland religion essentially defined and was identified with changes in political control and land ownership as Anglo-Protestant rule was extended throughout the country. Religion and language became signifiers of political and ethnic identity, the Catholicism of Gaelic Ireland distinguishing the Irish-speaking population from the English-speaking, Protestant minority who held political power and, particularly following the Cromwellian settlements in the middle of the century, owned most of the land. The result was a more profound hiatus than was the case in many European countries in which religious change was not allied with changes in both the language and cultural heritage of the dominant, land-owning class.

Music in seventeenth-century Ireland both echoed and transcended these divisions. The displacement of the native Irish aristocracy by a new English ruling class brought about the decline of Gaelic civilization and with it of the Irish harping tradition; but the seventeenth century is one of the earliest periods to which certain songs and melodies still in the aural tradition can be traced with any degree of confidence. It is also a century in which the patronage and practice of music among the ruling minority laid the foundations for the notable growth in the eighteenth century of musical practices based on European models, most particularly in Dublin. To identify any one of these aspects too narrowly with one or other of the cultural traditions within the country, Gaelic or Anglo-Irish, would be to ignore the extent to which, for all that they did often operate in contexts far removed from each other, they also interacted and enjoyed common patronage. The Irish harp, that most iconic emblem of the country's native musical heritage, was admired in the early seventeenth century not only within Ireland by the Anglo-Irish elite but also at the English court itself. By the close of the century the most famous of the harper-composers, Turlough Carolan, would already be establishing a reputation which would lead him to engage directly with European musical traditions and to be patronized by members of both the surviving Gaelic and the Anglo-Irish gentry.

15

Ireland's turbulent history during the seventeenth century, most particularly following the rebellion of 1641 and during the Cromwellian wars of the 1650s, has contributed to a singular paucity of sources available to the historian of music in Ireland. Although surviving documentary records are now acknowledged as being more extensive than had formerly been recognized, the destruction of the Public Record Office in the Custom House in 1922 notwithstanding, the position regarding notated music remains exceptionally poor. It is a sobering thought that not one music manuscript or other source of notated music of Irish provenance is known to survive from the nearly two-hundred-year period between the latest notated Sarum sources dating from the mid- to late fifteenth century (*IRL-Dtc*, MSS 78, 79) and a manuscript now in Durham, *GB-DRc*, MS B1 (the Hosier MS) copied at the Dublin cathedrals between 1660 and 1678.[1] Isolated later seventeenth-century musical sources with Irish connections are however beginning to be identified.[2]

Exceptional though the Hosier MS is as a manuscript originating from and including pieces of music composed in seventeenth-century Ireland, other examples or adaptations of Irish music exist in sources which are either later or originate outside Ireland. An anthem by Thomas Bateson almost certainly composed in Dublin in 1612 survives in two sources, but these were both copied in England in the 1620s.[3] Likewise, some anthems by Randall Jewett and Benjamin Rogers, both of whom served in the Dublin cathedrals in the 1630s and 1640s, may have been composed during their Dublin years although they only survive in later sources (including the Hosier MS).[4] A number of late sixteenth- or seventeenth-century manuscripts are held in Irish collections, notably the Ballet and Dallis lute books and the so-called Dublin Virginal MS in Trinity College library as well as viol consort, lyra viol and lute manuscripts in Marsh's Library, Dublin, but these did not originate in Ireland although they came here in the seventeenth century.[5] On the other hand, the consort music attributed to

1 On the TCD MSS see Patrick V. Brannon, 'The search for the Celtic rite', *IMS* 2, pp 13–40, and 'Medieval Ireland: music in cathedral, church and cloister', *EM*, 28 (2000), 193–202 at 195f. Fragments of untexted mensural notation survive, inscribed on slates probably in the later fifteenth century: see Frank Ll. Harrison, 'Polyphony in medieval Ireland' in M. Ruhnke (ed.), *Festschrift Bruno Stäblein zum siebzigsten Geburtstag* (Kassel, 1967), pp 74–8. On the Hosier MS see Boydell, *History of music*, pp 88–96.   2 Peter Holman first drew attention to the presence of Dublin musicians among the composers represented in *GB-Och*, MS Mus. 1183 (Holman, *Four and twenty fiddlers*, p. 321). Silas Wollston has recently identified one set of instrumental parts within this collection (fos. 34r–69v) and comprising fifty-five pieces – mostly short dance movements – as being entirely the work of musicians who were members of the Dublin city music (or 'waits') in 1669 or were otherwise connected with Dublin. Although the copyist of the manuscript was an Oxford man, this collection of music by Dublin musicians may be linked to the visit to Oxford of the Smock Alley theatre players in 1677. The theatre players would most probably have been accompanied by their violin band which may have included the musicians identified as members of the city music. I am grateful to Silas Wollston for sharing this information, which forms part of his doctoral research in progress (Open University).   3 Thomas Bateson, *Holy, Lord God almighty*. See Grindle, *Cathedral music*, p. 164; Boydell, *History of music*, p. 59.   4 *IMS* 6, pp 71–2; Boydell, *History of music*, pp 59–60, 89. See further ch. 9, below.   5 For MSS in Marsh's library (*IRL-Dm*) see Charteris, *Catalogue*. See also ch. 8, below.

Cormac MacDermott (d. 1618), who served as a harper in England to Robert Cecil and at the court King James I, and the harp consorts of William Lawes, very possibly written for a chromatic Irish harp, while again originating in England, are relevant to early seventeenth-century Irish music because of their associations with the use of the Irish harp abroad.[6] Likewise, a number of tunes with Irish titles form the basis for keyboard or lute variations in English manuscripts of the late sixteenth or early seventeenth century, as for example *The Hay* and *The Irish March* present in the Dallis Lute Book (*c.*1583) and My Lady Nevells Book (1591), or the anonymous *Irish Dump* and *Irish Ho-Hoane* and William Byrd's variations on *Callino casturame* in the Fitzwilliam Virginals Book (1609–19). Irish tunes appear in other seventeenth-century English collections (including twelve in the first 1651 edition of Playford's *The Dancing Master*), but otherwise most of the Irish harp and traditional repertoire of the period only survives in considerably later sources.[7]

A number of the chapters in this volume arise out of papers first presented at a conference on music in seventeenth-century Ireland held at NUI Maynooth in April 2005, a setting with particularly appropriate historical resonances. Adjacent to the main gates of the south campus of NUI Maynooth stand the ruins of Maynooth castle, stronghold of the Fitzgeralds, earls of Kildare, who had come to Ireland with the Anglo-Norman conquest in the twelfth century and established themselves by the later mediaeval period as one of the most powerful families in Ireland. Maynooth castle fell into ruin after the Cromwellian wars, but during the first half of the seventeenth century it witnessed the musical and cultural life of Ireland at a period which saw the rise to power of the country's new, Anglo-Protestant rulers following the Tudor conquest. The castle underwent restoration in the 1630s when George Fitzgerald, sixteenth earl of Kildare, married the eldest daughter of Richard Boyle, first earl of Cork (and subject of chapter 5 in this volume). This juxtaposition of new and old, of the established Gaelic and 'Old English' families such as the Fitzgeralds with the new English settlers of whom the earl of Cork was among the most powerful, epitomizes the complex social and cultural environment which is reflected in music in Ireland at this time.

A number of references to the musical patronage of the Fitzgeralds of Maynooth castle during the sixteenth and early seventeenth centuries emphasize the interaction of music associated with both the Irish and the Anglo-European traditions as well as hinting at the more often undocumented musical environment of leading Irish aristocratic households. When Maynooth castle was seized by the English in 1535 following the rebellion against English rule by 'Silken' Thomas, tenth earl of Kildare, most of its inhabitants were slaughtered, but it is reported that two singing men from the castle's chapel had their lives spared because they sang so beautifully a motet *Dulcis amica*.[8] A number of harpers are

---

6 See ch. 4, below.   **7** For tunes considered to be Irish and occurring in late sixteenth- and seventeenth-century British manuscript and printed sources see Fleischmann, *Sources*, i, passim.   **8** Fletcher, *Drama, performance*, p. 213; Fletcher suggests that this could possibly be the setting by the Franco-Netherlandish

recorded in the service of the earls of Kildare during the sixteenth century,[9] and the 'Fitzgerald-Kildare' harp, one of the finest extant seventeenth-century harps and thought to date from the later seventeenth century, carries the arms and crest of the Fitzgerald family.[10] Alongside the Irish harp, an undated letter written by Elizabeth Fitzgerald, sister of the same sixteenth earl of Kildare who married Joan Boyle in 1630, makes reference to an unnamed viol maker living and working if not in the vicinity of Maynooth then perhaps more likely in Dublin. The Fitzgeralds of Maynooth are also associated with two significant writers on music: William Bathe, author of the earliest printed treatise on music in the English language and who constructed a 'harp of a new device' which he presented to Queen Elizabeth I – possibly a chromatic Irish harp along the lines of the Dalway harp dating from 1621[11] – was a grand-nephew of the ninth earl of Kildare;[12] and John Birchensha, theorist, composer, music teacher (and the subject of a chapter in this volume), was associated with the earl of Kildare before he fled to England following the outbreak of rebellion in 1641.

The Kildare Fitzgeralds' patronage of both native Irish and European art-music traditions is reflected throughout early modern Ireland and emphasizes how misleading it would be to portray early seventeenth-century Ireland as a country exclusively divided along cultural lines. For example, an inventory from 1645 of Dunluce castle, Co. Antrim, seat of the MacDonnells, earls of Antrim, lists only two musical instruments, but significantly these are again an Irish harp and a bass viol, instruments which symbolize the two distinct but complementary cultures within which this old-Irish family lived.[13] Randall MacDonnell, born in 1609 and created second earl of Antrim after his father's death in 1636, had been brought up at Dunluce in a wholly unanglicized environment with Irish as his first language. He later spent nine years in London at the court of Charles I where his residence, York House, was regarded as one of the finest palaces, and he also maintained a country house and estate in Hampshire.[14] Equally, the first earl of Cork not only maintained what was clearly one of the most extensive musical establishments in early seventeenth-century Ireland including lutes, viols and organ, but he was also a patron of harpers, owned an Irish harp himself and on at least one occasion gave a harp as a gift, to the lord keeper of England.[15] Alan Fletcher has recorded a number of further inventories, payments and other contexts from the later sixteenth and early seventeenth centuries in which the harp is found alongside instruments of the European art music tradition such as

composer Johannis Prioris. **9** Fletcher, *Sources*, pp 205, 603. **10** NMI (it bears the inscription RFG fecit Anno 1*75); further on this instrument see Rimmer, *Irish harp*, pp 52–3, 76. **11** On the possible chromatic tuning of the Dalway harp see Billinge & Shaljean, 'Dalway'. **12** Rainbow, 'Bathe', 247; cf. Flood, *History*, p. 162. **13** Hector MacDonnell, 'A seventeenth-century inventory from Dunluce castle, Co. Antrim', *Journal of the Royal Society of Antiquaries of Ireland*, 122 (1992), 109–27. The paucity of primary sources for the understanding of music is paralleled in other fields. MacDonnell comments that 'In the whole of Ireland there is only one piece of furniture, a table datable to about 1600, now surviving to represent the entire century before the Restoration' (ibid., 109), the item in question belonging to the O'Briens of Clare and now in Dromoland Castle. **14** Ibid., 117. **15** See ch. 5, below; see also Fletcher, *Drama, performance*, pp 228–34.

the virginals, lute or bass viol.[16] Indeed, the Irish harp and bass viol were cited by Francis Bacon (1561–1626) as examples of instruments which sound particularly well together:

> Some consorts of instruments are sweeter than others (a thing not sufficiently yet observed) as the Irish harp and bass viol agree well, the recorder and stringed music agree well, organs and the voice agree well, etc. But the virginals and the lute, or the Welsh harp and the Irish harp, or the voice and pipes alone, agree not so well.[17]

The historiography of music in seventeenth-century Ireland has been influenced both by the relative absence of primary musical sources already referred to and by the negative image with which the period has been imbued by nationalist historiography. In his often detailed but frustratingly unreliable *History of Irish music* first published in 1904 Grattan Flood devoted three chapters to the seventeenth century, two on 'Irish music' and one on 'Anglo-Irish music'. Flood's labels enshrined a clear division between the two traditions and have cast a long shadow over Irish music history, and indeed Irish musicology. This has contributed to the often deep but surely unnecessary divide between the study of Ireland's indigenous musical traditions and that of its art music. Flood's implication that the term 'Irish music' excluded notated music in the European art music tradition composed and performed by Irish composers and musicians reflected the separatist mentality of late nineteenth- and early twentieth-century nationalism. In his *History*, as in several shorter articles relating directly or indirectly to music in seventeenth-century Ireland,[18] Flood espoused a nominally positivist, factual approach, citing information he had derived from his documentary research but often with little or no commentary, and that too often of a speculative and unsubstantiated nature sometimes unduly coloured by his partisan views. His two chapters on 'Irish music in the seventeenth century' place particular emphasis on the names and dates of Irish harpers and other 'minstrels' often accompanied by his emotive commentaries, and on his unquestioning attribution of seventeenth-century origins to certain extant Irish traditional tunes often based solely on their titles (an issue addressed in chapter 3, below). Flood opened the first of his chapters with the comment 'Politically, no more gloomy outlook could be imagined of any country than the state of Ireland during the last years of Queen Elizabeth's rule',[19] an attitude which permeates the ensuing pages. The harp, and indeed Irish music in general, is projected both as victim and as a civilizing influence on even the hardest of hearts during 'that dreadful period' of Cromwellian rule in the 1650s:

---

16 Fletcher, *Sources,* pp 278, 360, 419, 422–3, 427.   **17** Bacon, *Sylva sylvarum,* p. 72. On the combination of the wire-strung Irish harp and the bass viol see further ch. 4, below.   **18** E.g. W.H. Grattan Flood, 'Dublin "City music" from 1456 to 1786', *SIMG,* 11 (1909–10), 33–41; 'Dublin music printing from 1685 to 1750', *Bibliographical Society of Ireland Publications,* 2:1 (1921), 7–12.   **19** Flood, *History,* p. 181.

Yet in spite of the Cromwellian atrocities, the harp still was heard in tuneful lays, accompanying the dear old tongue of the Gael, in strains that appealed even to the Puritans themselves. Who will deny that the harp was a potent factor in softening the hearts of the grim Ironsides?[20]

In contrast, Flood's chapter on 'Anglo-Irish music in the seventeenth century' eschews such emotive language in its uncritical presentation of a positivist array of music-historical 'facts' relating to music within the Anglo-Irish, or English-speaking, population centred primarily in Dublin. But, as ever with Flood, the accuracy of the information he presents, wide-ranging and detailed though it may appear to be, is always open to question; likewise, he is ever alert to the opportunity to claim Irish credit sometimes in the most unexpected quarters, as when he writes that:

Although it is generally known that King Charles II, after the Restoration, introduced a band of twenty-four instrumentalists into the Chapel Royal ... few are aware that the frivolous monarch was indebted to an Irishman, Rev. Peter Talbot, S.J., for many of his musical ideas. When residing at Madrid in 1659, Father Peter Talbot was commissioned by King Charles to procure for him some Spanish music, which commission was duly fulfilled in January, 1660. The Irish priest also supplied the English monarch with French and Portuguese airs.[21]

Quite apart from representing an approach to historiography that is now hopelessly dated, Flood repeatedly frustrates by his lack of all but the most occasional source references; he renders himself untrustworthy by the fact that, where his sources can be checked, he sometimes misquotes or misinterprets them; and he is too ready to jump to conclusions which are presented as if they were fact. It is unfortunate that so many of Flood's original sources were lost in the Public Record Office fire in 1922, so that his unverifiable information is often all that survives.

A number of isolated studies in the mid-twentieth century touched on music in the seventeenth century, although little attention was focussed directly on that period. Donal O'Sullivan's study of the life and music of Carolan, published in two volumes in 1958, incidentally drew attention to the seventeenth-century harping tradition into which Carolan was born; likewise, O'Sullivan's 1960 collection *Songs of the Irish* made some reference to the period, although that was not its particular focus.[22] Joan Rimmer's book on the Irish harp, first published in 1969, discussed the surviving Irish harps of the late sixteenth and seventeenth centuries – the Ballinderry and the Dalway fragments, and the

20 Ibid., p. 200.   **21** Ibid., pp 215–16. In this instance Flood cites, without page number, as a source for this claim: Cardinal [Patrick Francis] Moran, *Spicilegium Ossoriense* [Dublin, 1874].   **22** O'Sullivan, *Carolan*; O'Sullivan, *Songs of the Irish* (Dublin, 1960).   **23** Rimmer, *Irish harp,* esp. pp 39–55.

Otway, O ffogarty and Fitzgerald-Kildare harps – not only within the Irish context but, perhaps most significantly, also within the wider European context.[23] However, aside from the work in particular of Frank Harrison and Aloys Fleischmann into the mediaeval period, it was the reputation of eighteenth-century Dublin as a 'golden age' in Irish music history, not to mention the increased survival of written records from that century, which attracted scholarly interest as musicology began to establish itself within Irish academic circles in the later twentieth century.[24] Suffering from its reputation as a 'troubled' century in Irish history and overcast by the perception that most of the documentary record had been lost, the seventeenth century has suffered from an unspoken reputation of itself being a 'lost' century in Ireland's musical history. The lack at that time of significant new research is reflected in the fact that Brian Boydell's contribution 'Music before 1700' published in 1986 in the *New History of Ireland* – the greater part of which concentrates on the seventeenth century – was, aside from the authors cited above, still obliged eighty years later to draw significantly on Flood's *History*, acutely conscious though the author was of its shortcomings.[25] Brian Boydell's particular contribution to the historiography of music in seventeenth-century Ireland was his recognition of the need to redraw the parameters for an understanding of the period by rejecting the partisan approaches which had applied to the study of the music of the Gaelic and of the European art music traditions. Stating that 'the disruption of Gaelic society during the seventeenth century is reflected in the musical activity of the period' and that 'these changes were associated with periods of violence, [a fact which] was not conducive to the cultivation of music', he noted that 'the music and many other cultural aspects of the older Irish culture had crystallized into what is usually termed the Gaelic tradition'. In marked contrast to prevailing attitudes to Irish musical traditions he roundly stated that this 'itself was undoubtedly the result of an amalgam of many streams of native and European fashions' while acknowledging that 'a sharp division was created between Gaelic music and what is usually referred to as Anglo-Irish music' since 'each tradition acted as a powerful symbol of rival political and cultural ideologies'.[26] He urged that 'an account of music and society in Ireland must face the problem of presenting a balanced treatment of the two separate streams of activity so sharply contrasted in social context and in methods of performance and dissemination', summing up his inclusive view when he wrote that:

the seventeenth century was a period in which there was frequent mixing of cultures brought about by the movement of armies, the flight of refugees, and the planting of settlers. Not only did Irish music spread its stylistic influence abroad, but the original style of the old Gaelic tradition must have been considerably modified by contact with outside influences.[27]

24 See for example Ita Hogan, *Anglo-Irish music 1780–1830* (Cork, 1966); Boydell, *Musical calendar*; T.J. Walsh, *Opera in Dublin, 1700–1798* (Dublin, 1973). **25** Boydell, 'Music before 1700'. **26** Ibid., p. 546. **27** Ibid., p. 565.

The essays in this present volume echo this call for a 'balanced treatment of the two separate streams of activity' and, indeed, argue for a greater understanding of the links, as much as the divisions, between those two traditions.

Although musicological activity in Ireland over the past two decades has largely been directed elsewhere, research into music in or associated with seventeenth-century Ireland has formed a small if important part of this activity. Since the 1980s Seán Donnelly has researched the use of the Irish harp both within Gaelic Ireland and among the new Anglo-Irish and English aristocratic circles, and of the bagpipes in early modern Ireland.[28] Barra Boydell's work on the Dublin city musicians, although not restricted to the seventeenth century, and on the musical patronage of Richard Boyle, first earl of Cork,[29] was subsequently to be significantly enhanced by Alan Fletcher's two important books on the performing arts (including music) in pre-Cromwellian Ireland, his narrative volume *Drama, performance and polity in pre-Cromwellian Ireland* (2000) and the sources volume *Drama and the performing arts in pre-Cromwellian Ireland* (2001).[30] These two publications together comprise one of the most significant contributions to medieval and early modern Irish musical history in recent years. Indeed, the wealth of material they contain relating to the practice of music in Ireland up to the mid-seventeenth century constitutes a primary resource, in particular in the 'source' volume of 2001, which has yet to be fully explored by Irish musicology.

Harry Grindle's *Irish cathedral music* (1989) drew the attention of modern scholarship to the sources available for the study of seventeenth-century cathedral music, as indeed for other periods too. The full extent of the documentary material relevant to music at Christ Church cathedral Dublin in the seventeenth century, first outlined in detail in Barra Boydell's edition (1999) of documents and anthems from before 1800,[31] together with the confirmation of the Hosier MS as having originated in Dublin in the 1660s and 1670s and thus of its importance to the history of music in Ireland, resulted in the sixty or so pages (almost one third of the narrative) devoted specifically to the seventeenth-century in his subsequent history of music at the cathedral (2004).[32] In the meantime Gillen and Johnstone had given further emphasis to the repertoire of seventeenth-century cathedral music associated with Ireland by including two early verse anthems by Randall Jewett in their *Historical anthology of Irish church music* (2001).[33]

The historical mapping and critical investigation of musical life in seventeenth-century Ireland has thus advanced significantly over recent decades, together with a growing recognition of the extent to which music acted as a

---

28 Donnelly, 'An Irish harper in the royal musick'; Donnelly, 'The Irish harp'; Donnelly, 'An Irish harper and composer'; Ua Suilleabháin & Donnelly, 'Music has ended'; Donnelly, 'A Cork musician'; Séan Donnelly, 'The Captain and the Harper – Two Mayo Brothers of Elizabethan Times', *Cathair na Mart: Journal of the Westport Historical Society,* 23 (2003), 18–34; Donnelly, 'Warpipes', i–iv; Donnelly, *Early history.*   **29** Boydell, 'Dublin city'; Boydell, 'Earl of Cork' (see also ch. 5, below).   **30** Fletcher, *Drama, performance*; Fletcher, *Sources.*   **31** Boydell, *Music at Christ Church.*   **32** Boydell, *History of music.* **33** *IMS* 6, pp 41–72.

common link between the country's two main cultural traditions. Against this background, a collection of essays on music in and related to seventeenth-century Ireland presents the opportunity both to challenge misconceptions of this period of Irish music history and to explore this complex and pivotal century as expressed through the music of both the native Irish and of the English-speaking cultures, both individually and in their interrelationships with each other.

This volume is not a history of music. A title such as 'Music in seventeenth-century Ireland' has therefore been avoided since this might misleadingly suggest an attempt to provide an inclusive study of musical practices in Ireland during the period. Rather, the essays collected in this volume explore a range of independent but interlinked topics which range from explorations of the place of music within different social and cultural contexts, through the documentation of musical practices, to the theory of music as an expression of the emerging Age of Reason. The themes adverted to earlier in these pages of the interdependence and interplay between the different cultural traditions underlie many of these chapters. Thus Raymond Gillespie and Adrian Scahill respectively question the prevailing paradigms of colonial and ethnic ideologies of music and culture in seventeenth-century Ireland. They variously examine those formations of musical identity which underpinned the transmission of music, and in the process they substantially revise our assumptions about the co-existence (and sometimes the cross fertilization) of distinct musical traditions at a period in which newly established political hegemonies not only subverted the remnants of the old order, but attempted to assimilate aspects of Irish musical culture within the new. Gillespie argues for a reading of music in seventeenth-century Ireland as a social art which provides an important but largely overlooked window into everyday life. Distinguishing between a high culture of Gaelic civilization and a popular musical tradition, Scahill presents a revisionist reading of 'traditional' Irish music founded on cultural theories of musical transmission.

The relationships between the colonial and the ethnic musical traditions come into focus no more clearly than through the patronage of Irish harpers by Anglo-Irish society but also beyond Ireland within courtly society, extending even to the heart of English musical life as members of the Royal Music. Thence it was but a logical progression for the Irish harp to be used in the performance of contemporary non-Irish music, as John Cunningham demonstrates in chapter 4. This engagement with the Irish harp in non-Irish contexts provides a link to chapters 5 and 6 which focus on the musical worlds of the new English settlers in early seventeenth-century Ireland. Barra Boydell's chapter on Richard Boyle, first earl of Cork and one of the wealthiest new English landowners, reveals both an attempt to replicate the musical world of English courtly circles at his seat in Lismore, Co. Waterford, and an engagement with indigenous musical traditions through his patronage of harpers. The presence of a substantial collection of music books primarily of theoretical interest within the library of Lord Conway in early seventeenth-century Ulster is documented and contextualized by Barra Boydell and Máire Egan-Buffet. This collection may be a reflection more of

Conway's desire to surround himself with the visible trappings of culture than of actual music making, but it highlights the presence of contemporary European musical thought in Ireland at the time. An emphasis on music-theoretical texts draws attention to the emergence in the seventeenth century of the scientific or mathematical approach to knowledge which was applied likewise to music by European philosophers and theorists including Descartes and Kircher. Chapters 7 and 8 focus on two very different people, both with Irish connections, whose thinking was shaped by the application of these rationalist theories to music. Christopher Field's chapter on John Birchensha – of English parentage but brought up and probably born in Ireland although he had moved to England by the time he developed his 'mathematical way of composure' – reflects the optimism of seventeenth-century rationalism: that the composing of music could successfully be reduced to mathematical principles. Andrew Robinson examines the musical interests of Narcissus Marsh whose career in some respects presents a mirror image of Birchensha: born in England, he spent the latter part of his life in Ireland first as provost of Trinity College Dublin, later becoming archbishop of Dublin and then of Armagh. Marsh's two short but incisive essays on acoustics developed Descartes' theories and proposed theoretical models for problems such as the transmission of a sound to a distance without being heard in between, problems whose realisation would have to await the electronic revolution of modern times. As Robinson reminds us, it is to Marsh that we owe the invention of words in common use today including 'acoustics' and 'microphone'.

As archbishop of Dublin and an active musician in his youth, Marsh would have taken a close interest in sacred music in the Dublin cathedrals and parish churches, topics which are examined in chapters 9 and 10. Focussing on the period following the Restoration of Charles II in 1660, the earliest period for which the Dublin cathedral repertoire is relatively well documented, Kerry Houston analyzes the repertoire in Dublin's two Anglican cathedrals, Christ Church and St Patrick's, drawing on sources including an anthem word-book specific to Dublin dating from 1662 and *GB-DRc*, MS B.1, the Hosier MS, which was compiled in Dublin in the decades following the Restoration. He draws particular attention to the dependence of the Dublin cathedral repertoire on English composers particularly of the Chapel Royal, the relative absence of local composers, and to the constant renewal of the Dublin repertoire with its strong preference for 'modern' compositions. In contrast to the rich musical tradition in the cathedrals, Denise Neary examines the evidence for music at parish level. With the subjugation of the Catholic church, all religious property being held by the established Anglican church by the late seventeenth century, and surviving parish records relating almost exclusively to Dublin, it is the musical practices in the Protestant churches of the capital, including the provision of organs, which provide the focus of this chapter. Information on the wider practice of music at parish level is nevertheless provided by writers including Edward Wetenhall and by the active debate in the 1690s concerning the place and role of music in worship. Founded by Queen Elizabeth I in 1594, Trinity College Dublin was one of the intellectual pillars of Anglo-Protestant Ireland. Its centenary was marked in 1694 by the performance of Henry Purcell's ode *Great parent, hail* to a text by the Irish-born poet laureate (and graduate of Trinity) Nahum Tate. Martin Adams reassesses Purcell's centenary ode in the concluding chapter, arguing that the largely negative views which this work has attracted within Purcell scholarship operate on faulty premises since they fail to engage with aesthetics and with the identification of the rhetorical concepts that have a primary role in shaping the material of seventeenth-century music: Tate's text and Purcell's music responded precisely, as Adams demonstrates, to the particular conditions appropriate to the centenary celebrations in late seventeenth-century Dublin.

Despite the paucity of sources of notated music and even of detailed evidence for the practice of music within both the Gaelic aural tradition and the predominantly Anglo-Irish context of music in the European tradition, the chapters in this volume offer a new understanding of the place and significance of music within seventeenth-century Irish life and culture. By challenging perceptions of the seventeenth century as a largely forgotten period of Irish music history, these essays should both stimulate a broader appreciation of the importance of music for an understanding of seventeenth-century Ireland, and encourage further research into this most intriguing if imperfectly understood era in Ireland's musical and cultural history.

Seventeenth-century Irish music and its cultural context

RAYMOND GILLESPIE

Seventeenth-century Irish music is notoriously difficult to talk about. However that has not prevented historians of the subject trying, particularly given the importance of music in understanding the social context in which it exists. Those who have written about music in seventeenth-century Ireland have chosen to concentrate on what might be described as the supply of music, and in particular the sort of institutions that made music making possible. Thus Barra Boydell's studies of the Dublin city musicians and the musical world of Christ Church cathedral have done much to elucidate the significance of music in the city.[1] In particular this has highlighted the cultural significance of cathedral music of the established church in establishing the cultural norms of Protestant Ireland.[2] Alan Fletcher's compilation of the surviving evidence for the practice of music before 1642 reveals much about the provision of music in great households, of both the lords deputy and magnates, and sets this against other forms of performance within Gaelic lordships.[3] New English settlers, it is clear, brought new musical contacts and repertoires with them to Ireland that marked them out as a cultural group. The well-known example of the dedication by the English composer John Dowland of one of his songs to 'my loving countryman Mr John Foster the younger, merchant of Dublin in Ireland' provides one example of this interaction of musical and geographical worlds.[4] Another is provided by Narcissus Marsh who, when he came to Ireland from Oxford in 1678, brought with him the music that he had played with his friends in England and continued to use these manuscripts to make music in Dublin.[5] Again, in the late 1680s the Irish poet Dáibhí Ó Bruadair in his triumphalist poem 'Caithréim Thaidhg' identified the new order with the older world of Gaelic Ireland since the settler women were supposed to be frightened by the Catholic Irish guards outside 'humming old tunes that they [the settlers] were not accustomed to'.[6] Such evidence, combined with studies of the availability of music, have highlighted the problem of cultural fragmentation and difference within the Irish polity in the seventeenth century and have suggested links between cultural changes and religious and political

1 Boydell, *History of music*; Boydell, 'Dublin city', 42–3.   2 Barra Boydell, 'Cathedral music, city and state: music in reformation and political change at Christ Church cathedral, Dublin' in Fiona Kisby (ed.), *Music and musicians in renaissance cities and towns* (Cambridge, 2001), pp 131–42.   3 Fletcher, *Sources*.   4 John Dowland, *The pilgrims solace* (London, 1612).   5 The manuscript music is now in Marsh's Library, see Charteris, *Catalogue*, pp 81–5, 99–126. See also ch. 8, below.   6 John Mac Erlean (ed.), *Duanaire Dháibhidh Uí Bhruadair*, 3 vols (London, 1910–17), iii, pp 136–7.

divisions in an age of dramatic colonization. As one authority on the subject has put it, 'a new wave of affluent and determined colonialism, which supported organized music of more recent European fashions, overwhelmed the older local tradition and a sharp division was created between Gaelic music and what is usually referred to as Anglo-Irish music'. The fact that each tradition acted as a powerful symbol of rival political and cultural ideologies ensured that the two streams had 'little contact with each other.'[7] What this chapter suggests is that the picture is more complex than this, with music forming both a bridge and a chasm between the various cultures that developed in Ireland in the seventeenth century.

* * *

Institutional changes, which have the merit of being easy to observe, are not necessarily the best guide to broader cultural shifts. Cultural fragmentation or absorption is better studied in the context of performance in which the survival and adaptation of older cultural traits, as well as the assimilation of new ones, can be more clearly observed. The problem with this approach is that such musical performances were an ephemeral art. No one from within Gaelic Ireland wrote down the music they heard in particular contexts, although some evidence is preserved in English contexts from the early seventeenth century.[8] That Irish 'folk' music should be preserved in the context of the English 'high' culture of printed music should cause historians to be wary of simple models of colonial replacement of one set of 'native' musical forms with those of colonists. Most music, like oral literature, was passed on through listening and remembering: it was not until 1714 that an Irish song with its air was printed.[9] At the popular level it seems highly likely that certain tunes were well known and could be brought to light as required rather than being notated, which required a certain level of literacy to understand. When in 1684 Bishop Wadding of Ferns published his book of songs, *A small garland of pious songs*, he did not provide any music but simply named the airs to which they were to be sung, presuming his audience would know or have access to them.[10] Again, the late seventeenth-century Kerry poet Seafraidh Ó Donnachadha directed that his poem 'Is brónach mo thocht' was to be sung to the air 'Iom bó agus um bo' which was, presumably, well known.[11] In the case of ballads the seller of printed sheets seems to have sung his product and by that means provided the music to go with the text he sold.[12]

The success of such a system of transmission depended on a level of social stability. How well this process of social reproduction of music worked in practice is difficult to say. One sixteenth-century song with an air, probably from north Dublin, certainly survived into the mid-twentieth century. Again, songs

7 Boydell, 'Music before 1700', pp 542–67 at 546. **8** Fleischmann, *Sources*, i, pp 1–37. **9** Breandán Breathnach, 'The first Irish song published', *Ceol*, 5:1 (1981), 2–3. **10** Pádraig Ó Súilleabháin, 'The airs in Bishop Wadding's "Small garland"', *Ceol*, 4:2 (1973), 51. **11** Pádraig Ó Duinnín (ed.), *Dánta Séafraidh Uí Dhonnchada an Ghleanna* (Dublin, 1902), p. 20. This is the earliest secular song attached to a contemporary air of which I know. **12** Hugh Shields, *Narrative singing in Ireland* (Dublin, 1993), pp 43–4.

from south Ulster by the late seventeenth-century poets Cathal Buí Mac Giolla Ghunna, Pádraig Mac Giolla Fhiondaín and Séamus Dall Mac Cuarta continued in the repertoire into the twentieth century and it now seems clear that more of this poetic corpus may have been sung. It is difficult to know if the airs that were collected with these songs are indeed traceable into the seventeenth century although it is now clear that some of these are older than previously thought.[13] Certainly the music historian Grattan Flood cited a number of airs that he claimed to be able to date to the sixteenth or seventeenth centuries.[14] If this evidence is to be trusted it does suggest that Irish music of the early modern period was successfully transmitted in this way despite the considerable political and social disturbance of the period.

Apart from problems with repertoire, the historian of Irish music in the seventeenth century is also faced with the lack of any real descriptions of musical events. Some contemporaries might complain in passing of the music they heard, such as the duke of Ormond's comment in 1678 that he had to 'entertain my lord mayor [of Dublin] and his brethren at noon and in afternoon at post and pair; and just now I am assaulted with drums, trumpets and fiddlers. God send us no more dangerous alarms.'[15] Such comments do not amount to an understanding of how music worked in seventeenth-century Ireland but they do point out the importance of music in the Anglo-Irish world. Unlike the music-making of much of Ireland, this 'classical' music was professional and therefore associated with centres of patronage: the vice-regal court, the church, civic entertainments or the great house. Reconstructing such patterns of patronage or what might have been performed in this context is problematic because of the nature of the sources.[16] However, as in the case of the music performed at a lower level in Ireland there appears to have been considerable cross over between a number of cultural traditions, with the harp being a favoured instrument in many Anglo-Irish houses into the eighteenth century.

All this suggests that music was a deeply social art. Indeed, when those in late seventeenth-century Ireland talked about their particular types of music the social context, rather than aesthetics or technicalities, was what they discussed. During the debate between the Presbyterian Joseph Boyse and Bishop King of Derry in the 1690s the discussion of the role of music in worship turned on social questions: who made music, when was it performed, what was it was called, how was it used, how was it to be sung, who were the participants in music making and who were the audience.[17] Indeed, men such as Edward Wetenhall, the

---

13 Gerard Murphy, 'A folksong traceable to Elizabethan times', *Éigse,* 7 (1953), 117–20; Pádraigín Ní Uallacháin, *A hidden Ulster: people, songs and traditions of Oriel* (Dublin, 2003), pp 44–58, 217–23, 337–47; Pádraigín Ní Uallacháin, 'A Drogheda list of melodies: implications for the song tradition of Oriel' in Anne Clune (ed.), *Dear far-voiced veteran: essays in honour of Tom Munnelly* (Milltown Malbay, 2007), pp 169–90.   14 For instance Flood, *History,* pp 189, 193, 195, 199, 201–6.   15 Historical Manuscripts Commission, *Report on the manuscripts of the marquess of Ormond* (old series, 3 vols, London, 1895–1909), ii, p. 266.   16 Fletcher, *Drama, performance,* pp 206–60.   17 For an outline of the debate see Phil Kilroy, *Protestant dissent and controversy in Ireland, 1660–1714* (Cork, 1994), pp 171–87.

precentor of Christ Church cathedral in the 1670s and later bishop of both Kilmore and Cork, urged that technical virtuosity or complex ideas about beauty had nothing to do with music in church.[18] Music in worship was not to be confused with art. The language that such men used about music was the same language they used when describing other aspects of everyday life. Music was described by the social context in which it was used; music, for instance, was dance music or worship music. At the beginning of the seventeenth century as Tadhg Ó Cianáin travelled through Europe with the Ulster earls who had fled from Ireland he encountered music performed in different contexts to those he had encountered in Gaelic Ireland. To deal with what went on in these new settings he borrowed the word *múisic* into Irish and used it alongside the more familiar *ceol*.[19] The implication of this is that it is not possible to understand music outside of the collective formation that was seventeenth-century society. This does not mean that music performed general society-wide functions, such as defining social values or relationships within the world of the seventeenth century, although it did perform other functions in that world, which will be considered below. Defining social relationships through musical activity would have been difficult in a society without the sort of public sphere, and middle class cultural participation, associated with the concerts that later became a feature of eighteenth-century Dublin.[20] Seventeenth-century music-making was almost always a private affair in the context of the household, albeit some rather large households, or else took place in very circumscribed public contexts, especially that of religious worship. Rather, the social and cultural context was apparent as the inhabitants of early modern Ireland listened to and understood their music through the interpretative skills and modes of thought they brought to it. It is that process which reveals a great deal about their world although it is difficult to reconstruct. Few have chosen to travel that path in understanding music in Ireland.

One example that makes this approach clearer for the seventeenth century is the case of the harp. In sixteenth-century Gaelic Ireland the harp and the harper were seen by many as central to social life. That status they shared in common with the *file*, or poet, at whose recitations they played. The crafts of harpist and poet were closely interconnected and each fed off the standing of the other. In some cases there are even hints that poets were also harpers and that they possessed harps.[21] The harpist also had other roles within the lordship, most especially as messenger and political propagandist. Harpers, for instance, moved easily between Ireland and Scotland in the sixteenth century. These harpers were

---

18 Wetenhall, *Of gifts and offices*, pp 239, 246–7. **19** For references to the borrowings and their context see Nollaig Ó Muraíle (ed.), *Turas na d'taoiseach nUltach as Éirinn: from Ráth Maoláin to Rome* (Rome, 2007), p. 643. **20** For the links between the rise of the concert and the 'public sphere' see T.C.W. Blanning, *The culture of power and the power of culture: old regime Europe, 1660–1789* (Oxford, 2002), pp 161–82. **21** Eleanor Knott (ed.), *The bardic poems of Tadhg Dall Ó hUiginn*, 2 vols (London, 1922–6), i, p. 184, ii, p. 123; Réamonn Ó Muireadhaigh (ed.), 'Marbhna ar Mhuiris Mac Torna Uí Mhaolchonaire', *Éigse*, 15 (1973–4), 129.

often regarded as politically subversive figures since it was they who aided the poet in encouraging lords to have an over-inflated view of their capacities.[22] The number of official pardons recorded in the late sixteenth-century fiants suggest that many escaped the severe sanctions which could have been imposed on them.

Two things are striking about harp music in Ireland in the course of the seventeenth century. The first is that harpists continued to be patronized by both Gaelic and Anglo-Irish lords, as they had been in the sixteenth century, while other features of lordly patronage, such as bardic poetry, fell into disuse. Even as the poetic craft declined, poets continued to praise the music or technical skill of harpers or castigate them for the noise that they made well into the seventeenth century.[23] The second feature is that settler gentry, even those of high social level, patronized harpers. In the late sixteenth century Lord Deputy Perrot employed a harper and in the early seventeenth century Lord Deputy Chichester and Richard Boyle, one of the wealthiest settlers in Ireland, kept harpers. By the beginning of the eighteenth century the harper Carolan produced music for families that spanned the social and ethnic divide, although technically the music was rather different to that performed in the sixteenth century.[24]

From this it might be concluded that the harp and its music fitted into the changing fabric of Irish society rather better than its poets did. It is not possible to know how the repertoire of the harp adapted since we have no contemporary copies of the repertoire and part of the adjustment process may have been a shift in the type of music played. However, given that Lord Deputy Perrot patronized a traditional harper, Richard Barrett, in the 1580s, this cannot have been a major factor. At an even more exalted level Irish harpers can be found among the royal musicians in London. How much Irish music they played in England is unclear but it may be worth noting that at the same time as Irish harpers begin to appear in London Irish harp tunes also begin to appear in English collections of music. Such references become less common from the 1630s perhaps reflecting the fact that Irish instruments, like the image of Ireland on stage, were becoming less exotic and more normal.[25]

The task of those who governed seventeenth-century Ireland was to create, from a disparate range of elements, a social order focused on the king. As early as 1605 a royal proclamation had declared that all the inhabitants of Ireland were now the immediate subjects of the king.[26] The implication of this was the abandoning of the Henrician scheme for forcing Ireland into cultural homogeneity,

---

22 Fletcher, *Drama, performance*, pp 32–3, 47–50, 52, 54; Colm Ó Baoill, 'Some Irish harpers in Scotland', *Transactions of the Gaelic Society of Inverness*, 47 (1971), 143–71.   **23** For examples, Osborn Bergin, *Irish bardic poetry* (Dublin, 1970), nos. 24, 54.   **24** Fletcher, *Drama, performance*, pp 211–12, 220, 222–3, 231–2; Joan Trimble, 'Carolan and his patrons in Fermanagh and neighbouring areas', *Clogher Record*, 10:1 (1979), 26–50; T.C. Barnard, *Making the grand figure: lives and possessions in Ireland, 1641–1770* (London, 2004), pp 399–400.   **25** For examples see Donnelly, 'An Irish harper in the royal musick'; Donnelly, 'The Irish harp'; Donnelly, 'An Irish harper and composer'; Donnelly, 'A Cork musician'. For the changing image of Ireland on stage see Tristan Marshall, *Theatre and empire: Great Britain on the London stage under James VI and I* (Manchester, 2000), p. 175.   **26** For some of the social implications of this see Raymond Gillespie, *Seventeenth-century Ireland* (Dublin, 2006), pp 6–15.

contained in the 1534 Act for the 'English order, habit and language', that had argued

[there is] nothing which doth more contain and keep many of the [king's] subjects of this his said land in a savage and wild kind and manner of living than the diversity that is betwixt them in tongue, language, order and habit, which by the eye deceiveth the multitude and persuadeth unto them that be as it were of sundry sorts, or rather sundry countries, where indeed they should be wholly together one body whereof his Highness is the only head under God.[27]

The retreat from this position seems clear in two acts of the Irish parliament of 1613–15, which removed sixteenth-century restrictions on Irish and Scots in Ireland, including prohibitions on intermarriage, trade and fosterage. All inhabitants of Ireland were now deemed to be the king's subjects 'without difference and distinction'.[28] Even this was not enough for the English privy council who in 1615 wrote to the Irish lord deputy requiring an even greater purge of such cultural legislation as might exist against the Gaelic Irish 'for they are in effect merely hostile and in no way agreeable with that obedience and loyalty wherein his majesty now beholdeth the whole of his subjects there'.[29] Apart from, briefly, in the 1650s no attempts were made to reintroduce legislation that distinguished between various cultural, as opposed to religious, groups in Ireland. In short, the various elements within Ireland were to be bound together into a new social world. This understanding of the world meant that, in order to imagine the sort of society that some social theorists aspired to, it was necessary to find symbols that would provide commonalities among all the inhabitants of Ireland. Undoubtedly the most important of these symbols was the king, but it seems that the harp and harp music may have been another. Thus the harp was both the symbol of the old Gaelic world and of a new order so that in 1688 it was possible for the English poet Aphra Benn to salute the duke of Ormond as he ceased to be lord lieutenant with the couplet 'The Irish harp which long abased had lain / Your skilful hand first brought in tune again'.[30] Finally, by 1689 Ireland was represented on the stage of the new world of Williamite London as dressed in linen with a wreath of shamrocks and in one hand a shield 'bearing the Irish harp'.[31] The passage may have been eased by the symbolic status of the harp, which had been used by the Dublin government since the latter middle ages as a representation of Ireland. In the 1640s the Kilkenny confederates adopted the same image suggesting the uniting effect the symbol may have had.[32]

As a symbol the harp may have had a long-lasting and stabilizing influence in Ireland, but as a musical instrument it did change and develop in the seventeenth

---

27 Philomena Connolly (ed.), *Statute rolls of the Irish parliament: Richard III – Henry VIII* (Dublin, 2002), p. 237. **28** Irish statutes, 11, 12 & 13 Jas I, c. 5, c. 6. **29** *Acts of the privy council of England, 1615–16* (London, 1925), p. 80. **30** Aphra Benn, *Poems upon several occasions with a voyage to the island of love* (London, 1697), p. 109. **31** Mathew Tauban, *London's great jubilee containing a description of several projects and speeches* (London, 1689), np. **32** Boydell, 'Iconography', pp 131–7.

century, reflecting new influences on Irish musical style. The instrument became larger and the number of strings grew throughout the century, adding to its range.[33] The process is recorded by John Lynch in the 1660s who noted that the Jesuit Robert Nugent increased 'to a great degree the melodious powers of the harp' by modifying its structure.[34] It is perhaps not difficult to detect Nugent's European experience, acquired as a Jesuit, in executing his changes. A similar process of borrowing may be detected with the fiddle. While bowed string instruments had existed in medieval Ireland, the fiddle (or violin) appears to have been a borrowing from a European, or probably English, tradition. The Irish word *fidil*, referring to the modern instrument, appears first in the late seventeenth century and this probably dates the introduction of the instrument into Irish traditional music. Fiddles also appear in association with popular dancing by the 1670s. However, the fiddle is mentioned in the early part of the century in Anglo-Irish records.[35]

A contrast to the experience of the harp and harp music in the social context of the seventeenth century is provided by piping and its musical repertoire. Whereas the harp flourished, the pipes as they had been known in the sixteenth century went into rapid decline and were replaced, probably in the early eighteenth century, by the uilleann pipes.[36] In the main this was a functional shift. The sixteenth-century pipes were war pipes intended to make a noise that contemporaries described as being the equivalent of a trumpet.[37] After the end of the Nine Years War in 1603 references to the use of the pipes become infrequent and it is only in the 1640s during the Confederate wars that mentions of piping again become common. These references are mainly in a military context with the pipes playing their normal function of enthusing soldiers. As the Cromwellian general Edmund Ludlow described the news of the surrender of Limerick in 1649, the Irish army 'sent me a defiance and sounded their bagpipes in contempt of me'.[38] The years after 1660 again see a reduction in references to pipes and piping, although there are some references to what are clearly outdoor dances that used pipes. That this may be an older tradition is suggested by the comment in Wexford in 1641 that the insurrectionists tore up the Bible and Book of Common Prayer, scattering the pages around the churchyard and then called a piper to play while they danced on the detritus.[39] References to the warpipes reappear in a number of contexts during the Jacobite period. In Dáibhí Ó Bruadair's triumphalist poem of 1690 'Caithréim Thaidhg' what is presented as characteristic of the newly restored Gaelic world is 'The dance of the withe and the strain of the three

---

33 Rimmer, *Irish harp*, pp 47–9, 55–7.   34 John Lynch, *Cambrensis eversus*, ed. Mathew Kelly, 3 vols (Dublin, 1848), i, pp 316–19.   35 Fletcher, *Sources*, pp 316, 417; Eugene O'Curry, *Manners and customs of the ancient Irish*, 3 vols (London, 1873), iii, p. 329; S. Ó Neachtain (ed.), *Stair Eamuinn Uí Chléire* (Dublin, 1918), p. 48; MacLysaght, *Irish life*, p. 36.   36 Most of the evidence is gathered together in Donnelly, 'Warpipes', i–iv. The reference by John Dunton in 1699 to the pipes being apparently played indoors may be the earliest recorded use of a set of pipes smaller than the warpipes. MacLysaght, *Irish life*, p. 359.   37 D.B. Quinn, *The Elizabethans and the Irish* (Ithaca, NJ, 1966), pp 41, 96 and plates 4, 13. 38 *Memoirs of Edmund Ludlow esq.*, 2 vols (Vivay, [1698]), i, p. 352.   39 *IRL-Dtc*, MS 818, fo. 8v.

droned pipe'.[40] However, the description of James II's entrance into Dublin in 1688 records that he was preceded by pipers but this time playing a song from the English Civil War: 'The king enjoys his own again'.[41] In the wake of the Williamite wars references to the war pipes again recede. This is a history strongly contrasting with that of the harp and its music. In part the disappearance of the warpipes was a practical matter. The harp could adapt to the consort music tradition in a way that the volume of the pipes could not. However, the association of the pipes with war is almost certainly another reason why they were deemed less appropriate certainly in the elite circles in which the politically aware moved. For that reason the pipes may have survived in an era of peace only as an outdoor dance instrument at a lower social level.[42]

It seems possible that music in seventeenth-century Ireland, irrespective of its ethnic context as the case of the harp suggests, was a cultural requisite and so could, presumably, be understood by the diverse inhabitants of that world. As such, the harp and at least some of the traditional music that was associated with it became part of everyday life alongside the more recent Irish musical canon at the level of those who could afford it. Thus, those who attended the theatre in Dublin might expect to encounter an eclectic range of music. The Dublin performance of Henry Burnell's play 'Landgartha' in 1640 included in its stage directions the use of what might be regarded as typically 'English' instruments including recorders and violins. Equally, one of the dances in the play was to the traditional tune 'The whip of Dunboyne'.[43] That bardic poetry, traditionally closely related to the social contexts of the harp and its music, failed to make the same transition is a reminder of the importance of considering the various strands of cultural evidence in their own terms. However, it may well be that the harp and its music are a special case.

* * *

If we are to approach the music of the seventeenth century at the level of other interpretative communities, understanding the functions of music and its ability to cross boundaries and adapt to new situations may appear in a rather different light. Music in seventeenth-century Irish society may not have fulfilled the same social functions as it did in the eighteenth century, but it was nonetheless important in shaping the ways that social groups formed and reformed around music and, in the case of song, the associated texts. At one level, Thomas Monck

---

40 Mac Erlean, *Duanaire Dháibhidh Uí Bhruadair*, iii, pp 130–1. **41** *Ireland's lamentation: being a short, but perfect, full and true account of the situation, natural constitution and produce of Ireland* (London, 1689), pp 26–8. **42** The decline of the warpipe may also be linked to a rise in the popularity of indoor entertainment, such as the alehouse, from the early eighteenth century, see Elizabeth Malcolm, 'The rise of the pub: a study in the disciplining of popular culture' in J.S. Donnelly & Kerby Miller (eds), *Irish popular culture, 1650–1850* (Dublin, 1998), pp 55–68. **43** Henry Burnell, *Landgartha: a tragie-comedy* (Dublin, 1641), sigs B1v, E4v, F2v. For other uses of music in the theatre see Christopher Morash, *A history of Irish theatre, 1601–2000* (Oxford, 2002), pp 28–9.

describing Co. Kildare in 1683 was inclined to identify a 'national' music. As he observed of the native Irish, 'they are great admirers of music, yet their own songs generally are doleful lamentations as those of a conquered people, or as the Jews in bondage or captivity (for what are brisk and airy are Old English or Scotch)'. John Dunton agreed some fifteen years later, seeing Irish music as 'melancholy and doleful as suiting the humours of a people always in subjection'.[44] Such comments are of limited enough use since they tend to reflect the perceptions of the observer rather than the workings of the social structure. However, what such comments do highlight is contemporary understanding of the emotional power of music in mobilizing senses other than purely rational ones. As the inscription on the Dalway harp, made in 1621, put it 'I am the queen of harps. I sound, I conquer, I rule … Music consoles the troubled mind'.[45] Indeed the emotional power of music was seen by some contemporaries as supernatural in origin, with some early seventeenth-century poets using a motif that described music as being inspired by fairies, or given by them.[46] One early seventeenth-century poem, for instance, described as magical the power of music to dispel an individual's ills.[47] In this context song can allow for the verbalization of feelings and ideas that it would not be possible to detect in other language contexts. Thus the songs of Cathal Buí Mac Giolla Ghunna, composed in the late seventeenth century and still sung in the early twentieth century, celebrate the joys of alcohol, chart love between a woman and a student priest, and proclaim the need for repentance before death. However, given the limited number of songs that are currently dateable to the seventeenth century it is difficult to provide any meaningful analysis of how contemporaries may have used this licence. We might also assume that songs had other social functions such as escapism or support for important social attributes, such as patronage, or criticism of undesirable ones, but evidence here is lacking.[48]

Perhaps the most important ways in which music worked in seventeenth-century Irish society was as a means of constructing and consolidating social groups. In some cases music formed a focus around which a particular group of people could gather to create what was, in effect, a micro-society within the larger social order. Once achieved, music, both in tunes and in songs, could act as a point of solidarity to integrate such a group. This might happen in a number of ways. The emotional power of music, for instance, could form a focus for a group. One instance of this is the 'keen' (*caoineadh*) or lament sung at funerals, as Sir William Brereton described in Wexford in 1635 with 'women and some other following making lamentation, sometimes as violent as though they were

---

44 Edited in MacLysaght, *Irish life*, pp 317, 344.   45 Rimmer, *Irish harp*, p. 75.   46 For examples of music said to be inspired by fairies see Ua Suilleabháin & Donnelly, 'Music has ended', 161; Cuthbert McGrath, 'Two skilful musicians', *Éigse*, 7 (1953), 88–90. For a folklore perspective see Ríonach Uí Ógáin, 'Music learned from the fairies', *Béaloideas*, 60–1 (1992–3), 197–214.   47 Eoin Mac Giolla Eáin (ed.), *Dánta, amhráin is caointe Sheathrúin Céitinn* (Dublin, 1900), p. 30.   48 For this in a later context see Breandán Ó Madagáin, 'Functions of Irish song in the nineteenth century', *Béaloideas*, 53 (1985), 130–216.

distracted, sometimes as it were in a kind of tune singing'.[49] The practice was condemned by the Catholic church but attempts to stamp out the practice met with limited success since the emotional power of the music bound the mourners together into a coherent group. More conventional songs could have a similar bonding effect where song texts would be given additional power by music. Unfortunately, few of these texts have survived but one example may be the earliest Irish printed ballad, 'Mount Taragh's triumph', of July 1626.[50] The context of this ballad was the discussion between the Old English gentry of the Pale and the king, which ultimately led to the granting of a number of concessions, or Graces, in September. The words are loaded with the sort of royalist sentiments that were the hallmark of the Catholic Old English and which they were at pains to demonstrate to others, especially to Ireland's New English provincial governors. From a different political perspective, in the 1690s Thomas Wharton's Williamite song 'Lillibulero' was so successful in bonding together William's Irish followers that the same tune was also ascribed to an Irish ballad of 1690.[51]

Perhaps the most powerful way in which music created shared experiences was through its use in religious worship. Here words and music interacted to create long-lasting emotional effects and formed rather different approaches to their world among those who sang the texts provided for worship. The text that lay at the centre of this experience and provided the materials for worship was the Bible, which the three main confessional groups in Ireland agreed to read in different ways. What flowed from those confessional differences, as expressed in liturgical terms, were rather different assumptions about how everyday life worked.[52]

The first dimension of these singing and reading groups is the world of religious dissent, illustrated in particular by Joseph Boyse's two hymn books of 1693 and 1701.[53] These were books produced for a particular religious community with specific views on how the everyday world should work. The dominant feature of the 1693 hymn book is that no music was provided. Congregations were simply expected to know the hymn tunes specified for each hymn although in the case of the 1693 text everything was sung to 'Old hundredth', which no doubt made things easier. This implies a society that already had a common musical bond and one that could be easily replicated over time. Moreover, it also presumed a society in which a sense of community was important, or, as Joseph Boyse himself told Bishop King of Derry during their dispute in the 1690s, they held that holiness was in the gathering of people not in the place. However, it is possible to move a stage further since Boyse's books were radically new in the

49 Edited in C. Litton Falkiner, *Illustrations of Irish history and topography* (London, 1904), p. 396. Further examples in MacLysaght, *Irish life*, pp 318, 349, 351.   **50** For the text see Andrew Carpenter, *Verse in English from Tudor and Stuart Ireland* (Cork, 2003), pp 183–5.   **51** Ó Buachalla, 'Lillibulero' **52** Raymond Gillespie, 'Reading the bible in seventeenth-century Ireland' in Bernadette Cunningham & Máire Kennedy (eds), *The experience of reading: Irish historical perspectives* (Dublin, 1999), pp 10–38. **53** For much of what follows on dissent see Raymond Gillespie, '"A good and godly exercise": singing the word in Irish dissent, 1660–1701' in Kevin Herlihy (ed.), *Propagating the word of Irish dissent, 1650–1800* (Dublin, 1998), pp 24–45.

1690s. Most Presbyterian communities used the metrical psalter with the practice of lining out, or announcing the line of the psalm before it was sung. This was certainly the practice in Ulster where the Presbyterian minister at Derry, Robert Craghead, was clear in the 1690s that this was the only acceptable form of singing. However in Dublin the situation is rather less clear. William Barton's 1697 edition of the psalms was reprinted in Dublin in 1698 and 1706, and included music, and it may be that these publications were for worship. At any rate, the use of music in the manner of Boyse's congregation, through the hymnbook, reflects the rather different sort of society that was emerging in Dublin which rejected the sort of standardisation that had become characteristic of Ulster Presbyterianism with its requirement to use the metrical psalter. Thus, liturgical musical practice can be interpreted as reflecting the views of local society as community and also as illustrating the fact that one community was not like another.

A rather similar sort of explanation can be invoked for the somewhat different musical practice found in the Church of Ireland in Dublin as compared with Presbyterianism. In the 1670s, Edward Wetenhall had highlighted one difference between the worlds of the established church and dissent as being that of singing practices. Whereas the musical practices of the Presbyterians were akin to what might be described as 'folk music', reflecting the community-based nature of Presbyterian society, those of the Church of Ireland were decidedly what might be called 'classical'. Again, this musical difference reflects a social and theological one. The Church of Ireland at prayer was a world of hierarchy – a dialogue between priest and people but with clear messages about where authority lay – whereas Presbyterian prayer was more egalitarian.[54] Wetenhall, in fact, was sensitive to the 'folk' character of Presbyterian music noting that singing

> is better approved (indeed strangely doted upon) by those of our nation who dissent from the church for no other reason more than I can imagine but that one is of the Church's constitution, the other the people's creature, and of their own voluntary taking up.[55]

In the course of the seventeenth century, the Church of Ireland began to think about singing as more of a communal activity with music that could be reproduced by congregations. One indication of this is the installation of organs in the Dublin churches from the 1680s onwards: St Werburgh's in 1676, St Catherine's 1678, St John's 1684, St Peter's 1686 and St Bride's *c*.1686.[56] It may be worth reflecting that in some, though not all, of these churches the organ was inserted as part of more general works to the building, works that included the raising up

54 I have argued this case on the basis of liturgical evidence in Raymond Gillespie, 'Differing devotions: patterns of religious practice in the British Isles, 1500–1700' in S.J. Connolly (ed.), *Kingdoms united? Great Britain and Ireland since 1500* (Dublin, 1998), pp 67–77.   **55** Wetenhall, *Of gifts and offices*, p. 404.   **56** Denise Neary, 'Music in late seventeenth- and eighteenth-century Dublin churches' in *IMS* 4, pp 103–10.

and railing in of the altar, often tiling the sanctuary in a different way to the main body of the church. This sort of work, and particularly changes to the altar, can be characterized as the outworking of the theological ideas of the Caroline divines, Jeremy Taylor and others, who had jettisoned the Calvinism that had shaped the Church of Ireland in the early part of the seventeenth century and began to move that church to a more Arminian position. This saw the downgrading of the word in favour of sacrament and the replacement of the idea of an elect with the idea that all the parish community could be saved.[57] The communion service was thus to be a liturgical event in which all would participate. It seems reasonable to associate this shift in the understanding of local society with the deployment of music to draw those who might be regarded as outsiders into that parish community.

Finally, to turn to Catholicism and its use of music to reflect the society built around it: here, unfortunately, the evidence is pitifully thin. Almost no evidence has survived about Catholic liturgical music or the context of its use in seventeenth-century Ireland. In 1597 the Jesuit Henry FitzSimon celebrated High Mass in the house of a nobleman in Dublin 'with full orchestra, composed of harps, lutes and all kinds of instruments except the organ'. This he notes was the first High Mass celebrated in Dublin for forty years.[58] The description is significant since the instruments were those that might be normally be found in one of the great houses of the Pale during the period. The music must therefore be seen as an extension of domestic music-making. It may be that this was occasionally replicated in at least some other houses, but no descriptions of such events have survived. In part, this lack of evidence for a Catholic liturgical tradition is the result of the sort of sources that have survived, but the use of liturgical music was certainly limited by the political and economic conditions under which Mass could be said in the seventeenth century. Local religious communities certainly had periods in which they were little disturbed and local traditions of religious music may have existed. In 1677, for instance, the prior of the Galway Dominicans died on his way to Dublin where he was to purchase an organ for the convent in Galway.[59] Only in the 1640s and then again in the late 1680s with James II briefly on the throne might a tradition of Catholic liturgical music have flourished in any real way. Such an absence of music undoubtedly influenced the experience of Mass in the Irish context, making it a more intimate though less dramatic liturgical celebration than in other places in Europe. By limiting participative singing, attention was focussed on the priest. While music became interwoven into most Protestant worship traditions in seventeenth-century Ireland, serving to validate and reinforce those traditions by articulating orthodox belief, it did not fulfil the same role in Catholic worship, leaving the

57 Raymond Gillespie, *Devoted people: belief and religion in early modern Ireland* (Manchester, 1997), pp 97–8; F.R. Bolton, *The Caroline tradition of the Church of Ireland* (Dublin, 1958). **58** Henry Fitzsimon, *Words of comfort to persecuted Catholics* ed. Edmund Hogan (Dublin, 1881), p. 207. **59** John O'Heyne, *The Irish Dominicans of the seventeenth century*, ed. Ambrose Coleman (Dundalk, 1902), p. 142.

Catholic tradition distinctive even within Ireland. However, outside the liturgical sphere music was used, as it was in other European countries, to promote moral reform. In 1616 the Jesuit Edward Nugent was said to have composed hymns when a prisoner in Dublin Castle and these, it was claimed, became popular.[60] What they said is not known. No music was provided for the morally-improving songs and pious hymns in Bishop Wadding's *A small garland of pious songs* (1684) although tunes were named. The same tradition of using popular tunes associated with carols was later used in the early eighteenth century in Wexford by Fr Devereux. The importance of these texts is not that music was a reflection of society but that it was being actively used to change that society. The songs of Wadding, Devereux and, later, Tadhg Ó Súilleabháin's *Pious miscellany* in the early nineteenth century, were intended to introduce the ideas of the Council of Trent, particularly in the area of moral reform and acceptance of political conditions, to a wide range of hearers and singers by providing a well-known point of contact in music. By linking words and music, memorization was made easier and the songs achieved a much wider circulation than simply the literate minority. As such, music was used by one group to reshape another and create a new order.

* * *

This chapter has tried to suggest that, in the minds of those who lived in the seventeenth century, music was inseparable from its social context. That case has rarely been made in the history of music in Ireland. A related approach is found in Harry White's account of the period 1770–1970 which attempted to utilize the paradigm of 'the dialectic between the ethnic and colonial ideologies of culture, which history itself provides' as a way of understanding the development of music in society.[61] This may well be true, but, in the case of the seventeenth-century, music of different types was even more tightly woven into the social fabric than White's generalization would suggest. In fact, music was part of everyday life and not simply that of the great house or cathedral, and it was discussed as such by contemporaries. This reality goes some way to explaining the complexities of the history of music in seventeenth-century Ireland. As with the society around it there was no simple pattern of replacement of one set of music practices with another as a result of colonisation and the introduction of new cultural norms. Rather, the experience of music was a complicated one. At one level parts of an older tradition, especially the harp and its music, survived not simply by becoming part of a hidden Ireland but by integrating itself into smart society. Other traditions, such as that of piping, declined fitfully as the warpipes lost their function. In the early eighteenth century the pipes quietly adapted themselves to a new piping tradition. Music could absorb and reject elements of older traditions and repertoires. Equally, music could be used both to

60 Edmund Hogan, *Distinguished Irishmen of the sixteenth century* (London, 1894), p. 476.   **61** Harry White, *The keeper's recital: music and cultural history in Ireland, 1770–1970* (Cork, 1998), p. 2.

include and exclude people in particular types of society. Political and religious song had the power to mobilize emotion and create bonds of belonging through the communal singing of particular words. While one song brought people together it could, at the same time, exclude others. If these generalizations are even partly true, then music is an important window into everyday life and deserves a much greater place in the general histories of Ireland than historians have been prepared to concede.

Irish traditional music and the seventeenth century

ADRIAN SCAHILL

The title of this chapter reflects the uneasy relationship between the music of the seventeenth century and the body of music and practices currently defined as 'Irish traditional music'. It deliberately separates the two, because although the earlier period is a source for the transformations of the modern tradition, to write of traditional music *in* the seventeenth century would be to assume a continuity and a sameness between them. This would erroneously extend and apply contemporary concepts of traditional music to a more distant past. To dehistoricize the notion of traditional music risks misrepresenting it as a monolithic, unyielding structure, ignoring the changes and developments that have accrued over time in Irish musical culture, prompted by both internal and external stimuli.[1] As the ethnomusicologist Lauren Aubert has noted:

> Far from constituting fully preserved survivals of old times, the arts we consider today as traditional – those adorned with the most archaic appearance as well as those that appear to reveal modernity – are thus the products of multiple contents and events, of convergent influences whose fusion was achieved through long periods of assimilation.[2]

It is more accurate, therefore, to posit that a particular Irish music tradition existed in the seventeenth century, one which informed, to different extents, all subsequent music traditions in Ireland. The totality of these exists in a continuum reaching back to prehistory, and extending forward to the current agglomeration of music, musicians, and practices known as Irish traditional music.

It is important to establish from the outset that the musical culture of the seventeenth century itself was hardly homogenous. To generalize, this chapter is mainly concerned with the instrumental music of Gaelic Ireland, within which two broad strata have been distinguished: an élite musical culture centred on the wire-strung harp, and its coexistent vernacular culture. While musically both were orally transmitted, the former was learned and literary, and dismissive of vernacular culture, which was predominantly located within community-based rituals and practices.[3] From a modern perspective this division is now often

---

1 See Britta Sweers, 'Bach in a Venda mirror: John Blacking and historical musicology', in Suzel Ana Reily (ed.), *The musical human: rethinking John Blacking's ethnomusicology in the twenty-first century* (Aldershot, 2006), p. 182. 2 Laurent Aubert, *The music of the other: new challenges for ethnomusicology in a global age* (Aldershot, 2007), p. 20. 3 Sean Connolly, '"Ag déanamh *commanding*": élite responses to popular culture', in James S. Connolly & Kerby A. Miller (eds), *Irish popular culture, 1650–1850* (Dublin, 1998), pp 8–16.

obscured, in the sense that the harp and its music are now usually subsumed under the rubric of 'traditional music', which provides an excellent example of the reinterpretive strategies that occur as part of the construction of a tradition. It would also be wrong, though, to consider the music cultures of Gaelic Ireland in the seventeenth century as rigid and isolated: within the seventeenth century itself both élite and vernacular music responded to external pressures through the abandonment of the outmoded and the absorption of the new. Both the élite and vernacular traditions were thus transformed during the period. Both ultimately contribute to the confluence of practices, materialities and knowledge that were continually drawn on in the formation of the different stages of traditional music throughout its history.

A consideration of current traditional music as a product facilitates a more accurate representation of the significance of the seventeenth century as a constituent part of its interwoven musical fabric; and to discuss seventeenth-century musical culture within the framework of 'Irish traditional music' means posing the question of what imprint it has left on the tradition. This implies that there is a continuity between the two periods, one which can be real, imagined, or perceived.[4] The fact that most discussions of the concept of tradition highlight the necessity of continuity is hardly revelatory; typically representative of this is the phrase 'handed down', commonly used among traditional musicians to denote the inter-generational transmission of material, emphasized by Na Píobairí Uilleann's description of traditional music as having 'a direct stylistic lineage from the music of the past'.[5] An investigation of such a lineage cannot be simply restricted to the musical domain, but must encompass a wider scope. As Aubert has outlined:

> To refer to a musical tradition means to consider the set of knowledge, prac-
> tices and musical repertoires of a society as a coherent and identifiable cultural
> field, to evoke their role and significance within their context, historical
> development or stages of evolution, noting marked mutations, significant
> events and major influences.[6]

The relevance of the music of the seventeenth century to later traditional music and its imprint varies considerably within each of these fields. As discussed in more detail below, apart from the vague notion of 'ancientness' the seventeenth century is mainly absent from the conceptualization of traditional music, whereas, somewhat paradoxically, there are items from that repertoire which have filtered down through to the present day. So, while a lineage is perceptible, arguably even more so are the discontinuities, although not to the extent

---

4 David Atkinson, 'Revival: genuine or spurious?', in Ian Russell & David Atkinson (eds), *Folk song: tradition, revival and re-creation* (Aberdeen, 2004), p. 148. **5** Na Píobairí Uilleann, 'Submission to the joint committee on heritage and the Irish language on the traditional music of Ireland', *Ceol na hÉireann*, 3 (2001), 108–9. **6** Aubert, *The music of the other*, p. 16.

suggested by Diarmuid Ó Giolláin who argues that 'the unprecedented losses of the modern age have called the whole notion of tradition into question. The loss of cultural continuity has involved the loss of the shared past which is a foundation of identity'.[7]

Despite this reservation, an overview of seventeenth-century culture in Ireland reveals 'the beginning of the decay of all native learned traditions and ... a slower decline of the Irish language and of popular Gaelic traditions'.[8] Connolly dates the transformation in popular culture to 1650, saying that

> in the broadest sense these developments reflected the general European processes of 'modernization' associated with the expansion and transformations of capitalism, of centralized legal and religious administrations, of education and literacy, and, perhaps especially, of the growing hegemony of the bourgeoisie.[9]

A more specific reason for change, at least in the domain of élite Gaelic culture, was the disappearance due to colonialization of the patronage which underpinned the bardic system.[10] Modernization also occurred as part of the colonial process itself and for centuries after would be equated with Anglicization and perceived as a damaging imposition from without.[11] These twin dynamics, the final decline of a pre-modern, Gaelic culture, and its attendant modernization, affected (to varying degrees and at different rates) the broad spectrum of music in Ireland. To balance the portrayal of the seventeenth century as a period of foreclosure, it needs also to be identified as an originating moment for traditional music.[12] This is especially important as this century marks the beginning of a long process of assimilation of elements from the wider European musical culture into traditional music.[13] To view this in terms of an embracing of the other may be an overstatement, but certainly one of the key traits of the tradition has been the ability of musicians to draw from the musical others that they encounter and to successfully integrate this into their music.

In a different sense, what emerges in this chapter is that the music of the seventeenth century can be thought of as a temporal other; as Britta Sweers describes it, this is 'the other of the past' or the 'historical other', where the 'marker of otherness' is that of 'temporal differentiation' or distance.[14] The following overview of the musical practices and materialities of Gaelic

7 Diarmuid Ó Giolláin, *Locating Irish folklore: tradition, modernity, identity* (Cork, 2000), p. 17. **8** Ibid., p. 15. **9** James S. Connolly, 'Introduction', in Connolly & Miller (eds), *Irish popular culture*, p. xii. **10** See for example Pádraigín Ní Uallacháin, *A hidden Ulster* (Dublin, 2006), p. 19; Boydell, 'Music before 1700', pp 542–67. **11** Joe Cleary, 'Introduction: Ireland and modernity', in Joe Cleary & Claire Connolly (eds), *The Cambridge companion to modern Irish culture* (Cambridge, 2005), p. 3. **12** The formulation 'originating moment' is from Middleton, 'The popular music intertext', in Michael Talbot (ed.), *The musical work: reality or invention?* (Liverpool, 2000), p. 83. **13** Frank Harrison, 'Tradition and acculturation: a view of some musical processes', in Jerald C. Graue (ed.), *Essays on music for Charles Warren Fox* (Rochester, NY, 1979), p. 120. **14** Sweers, 'Bach in a Venda mirror', pp 181–3.

seventeenth-century Ireland aims to develop this idea of the 'historical other', while at the same time identifying those originating moments which left a lasting imprint on traditional music. This is contrasted with the relative absence of the seventeenth century in the conceptualization of traditional music which reveals that, as Caroline Bithell has noted, 'musical practices in the present are shaped not only by past experience but also by ideas, feelings and beliefs about the past'.[15] So, although traditional music draws on the totality of its past, 'what is remembered about the past is the outcome of a selective process that takes place in the present, reshaping the past in terms of present concerns'.[16] On a more fundamental level, the study of seventeenth-century Ireland is compromised by a lack of source material and by the representation of Ireland and Irish culture as an other. Thus, to an even greater extent than applies to the succeeding centuries, the musical culture of the period can only be accessed through highly mediated and translated forms: through print collections, unsympathetic commentators writing from the position of encountering the other, or performers.[17] In other words, what we hear in today's tradition is the music of the seventeenth century refracted through the totality of the transmission, change and development that has occurred since that time. The final section of this chapter explores these 'ways in which echoes and legacies from the past can still be heard in the present'.[18]

PRACTICES AND CONTEXTS

The transformations in Ireland during the course of the seventeenth century resulted in a relative strengthening of vernacular culture at the expense of that associated with the poets. The stratification of Gaelic society began to dissolve and was replaced by a new stratification based upon colonial and religious foundations. The consequences of the loss of typical performance contexts for the harpers are well documented, even though up to the eighteenth century they attempted to maintain some vestige of their status and that of their patrons.[19] The re-ordering of Gaelic culture from this time can also be seen in the attempts of the harpers to accommodate their new audiences through their later embracing of the music of the Italian Baroque.[20] They also extended their audience downwards, so to speak, towards the peasant classes in order to compensate for the declining

15 Caroline Bithell, 'The past in music: introduction', *EF*, 15:1 (2006), 3–16 at 4.   **16** Suzel Ana Reily, 'Remembering the baroque era: historical consciousness, local identity and the holy week celebrations in a former mining town in Brazil', *EF*, 15:1 (2006), 39–62 at 41.   **17** Fletcher, *Drama, performance*, p. 60; Boydell, 'Music before 1700', pp 547–8; Joep Leerssen, *Mere Irish and fíor-Ghael: studies in the idea of Irish nationality, its development and literary expression prior to the nineteenth century* (Cork, 1996), pp 50–61.   **18** Bithell, 'The past in music: introduction', 4.   **19** See for example the descriptions of harpers in Campbell, 'An account'; Arthur O'Neill, 'The memoirs of Arthur O'Neill', in O'Sullivan, *Carolan* (2nd ed. 2001), p. 316; Edward Bunting, *The ancient music of Ireland* (Dublin, 1840), p. 4.   **20** See Joseph C. Walker, *Historical memoirs of the Irish bards* (Dublin, 1786), p. 326; O'Sullivan, *Carolan* (2nd ed. 2001), pp 88–90; Bunting, *The ancient music of Ireland*, pp 9, 71; O'Neill, 'The memoirs of Arthur O'Neill', pp 319, 331.

interest in their music among the élite.[21] That this may have begun in the seventeenth century is indicated in John Dunton's letters which describe how, after a wedding 'we had a bagpiper and a blind harper that dinned us with their music to which there was perpetual dancing'.[22] This reference collates two constants of vernacular music in Ireland: the presence of dancing, and the location of music and dance within a social event or gathering. Termed 'traditional performance contexts' by Timothy Rice, these were common throughout almost all of Europe and in general terms remained reasonably stable during the following two centuries.[23] Evidence from the seventeenth century points to the importance of music within life-cycle rituals: Dunton mentions music in the context of a wedding and a baptism, and music was also an essential part of death and burial rituals with the practice of keening a focal point within these ceremonies.[24] Wakes also included music and dance of a more boisterous nature, and the church's role in the modernization of Irish society is evident in their condemnation of what was perceived to be uncivilized and premodern: the proclamations of synods issued in the seventeenth century censured the performance of 'obscene songs and suggestive games', 'improper songs and gesticulations … which would even be unlawful in festive rejoicings', and prescribed excommunication for those 'indulging in such musical merriment, just as it was for those indulging in the provision or consumption of *poitín*'.[25] Thomas Dineley, an English gentleman travelling in Ireland in 1681, described how the participants at a wake 'revel and dance the night throughout, make love and matches', a practice that was also criticized by the church.[26] Despite the denunciations of the Catholic church, music and dance persisted as vital components of the wake until the early twentieth century. Indeed, within the traditional music community the practice of playing music over the coffin at the wake is still found.[27] Calendrical rituals formed another important context for music and dance, of which the most important were the pattern and similar May day celebrations. The poets Aogán Ó

---

21 For examples see Bunting, *The ancient music of Ireland*, p. 82; O'Neill, 'The memoirs of Arthur O'Neill', p. 315.   **22** 'John Dunton's letters: letter no. 4: Co. Kildare; a wedding', quoted in MacLysaght, *Irish life*, p. 359.   **23** Timothy Rice, 'Traditional performance contexts', in Timothy Rice, James Porter, & Chris Goertzen (eds), *The Garland encyclopedia of world music*, viii: *Europe* (New York, 2000), p. 139. Lillis Ó Laoire, 'Irish music', in Cleary & Connolly (eds), *Cambridge companion*, p. 272.   **24** See Clodagh Tait, *Death, burial and commemoration in Ireland, 1550–1650* (New York, 2002), pp. 35–6; Ní Uallacháin, *A hidden Ulster*, pp 141–7; Breandán Ó Madagáin, *Caointe agus seancheolta eile* (Indreabhán, 2005), pp 81–9; Ó Súilleabháin, *Irish wake amusements* (Cork, 1976), pp 130–45; Patricia Lysaght, '*Caoineadh os cionn coirp*: the lament for the dead in Ireland', *Folklore*, 108:1 (1997), 65–82.   **25** Synod of Armagh (1614), quoted in Gearóid Ó Crualaoich, 'The "merry wake"', in Connolly & Miller (eds), *Irish popular culture*, p. 174; synodol statutes of Bishop David Rothe, Armagh (1618), quoted in Fletcher, *Sources*, pp 432, 584; Synod of Tuam (1660), quoted in Ó Crualaoich, 'The "merry wake"', p. 175.   **26** Thomas Dineley, *Observations in a voyage through the kingdom of Ireland*, ed. E.P. Shirley (Dublin, 1870), pp 21–2, quoted in Patricia Lysaght, 'Hospitality at wakes and funerals in Ireland from the seventeenth to the nineteenth century: some evidence from the written record', *Folklore*, 114:3 (2003), 406; Synod of Meath (1686), quoted in Lysaght, 'Hospitality at wakes and funerals', 406.   **27** Tait, *Death, burial and commemoration*, p. 34; Peter Woods & Christy McNamara, *The living note: the heartbeat of Irish music* (Dublin, 1996), p. 58.

Raithille and Dáibhí Ó Bruadair described the simultaneous performance of music and dance at such celebrations, and consequently it has been suggested that the traditions had their origin in the medieval *carole*.[28] A much less favourable description by Henry Piers describes the conclusion to a pilgrimage in Westmeath, when the participants

> return to a certain green spot of ground and here fall to dancing and carousing; for ale sellers in great numbers on these days have their booths as in a fair and to be sure the bagpipes fail not to pay their attendance. Thus in lewd and obscene dances with excess of drinking the day of their devotion is ended.[29]

Pattern customs, like those of the wake, were disapproved of by the church which forbade 'dancing, flute-playing, bands of music, riotous revels and other abuses in visiting wells and other holy places'.[30] The campaign against these calendrical rituals continued but was ineffectual. The pattern and May traditions survived until at least the end of the nineteenth century and in some places past this.[31]

Music and dancing featured more generally as a form of non-seasonal recreation, as evidenced by the description of Richard Head quoted below and, for example, in the fascinating portrayal by George Creichton, who related that Fingallian refugees in Virginia, Co. Cavan were 'A sort of profane wretches, after they had chopped up their Mass in the morning, they spent all their time in playing at tennis [and] in drinking, piping and dancing'.[32] It has been suggested that later traditional dances maintained many of the formations of their precursors, most of which did not survive into the eighteenth and nineteenth centuries; these dances which disappeared might be described as pre-modern (for example the sword dance and the withy dance).[33] The country dance was already current in Ireland by the early seventeenth century, as described by Fynes Moryson and others. Contemporary accounts name 'Balrothery' and 'The whip of Dunboyne' as examples, but no tunes have survived for these.[34] 'Trenchmore'

---

28 Ní Uallacháin, *A hidden Ulster*, pp 103–4; see also Breandán Breathnach, *Dancing in Ireland* (Miltown Malbay, 1983), pp 10–11.   **29** Sir Henry Piers, *IRL-Dtc*, MS I. I.2, p. 306, quoted in MacLysaght, *Irish life*, p. 164.   **30** *Tibicines* is translated by Danaher as flute players but probably is a reference to the bagpipes. Synod of Tuam (1660), quoted in Kevin Danaher, *The year in Ireland* (Cork, 1972), p 181; see also Diarmuid Ó Giolláin, 'The pattern', in Connolly & Miller (eds), *Irish popular culture*, p. 214.   **31** See for example Mary Friel, *Dancing as a social pastime in the south-east of Ireland, 1800–1897* (Dublin, 2004), pp 28–31; Ní Uallacháin, *A hidden Ulster*, p. 99; Helen Brennan, *The story of Irish dance* (Dingle, 1999), p. 116.   **32** Deposition of George Creichton, 15 Apr. 1643 (*IRL-Dtc*, MS 833, fos. 236–7), in John T. Gilbert (ed.), *A contemporary history of affairs in Ireland from A.D. 1641 to 1652*, i (Dublin, 1879), part 2, p. 542, cited after Maighréad Ní Mhurchadha, *Fingal, 1603–60: contending neighbours in north Dublin* (Dublin, 2005), p. 140.   **33** Brennan, *The story of Irish dance*, p. 89; for contemporary descriptions of dances see Fletcher, *Sources*, pp 187–8, 191, 214. The sword dance may have disappeared along with the kerne, with whom it was associated: Donnelly, *Early history*, p. 24.   **34** Fletcher, *Sources*, p. 191; see also Breathnach, *Dancing in Ireland*, pp 14–16. Both dances are named in 'Purgatorium Hibernicum: or, the sixt booke of Virgills Aeneis; travestie burlesque a la mode de Fingaule, c.1670', quoted in Mhurchadha, *Fingal, 1603–60*, p. 159; Graham Kew, *The Irish sections of Fynes Moryson's unpublished itinerary* (Dublin, 1998), p. 112. 'The whip of Dunboyne' is additionally named in Henry Burnell, *Landgartha: a*

was also popular from the sixteenth century onwards both in Ireland and Britain, occurring in several English collections of country dances.[35] In Seán Donnelly's estimation

> there would have been nothing particularly Irish, in the sense of Gaelic, about the dance; along with the dances found in the Pale, it is more likely to have been one of the old types that survived in Ireland after dying out elsewhere.[36]

In general, there is no agreement as to whether the country dance had a particularly Irish form or was practiced in Gaelic society at this time.[37] Helen Brennan suggests that 'Rinnce treasach le malartaibh ceolta' ('The dance in ranks with change of tempo') may indicate that it was common among the native Irish by the seventeenth century.[38] Another possible indicator is seen in a long description of music and dancing in the *Purgatorium Hibernicum*:

> There was Mulrony with his trump too
> And Gillegelagh his brother plump too
> And old Tadhg dall and Hugh O'Darcy
> Did sing all weathers at the clarsy,
> The Irish harp, whose airy mettle
> Sounds like the patching of the kettle.
> Mageen, yea, and be he did play
> Whip of Dunboyne and Irish Hay
> Skipping of Gort, Tripping of Swords
> Frisk of Baldoyle, best he affords,
> And for variety cronaans
> Ports and portrinkas and strinkaans
> Oraans and conies and gratulations.[39]

Although it may be reading too much into this poetic description, there does appear to be a clear separation made between the country dance tunes and Gaelic music, possibly revealing that the author considered these to be different types of music, albeit coexisting within a single performance space. That they existed together illustrates how the different vernacular musical cultures on the island had begun to coalesce and emphasizes the importance of assimilation as a foundational process of Irish traditional music. Furthermore, the country dance certainly had penetrated all levels of Irish society by the eighteenth century and

---

tragie-comedy (Dublin, 1641), quoted in Maighréad Ní Mhurchadha, *Fingal, 1603–60*, p. 160. **35** See Fleischmann, *Sources*, i, pp 2ff **36** Seán Donnelly, 'Trenchmore: an Irish dance in Tudor and Stuart England?', *The Dance Journal*, http://www.setdance.com/ journal/trenchmore.html, accessed 1 July 2007. **37** Brennan, *The story of Irish dance*, pp 16–17; Breathnach, *Dancing in Ireland*, pp 14–15. **38** Domhnall Garbh Ó Súilleabháin, 'Caoineadh' (1669), cited after Brennan, *The story of Irish dance*, p. 17. **39** 'Purgatorium Hibernicum', cited after Ní Mhurchadha, *Fingal, 1603–60*, p. 160.

survived in modified forms up to the late nineteenth century.[40] The 'Haymaker's Jig', ultimately repopularized by the Gaelic League, is in the longways form of a country dance, and in Kerry in the 1800s the dance 'An Country Deireanach' was common at crossroads dances.[41] An additional antecedent for céilí dances may have been the *Rinnce Fada* ('The Long Dance'), a ceremonial dance which was more closely associated with 'occasions of public rejoicing and merriment' and which survived into the nineteenth century.[42] An earlier dance, the hey or hay, dates back at least to the sixteenth century and is thought by some to be related to the reel, but it was not maintained within later musical traditions.[43]

It is evident then that a certain degree of continuity was preserved in terms of the contexts in which music and dancing took place in the seventeenth century, even if these were eventually to disappear in the early twentieth century to be succeeded by a plethora of new spaces for music. These spaces are important in that they facilitate a bringing-together of the traditional music community. Perhaps this indicates a fundamental continuity in the importance of music in creating a traditional music community,[44] and more generally as a marker of social gatherings. On the other hand, the dances themselves disappeared or became transformed over time, blending with or being replaced by newer assimilations.

INSTRUMENTS AND MUSICIANS

The seventeenth century was unquestionably a transitional period for the established instrumentarium of Irish music. This was due to the erosion of the functions of instruments and of musicians within Irish society, new arrivals from the mainstream European tradition, and the disappearance of audiences and contexts. The division between a pre-modern and a modern Ireland is markedly noticeable here, as none of the established instruments associated with the Gaelic élite would have a prolonged existence, and the harp only endured (for about a century more) through a limited adaptation to these changes. The *tiompán*, a stringed instrument and the other court instrument of the time, disappeared within the century. The last reference to it occurs in a seventeenth-century poem which illustrates the general erasure of the musical culture of the Gaelic élite: 'Big fires on the floors, the sound of tiompáns and harps, / Since these have gone and the feasts, Ireland is a desert'.[45]

---

40 See for example Breandán Breathnach, 'Dancing', in Hugh Shields (ed.), *Popular music in eighteenth-century Dublin* (Dublin, 1985), pp 32–5; Friel, *Dancing as a social pastime*, pp 7–9.   41 Brennan, *The story of Irish dance*, p. 93; Eibhlín Ní Murchú, *Ceol agus rinnce mo cheantair dúchais ó 1800–1880* (Baile an Fheirtéaraigh, 1990), p. 118, quoted in Brennan, *The story of Irish dance*, p. 117.   42 Breathnach, *Dancing in Ireland*, pp 22, 10; see also Brennan, *The story of Irish dance*, p. 19.   43 Breathnach, *Dancing in Ireland*, pp 12–13; Seán Donnelly, 'Trenchmore'; Boydell, 'Music before 1700', p. 545; Brennan, *The story of Irish dance*, pp 21, 94.   44 Helen O'Shea, 'Getting to the heart of the music: idealizing musical community and Irish traditional music sessions', *Journal of the Society for Musicology in Ireland*, 2 (2006–7), 3. www.ucc.ie/JSMI, accessed 28 Apr. 2007.   45 From the satirical poem 'Do rinneas mo thiomna, a Shéamais' ('Séamas, I made my will') by Thomas Dease, a Catholic bishop of Meath

The bagpipe, or warpipes, was also associated with aristocratic Ireland and, like the harp and tiompán, its musicians were professional.[46] Within the stratified structure of Gaelic society they had a much lower status than the court musicians, to the extent that the bagpipe was almost entirely ignored by the bardic poets.[47] The inclusion of twenty-six pipers in the fiants of Elizabeth I and James I between 1601 and 1605 attests to the prevalence of the instrument and to its primary role within a military context.[48] In particular it was considered an instrument of the kerne and galloglass, and its significance can be inferred from its positioning at the forefront of the soldiers and officers where it was used to signal movements to the troops.[49] Outside a military context it appears to have been played at funerals from the late sixteenth century, and in the seventeenth century its use as an instrument to accompany dancing appears to have been common.[50] John Dunton's letters include several descriptions of the bagpipes in this role, suggesting that the instrument had a currency among the general populace as well as within élite society:

In some towns these trees [ash] are old and very great, and hither all the people resort with a piper on Sundays or Holydays in the afternoon, where the young folks dance till the cows come home ... If in the dance the woman be tired, the man throws her to the piper, whose fee is half a penny, and the man if tired is served after the same manner.[51]

According to Donnelly, 'the píb mhór [warpipes] is last heard of to any great extent in the wars of 1689–90' and it appears to have been superseded by the union (uilleann) pipes early in the eighteenth century, when both instruments co-existed for a short period.[52] Some repertoire associated with the instrument is still current within traditional music, but the modern bagpipe (originally referred to as the Brian Ború bagpipes) is a peripheral instrument within the tradition. As an invention of the Gaelic revival modelled on the Highland and Scottish pipes it has only an imagined continuity with the older instrument.[53]

Outside élite culture, probably the only instrument that would have been available to the peasantry was the trump or Jew's harp. Archaeological evidence suggests it was well-established and common in the seventeenth century, but as a 'folk instrument' it was mostly ignored by writers as not meriting attention.

(1622–50), member of the Confederation of Kilkenny, and famous also, according to O'Curry, as a tiompán player and song-writer, to cite Ann Buckley, 'What was the tiompán? A problem in ethnohistorical organology: evidence in Irish literature', *Jahrbuch für Musikalische Volks- und Völkerkunde,* 9 (1978), 83. See also Carolan, 'O'Sullivan Beare', 56. **46** Seán Donnelly's use of the term 'warpipes' derives from the Irish *cuisleanna catha* (battle pipes): Donnelly, *Early history*, pp 1, 21. **47** Donnelly, 'Warpipes', iv, 55. **48** The majority were from Munster or Leinster, but pipers from Connacht and Ulster are also mentioned; see Fletcher, *Sources*, passim. **49** Donnelly, *Early history*, pp 13, 19. **50** Ibid., p. 23; Donnelly, 'The warpipes in Ireland, iv', 55. **51** John Dunton's letters: letter no. 3: a baptism, a wake and a funeral', cited after MacLysaght, *Irish life*, pp 354–5. **52** Seán Donnelly, 'Some glimpses of pipers in diaries and memoirs 1700–1998', *The Pipers' Review,* 24:4 (2005), 14. **53** Wilbert Garvin, 'Bagpipe', in Fintan Vallely (ed.), *The companion to Irish traditional music* (Cork, 1999), p. 15.

There is no information about what type of music might have been played on it.[54] Again, Dunton's letters provide evidence for the instrument's use in a typical domestic celebration: 'After the ceremony of baptism was over we had four persons who fell to play on their Jews Trumps, each playing on two at once.'[55] Apart from the fiddle, it is the only seventeenth-century instrument which remained a constant in Irish musical life until the late nineteenth century. However, the surge of new instruments available to musicians from then has led to its almost complete obsolescence.[56]

The harp, *tiompán*, bagpipe and trump can safely be grouped together as pre-modern instruments whose existence in current traditional music is either symbolic, peripheral, or as (re)invented instruments.[57] The opposite is the case with the fiddle, almost certainly the earliest of current traditional instruments, whose integration began in the seventeenth century. It probably appeared initially among the English in Ireland, almost certainly within urban contexts, there being records of payments to fiddlers in both Dublin (1613) and Kilkenny (1630) and also a literary reference to 'town-fiddlers' in 1640.[58] The fiddle had penetrated into Gaelic Ireland by the late seventeenth century[59] and appeared to be widespread by 1674, as attested in the commonly-quoted description by Richard Head:

Their Sunday is the most leisure day they have, on which they use all manner of sport; in every field a fiddle and the lasses footing it till they are all of a foam, and grow infinitely proud with the blear eye of affection her sweetheart casts on her feet as she dances to a tune, or no tune, played on an instrument that makes a worse noise than a key upon a gridiron.[60]

One important structure of traditional music practices which appears to have been established in this century is that the playing of music for dancing was the preserve of what Reg Hall calls artisan musicians. These were essentially professional in that their presence at social gatherings depended on their receiving payments from participants: they travelled around particular regions and localities playing at fairs, at patterns, and for outdoor dances. This system

54 Ann Buckley, 'A note on the history and archaeology of Jew's harps in Ireland', *North Munster Antiquarian Journal*, 25 (1983), 31. 55 'John Dunton's letters: letter no. 3', p. 344. 56 Reg Hall, 'Irish music and dance in London, 1890–1970: a socio-cultural history' (PhD, University of Sussex, 1994), pp 30–1; Anthony McCann, 'Jew's harp', in Vallely (ed.), *Companion*, p. 200. 57 The *tiompán* is almost wholly absent from the modern tradition; Derek Bell's appropriation of the name for the hammer dulcimer or cimbalom was entirely fictitious. See Christie M. Burns, 'Out of obscurity: discovering the dulcimer in Ireland' (Diss., UCC, 2002), p. 14 (See http://www.corkdulcimerfest.org/Dulcimer_Thesis.pdf. Accessed 17 June 2006); The Chieftains, *The Chieftains 5* (LP, Claddagh CC 16, 1975). 58 Francis Rogers, 'Journal of Francis Rogers', in *Three sea journals of Stuart times*, p. 196, quoted in MacLysaght, *Irish life*, p. 226; Fletcher, *Sources*, pp 316, 417 (these references are earlier than are cited in Ríonach Uí Ógáin, 'Traditional music and Irish cultural history', in *IMS 3*, p. 84); Burnell, *Landgartha*, pp 19, 34 quoted in Ní Mhurchadha, 159. 59 'Is amhlaidh mar tá sin – ní fearr liomsa gearán is caoine', Ag gabháil romham 'un a' teampaill ná cláirseach, fidil is píob'; Cathal Buí Mac Giolla Ghunna, 'Na briathra beacht', quoted in Ní Uallacháin, *A hidden Ulster*, pp 55–6. 60 Richard Head, *The western wonder* (London, 1674), p. 37.

faded with the advent of large-scale participation in traditional music in the late nineteenth century.[61]

CONSTRUCTING TRADITION

Definitions and conceptualizations of Irish traditional music emphasize the importance of certain phases of its past. This can be examined by first looking in more detail at the complexities of the notion of tradition, and then focusing on how traditional music has been imagined and represented. Bridging the gap between modern concepts of Irish traditional music and the music of the seventeenth century is not simple: no clear thread connects that liminal musical culture to the commodified, classicized, and fragmented tradition of today, which itself resists easy classification. Indeed, recent conceptualizations of traditional music in neologistic terms such as metatrad, poptrad and newtrad suggest a theorization of Irish traditional music which is predominantly centred on the present.[62]

A preoccupation with the new and the current is not surprising as one of the recurring tropes in the theorization of tradition is its currency and how its presentness is informed by a recourse to its past. This is clear in Henry Glassie's description of tradition as 'a continuous process situated in the nothingness of the present'. David Atkinson echoes this in his comments that the canon of folk or traditional music 'is *perceived* as reaching from the present, more or less continuously, back into the past'.[63] The interrelationship between past and present is central to the interpretation of tradition as a construct, something formed through selection, or as an invention.[64] It is important, therefore, in discussing the relevance of the seventeenth century to traditional music (or its condition as a historical resource for traditional music) to begin from a standpoint that recognizes the ongoing construction of the tradition, and to interrogate how its construction and conceptualization in the more scholarly domain has privileged, through the process of selection, a particular temporal space as having a special symbolic value. Equally important in the construction of a concept of Irish traditional music has been its identification with a distinct social group or geographical space. This has its roots in Herder's formulation of 'folk song', whereby the term 'folk' became synonymous with the rural lower classes, so that traditional music (or folk music) began to be conceived as that practiced, maintained and transmitted within the confines of that specific social group.[65] By

---

61 Hall, 'Irish music and dance', pp 29, 34–7.   **62** Fintan Vallely, 'Tiger Ireland, turd-sniffers and metatrad', *Journal of Music in Ireland*, 7:2 (2007), 13; Colin Hamilton, 'The role of commercial recordings in the development of Irish traditional music, 1899–1993' (PhD, UL, 1996), pp 214–15.   **63** Henry Glassie, 'Tradition', *JAF,* 108:430 (1995), 395; Atkinson, 'Revival: genuine or spurious', p. 148. **64** Glassie, 'Tradition', 399 (for a critique see Barry McDonald, 'Tradition as personal relationship', *JAF,* 110:435 (1997), 47–67); Zofia Lissa, 'Prolegomena to the theory of musical tradition', *International Review of Music Aesthetics and Sociology,* 1:1 (1970), 36–7; Atkinson, 'Revival: genuine or spurious?', pp 147–9; Eric Hobsbawm, 'Introduction: inventing traditions', in Eric Hobsbawm & Terence Ranger (eds), *The invention of tradition* (Cambridge, 1983), pp 1–14.   **65** Ó Giolláin, *Locating Irish folklore,*

extension, Irish traditional music has consistently been defined in homological terms where the 'music reflects or enunciates underlying social relations and structures'.[66] In general, a recourse to homology produces reductionist and static views of the relationship between Irish traditional music and society. However, it must be stressed that much of the commentary and discourse on the tradition has moved away from such a position, as evidenced by Helen O'Shea's study of the session and Colin Hamilton's critique of the 'monolith theory' of Irish traditional music.[67]

Drawing together these disparate strands, what is argued here is that in a discourse which forwards particular constructions of what Irish traditional music is, a selectivity operates which foregrounds a particular interpretation of the past both in terms of its temporal and socio-cultural dimensions. Scott Reiss has remarked on how this occurs as a response to change, arguing that a tradition can be thought of as invented 'when one point in the continuum is idealized' and the term traditional becomes restricted to that form.[68] However, his subsequent argument that the 'link to the past is activated by reference to "ancient Irish music", an authenticating trope often used to validate a claim of heritage', skims over the fact that the term 'ancient music' would rarely be used in current constructions of the tradition. Instead, as will be seen, concepts of Irish traditional music are more usually constructed with reference to much later (idealized) periods in this continuum, most commonly the late nineteenth and early twentieth century. Thinking of tradition, then, as an ongoing dialogue between the present and the past, what emerges from the following overview is the relative silence of the seventeenth century in this exchange. To pose the question succinctly: what presence has the music of the seventeenth century had in the definition and theorization of Irish traditional music?

The conceptualization of an Irish traditional music which emanated from the folk or peasantry might be said to have originated with George Petrie and P.W. Joyce, even if they did not advance this theory explicitly. Although Petrie's is a transitional collection related to Bunting's antiquarian approach by its designation as 'ancient music', the majority of his music was collected from the singing and playing of the peasantry.[69] Similarly, the collections of Petrie's collaborator and successor P.W. Joyce were also compiled from 'the people', whose music was associated with their 'pastimes, occupations, and daily life'.[70] The identification

p. 23; Dan Ben-Amos, 'The seven strands of tradition: varieties in its meaning in American folklore studies', *JAF*, 21 (1984), 105.   **66** Georgina Born, 'Introduction: On difference, representation, and appropriation in music: iv. Music and the representation/articulation of sociocultural identities', in Georgina Born & David Hesmondhalgh (eds), *Western music and its others: difference, representation, and appropriation in music* (Berkeley, 2000), pp 31–7.   **67** O'Shea, 'Getting to the heart of the music'; Hammy Hamilton, 'Innovation, conservatism, and the aesthetics of Irish traditional music', in Fintan Vallely et al. (eds), *Crosbhealach an cheoil, 1996, the crossroads conference: tradition and change in Irish traditional music* (Dublin, 1999), p. 83.   **68** Scott Reiss, 'Tradition and imaginary: Irish traditional music and the Celtic phenomenon', in Martin Stokes & Philip V. Bohlman (eds), *Celtic modern: music at the global fringe* (Lanham, MD, 2003), p. 153.   **69** See Aloys Fleischmann, 'Aspects of George Petrie: iv. Petrie's contribution to Irish music', *Proceedings of the Royal Irish Academy*, Section C, 72:9 (1972), 203.   **70** P.W. Joyce, *Old Irish folk music and songs* (Dublin, 1909), p. vii.

of Irish music with an innocent, rural, and Gaelic culture is more overt in Francis O'Neill's musings on folk music. Describing it as 'a melodious poetic expression of the sentiments and feelings of the people', he adds that it 'has been preserved from generation to generation among the peasantry', thereby advancing the notion of a communal music, one which is a reflection of a particular socio-cultural group with which it is explicitly identified.[71] The broad-ranging, but scattershot, survey of the history of Irish music in *Irish minstrels and musicians* touches on the seventeenth century in places, but predominantly O'Neill's is a representation of a musical tradition grounded in a constituency of nineteenth- and twentieth-century musicians. Following O'Neill's lead Donal O'Sullivan described the music as being 'an emanation of the people: the result, no doubt, of a corporate urge for self-expression'; yet he cast doubt on his predecessors' use of the term ancient, and Breathnach's definition similarly terms it as 'the product of the folk' and 'the property of the community'.[72]

More modern commentary maintains this mode of construction and is in fact more explicit in identifying particular social, geographic, and temporal roots for the modern tradition. The importance of rural Ireland, its land and landscape, to the tradition and to the identity of musicians is repeatedly emphasized in discourse; and it has been argued that the root of the tradition lies 'in the music of the peasant, tied to the land itself'.[73] Vallely confirms the significance of rurality to the identity of the music, but more importantly, he identifies the core of the tradition as being 'the soundscape of the nineteenth century and beyond'; essentially, when he describes traditional music as being 'the retrieval and re-presentation of Ireland's immortal tonic soul' he locates its essence in the recent past.[74] Both rurality and a specific time frame are considered essential by Reg Hall to the authenticity of the tradition: his contention is that there was a 'heyday' between 1850 and 1950 when 'traditional music-making belonged almost exclusively to the rural working population' and produced 'a great flowering of traditional music-making'.[75] This period is also central to Séamus Tansey's construction of a traditional music heritage as, despite his comment that the music was 'handed down to us by our ancient forefathers', the musicians he identifies with are all from the late nineteenth to early twentieth century.[76] Seán Corcoran posits a similar framework, describing the music as being 'a reflection … of the world view of a specific social class', that which is situated in a rural community, belonging to the recent past.[77] A more radical reading has been forwarded by Martin Dowling who is unequivocal in his depiction of the tradition

71 Francis O'Neill, *Irish minstrels and musicians* (Chicago, 1913; facs. repr. Darby, PA, 1973), pp 100–2. **72** Donal O'Sullivan, *Irish folk music and song* (Dublin, 1961), pp 7–8; Breandán Breathnach, *Folk music and dances of Ireland* (Cork, 1971), pp 1–2. **73** Sally Sommers Smith, 'Landscape and memory in Irish traditional music', *New Hibernia Review,* 1:1 (1998), 134–5. **74** Fintan Vallely, 'Authenticity to classicization: the course of revival in Irish traditional music', *Irish Review,* 33 (2005), 53, 55. **75** Reg Hall, 'Heydays are short lived: change in music making practice in rural Ireland, 1850–1950', in Vallely et al., *Crosbhealach an cheoil,* p. 79. **76** Séamus Tansey, 'Irish traditional music – the melody of Ireland's soul: its evolution from the environment, land and people', in Vallely et al., *Crosbhealach an cheoil,* p. 213. **77** Seán Corcoran, 'What is traditional music?', in Peter McNamee (ed.), *Traditional music: whose music?*

as modern, claiming that 'traditional music is a modern phenomenon, born along with Irish music itself' and that it is not 'the survival of some ancient and timeless manifestation of the essence of Irishness or the Celtic spirit, but rather a modern pursuit that kept time with the dramatic and often violent modernization of Irish society in the late eighteenth and nineteenth centuries.'[78]

This (admittedly selective) group of writings reveals that traditional music is most commonly defined in relation to quite narrow temporal and geographical spaces. These definitions may not explicitly locate an originating moment for the tradition in these spaces, but they do idealize them to a certain extent, leaving the seventeenth century at the edge of Irish traditional music and reinforcing its condition as a temporal other. This is a justifiable and reasonable position given that so much of it derives from later periods and because of the discontinuities outlined above. On the other hand, the previous section does identify continuities between the seventeenth century and the following centuries. To return to Aubert's notion of a tradition being a product and a confluence of influences, the imprint of the musical tradition of the seventeenth century is perceivable in its later transformations, even if this imprint has significantly faded into the twentieth and twenty-first century.

THE SEVENTEENTH CENTURY AS SOURCE

A recurring trope in earlier commentaries on the repertoire accumulated over history which has been drawn on by traditional musicians is the overt (and often strident) attempt to establish the national identity of tunes. The archetypal figure here was W.H. Grattan Flood who devotes a significant portion of his writing on Irish music in the seventeenth century to what he perceived as the appropriation of Irish tunes by Scottish and English songwriters and publishers.[79] Flood's agenda befits the Gaelic Revival period in which this history was written, being a construction of tradition which served a nationalistic ideology. It is largely unimportant whether Flood was correct or not in his speculations; instead we must acknowledge that it is often impossible to be authoritative about the ultimate origin of a tune and, as already stated, one of the defining characteristics of Irish traditional music is the ease with which items of repertoire have been assimilated. The difficulty in asserting a tune's 'nationality' is further increased in the case of the seventeenth century because the only notated sources from the period itself are English and Scottish; these include lute books, virginal books, manuscripts, and various printed collections.[80] Several interrelated complications are identified here. It is not possible to determine whether a tune originated in Ireland and was transmitted to Britain prior to printing or travelled in the other direction. Stylistic criteria cannot be used to solve this problem as 'a tune transmitted from one country

(Belfast, 1992), p. 5.   **78** Martin Dowling, 'Rambling in the field of modern identity: some speculations on Irish traditional music', *Radharc: a journal of Irish and Irish-American studies*, 5–7 (2004–6), 124–5. **79** See for example Flood, *History*, pp 183–207.   **80** See Fleischmann, *Sources*, i, pp 1ff.

to another is liable to take on the characteristics of its new environment'.[81] More than this, though, to describe a tune as Irish means 'judging it by criteria derived from the idiom which crystallized in the eighteenth century', and those that appear to have some Irish connection 'are quite unlike those of the succeeding century, and too few tunes have as yet been assembled to allow new stylistic criteria to be established'.[82] Although an invaluable anthology, Aloys Fleischmann's *Sources* creates a potential additional difficulty by including material 'which has been introduced to demonstrate the sort of folk tune typical of a particular period in Scotland, England or Wales'.[83] As these are not clearly identified in the notes to the tunes it may appear to render it ineffective as a basis for investigating the repertoire of the seventeenth century. On the other hand, the inclusion of material from this wider field can also be read as a recognition of the diverse origins of the tunes which form part of the wider corpus of traditional music. To return to the notion of the construction of tradition, the repertoire of the seventeenth century is best considered as a source and is part of 'a canon of texts that provides a cultural identity for its practitioners largely as a consequence of its perceived continuity with the same texts and their practitioners in the past and/or in other places'.[84] This canon of texts is constantly changing so that, if we classify the seventeenth century as an originating period for a portion of this canon, there has been as much discontinuity as there has been continuity in the transmission and maintenance of these texts.

My contention here is that there are two categories of repertoire within the canon which can be related to the seventeenth century: tunes that are documented within the period itself, and those that are found in later sources but which are perceived to be either from or evocative of the period. Evidence exists to allow the first category to be classified as actual remnants from the seventeenth century (or earlier – the appearance of a notated representation of a tune only indicates its currency at a particular moment and does not preclude that tune from having a longer history within an oral tradition). What is important about this repertoire is that, in tracing its history using the *Sources*, it becomes evident that these tunes have mostly disappeared from the canon. Admittedly this is rather a brute force method, but it is useful in highlighting the discontinuity between what was deemed popular enough to have been recorded in this period and what was maintained by traditional musicians over the following centuries. About 200 tunes which were notated in the seventeenth century are included in the collection,[85] but few of these can be directly related to specific tunes which had a durable presence – tunes that were documented consistently by later collectors and/or are part of the contemporary canon of traditional music. The correspondences outlined in the following table are mostly drawn from those included in the *Sources*, but some additional relationships are posited here, loosely based upon James Cowdery's principles of outlining and recombining.[86]

81 Ibid., p. xviii.   **82** Ibid.   **83** Ibid., p. xvii.   **84** Atkinson, 'Revival: genuine or spurious?', p. 149. **85** An exact figure cannot be identified because of the approximate dating of some of the sources. I have limited the scope of this survey to instrumental music excluding harp tunes, which have received detailed attention elsewhere.   **86** James Cowdery, *The melodic tradition of Ireland* (London, 1990), pp 87–94.

No. in Sources	Title	Source	Later Titles
4	'Greene sleves'	Ballet lute book (c.1593–1603)	'Larry Grogan', 'Coppers and brass'[87]
13	'A daunce: grien greus ye rasses'	Straloch MS (1627–9)	'Green grow the rushes O'[88]
21	'Adew Dundee'	Skene MS (1630–3)	'Laccarue boys'[89]
36	'Sedauny, or Dargason'	Playford, *The English dancing master* (1651)	'The Irish washerwoman'[90]
37	'An old man is a bed full of bones'	Playford, *The English dancing master* (1651)	'The priest and his boots'[91]
42	'Trenchmore'	Playford, *The dancing master*, ii (1652)	'The Kilfenora jig', 'Is fearr paidir ná port', 'Mullowny's jigg', 'Malowney's wife'[92]
44	'The Irish rant'	Benson & Playford, *A booke of new lessons for the cithern and gittern* (1652)	'O'Sullivan's march'[93]
54	Untitled ['Highland laddie']	*Seventeen pieces for keyboard* (c.1663)	'The high-caulled cap'[94]
60	'A new dance or Maheney'	Playford, *The dancing master*, iii (1665)	'Con Cassidy's jig', 'The sit-in jig'[95]
61	'Washington's march'	Playford, *The dancing master*, iii (1665)	'Rory O Moore – King of Leix's March'[96]
81	'Green stockens'	Playford, *The dancing master*, v (1675)	'Cailleacha ó thuaidh'[97]
100	'The rummer'	Playford, *The dancing master*, vii (1686)	'The top of Cork road'[98]
101	'Miller's jigg'	Playford, *The dancing master*, vii (1686)	'Who'll come fight in the snow'[99]
112	'Cold and raw'	Playford, *The dancing master*, vii (1686)	'The barley grain'[1]
117	Duke of Bucclugh's tune	Playford, *Apollo's banquet* (1687)	'The white cockade'[2]
121	'A new Irish tune'	Playford, *The second part of musick's hand-maid* (1689)	'Lillibulero'[3]
125	'Roger the cavoleyr'	Atkinson MS (1694)	'Sir Roger', 'Sir Roger de Coverly'.[4]
142	'Weells me I gott ever shott on her'	Atkinson MS (1694)	'Fairly shut of her'.[5]
145	'Leshly's march'	Atkinson MS (1694)	'Leslie's march', 'Dirty James'[6]
152	'Galloway Tom'	Atkinson MS (1694)	'Galway Tom', 'The lark in the morning'[7]
157	'Over the mure to Maggie'	Leyden MS (c.1695)	'Come west along the road'[8]
174	'Mad Moll'	Playford, *The second part of the dancing master* (1696)	'Here we go up, up, up', 'Yellow legs'.[9]

87 John Walsh, *Caledonian country dances …* (London, 1737–40), ii, p. 23; 'Green Sleeves', P. W. Joyce, *Old Irish folk music and songs* (Dublin, 1909), p. 72; Breathnach, *Ceol rince na hÉireann*, i (Dublin, 1963), p. 4.   88 Michael Tubridy & Méabh Ní Lochlainn, *Irish traditional music* (Dublin, 1995), p. 12.   89 Francis O'Neill, *The dance music of Ireland* (Chicago, 1907), no. 239.   90 For a very close version see 'Jig', *The Petrie collection of the ancient music of Ireland*, p. 104.   91 O'Neill, *The dance music of Ireland*, no. 188.   92 Breandán Breathnach & Jackie Small, *Ceol rince na hÉireann*, 5 (Dublin, 1999), p. 3; S. and C. Thompson, *Thompson's compleat collection of 200 favourite country dances …* 4 vols (London, 1770–85), iv, p. 71; O'Neill, *The dance music of Ireland*, no. 11.   93 Breandán Breathnach, *Ceol rince na hÉireann*, 2 (Dublin, 1976), pp 9–10.   94 O'Neill, *The dance music of Ireland*, no. 1000.   95 Caoimhín Mac Aoidh & Róisín Harrigan, *Cairdeas na bhFidléirí: an ceol*, 3 (Donegal, 1996), p. 37.   96 Edward Bunting, *A general collection of the ancient music of Ireland* (London, 1809), p. 32.   97 C.V. Stanford, *The complete collection of Irish music as noted by George Petrie*, 3 vols (London, 1902–5), no. 1109. This is suggested in Fleischmann, *Sources* but the correspondence between the two seems to be minimal.   98 O'Neill, *The dance music of Ireland*, no. 244.   99 R.M. Levey, *The first collection of the dance music of Ireland* (London, 1858), no. 68.   1 Francis O'Neill, *O'Neill's music of Ireland* (Chicago, 1903), no. 100.   2 Ibid., no. 1803.   3 Ibid., no. 19.   4 Francis Roche, *Collection of Irish airs, marches & dance tunes*, 3 vols (Cork, 1927), ii, no. 295; Colette Moloney, *The Boss Murphy musical legacy: Irish music from the Churchtown area of North Cork* (Churchtown, 2003), p. 29.   5 O'Farrell's pocket companion for the Irish or union pipes … 4 vols (London, 1804), i, p. 49.   6 Bunting, *The ancient music of Ireland*, p. 50.   7 O'Neill, *O'Neill's music of Ireland*, no. 744.   8 O'Neill, *The dance music of Ireland*, no. 786.   9 Stanford, *The complete collection of Irish music*

My aim is not to tease out in full tune families nor analyze how later tunes and variants emerge from older models, but instead to draw attention to instances where there is a documented continuity from the seventeenth century. A few of these connections merit additional commentary, but it must be acknowledged that these are tentative suggestions and that, in making these associations, I am myself in a sense 'reconstructing tradition'. The earliest of the tunes is 'Greene sleves' which is almost certainly an antecedent of the common jig 'Coppers and brass'. This is elsewhere described as a descendant of 'Larry Grogan', a popular eighteenth-century tune,[10] but the parallels between the tunes suggest that both have a common origin in the seventeenth century. Another common jig with an antecedent in the seventeenth century is 'The Irish washerwoman', whose first part is comparable to the single-strain tune 'Sedauny, or Dargason'.[11] The tune of 'Trenchmore' is minimal enough to allow a comparison with dozens of tunes;[12] two later tunes which seem to be particularly closely related are 'Mullowny's wife' and 'Is fearr paidir ná port'. An admittedly more speculative connection proposed here is that between 'A new dance or Maheney' and 'The sit-in jig', but the higher parts of both tunes share the same contour. 'The rummer' is a good example of how elements are combined from old tunes to form new tunes: in this case, the final four bars correspond to 'The top of Cork road' but otherwise the tunes are different. I have omitted from the table some tunes which appear in later Irish collections but are distinguished as being not Irish. One borderline case is included, namely the tune 'Fairly shut of her' which was printed up to the nineteenth century but, as O'Neill comments, 'was not known to our traditional musicians'.[13] A number of the tunes have a historical relevance or have acquired one over time, an aspect of the music which is dealt with in more detail below. 'The Irish rant' is better known today as 'O'Sullivan's march' which appears to be named after the Donal Cam O'Sullivan Beare, the 'leader of that astonishing retreat in which with a great price on his head, he in January 1603 literally hewed his way from Glengariff, Co. Cork, into O'Rourke's country: an exploit which lives in the well-known Munster pipe-tune "O'Sullivan's march to Leitrim"'.[14] Breathnach does not make this association in his detailed treatment of the tune which may have been originally played on the bagpipes, a belief which persists among players today.[15] The later title of 'Washington's march' places the tune in the mid-seventeenth century, but it is doubtful whether this tune survived in the tradition after the eighteenth century as it was never published in the interim.[16] Its

music, no. 101; O'Neill, *O'Neill's music of Ireland*, no. 1130. **10** See Seán Donnelly, 'A Wexford gentleman piper: "famous Larry Grogan"', *Journal of the Wexford Historical Society*, 16 (1996–7), 58. **11** Breandán Breathnach, 'An cnuasacht iomlán den cheol damhsa' (Bailiúchán tasclainne ceoil, Dublin, 1977), jigs, card 1449; Samuel P. Bayard, *Dance to the fiddle, march to the fife: instrumental folk tunes in Pennsylvania* (Pennsylvania, 1982), pp 419–20. **12** Donnelly, 'Trenchmore'. **13** Francis O'Neill, *Waifs and strays of Gaelic melody* … (2nd ed. Chicago, 1922 [1924]), p. 97. **14** Standish Hayes O'Grady, *Catalogue of the Irish manuscripts in the British Museum*, 3 vols (London, 1926), i, p. 362; quoted in 'O'Sullivan's march', *An Píobaire*, 2:44 (1989), 8. **15** Breathnach, *Ceol rince na hÉireann*, ii, pp 9–10; Mick O'Brien, *May morning dew* (ACM CD 101, 1996). **16** Donal O'Sullivan, 'The Bunting collection of Irish folk music and songs: part v', *Journal of the Irish Folk Song Society*, 27 (1936), 22–3; a later

popularity today is more than likely due to its revival by Seán Ó Riada and Ceoltóirí Chualann in the 1970s.[17] Of tunes evocative of the later seventeenth century, 'Lillibulero' has been discussed elsewhere and 'Lesley's march', named after a general of the Scottish Rebel Army in 1640, was collected by Bunting as 'Dirty James', a reference to the behaviour of James II after the Battle of the Boyne.[18] Considering these tunes in totality, they form only a miniscule portion of the repertory and in general have been considerably transformed in their transmission.

The second category of tunes was identified above as those that are found in later sources (both printed and recorded) and which are perceived and projected in their discourse to be either from, or evocative of, the seventeenth century. The investigation of these involves a retrospective approach, a working backwards from a later source towards the earlier period. The music discussed here epitomizes the role traditional music plays in the construction, maintenance and performance of a shared, collective cultural memory.[19] In its every-day form, acts of remembrancing take place as part of the informal actuation of the tradition within which a social memory is maintained through performance, transmission, repetition, and their accompanying discourse.[20] This repertoire furnishes a representation of the seventeenth century 'constructed upon a grid of talismanic dates' and forms part of what Joep Leerssen terms 'community remembrancing', an unofficial and folkloristic history perpetuated by repetition and transmission and situated within oral tradition.[21] These tunes act as resonances of the seventeenth century and their performance 'reaffirms the past and keeps it alive'.[22] The word 'resonance' deliberately aims to express the tunes' ambiguous relationship with the seventeenth century – they commemorate events from the period but may not actually be from it. There is a disjuncture here between the music's documented history and the folk or social memories which it generates, where tunes are popularly perceived to date from a particular period or are persistently associated with a period or event despite there being no evidence to support this.[23] In some cases, there can be said to be an archaizing process at work here, where music is reconfigured to allude to more distant historical events or personalities so that the memory encapsulated in the music is in fact a construction of the present.[24]

Three periods in particular are commemorated in this music: the Nine Years War, Confederate Ireland and the Williamite Wars, and because the music reflects

version probably prompted by the tune's revival is in Dave Bulmer & Neil Sharpley, *Music from Ireland* (South Shields, 1974), ii, no. 81.   **17** Seán Ó Riada agus Ceoltóirí Chualann, *Ó Riada sa Gaiety* (Gael-Linn CEF 027, 1970), B3.   **18** Ó Buachalla, 'Lillibulero'; Donal O'Sullivan & Mícheál Ó Súilleabháin (eds), *Bunting's ancient music of Ireland* (Cork, 1983), pp 107–8.   **19** Kay Kaufman Shelemay, 'Music, memory and history', *EF*, 15:1 (2006), 17–37 at 32.   **20** Paul Connerton, *How societies remember* (Cambridge, 1989), p. 4.   **21** Ian McBride, 'Introduction: memory and national identity in modern Ireland', in Ian McBride (ed.), *History and memory in modern Ireland* (Cambridge, 2001), p. 2; Joep Leerssen, 'Monument and trauma: varieties of remembrance', in McBride (ed.), *History and memory*, p. 215.   **22** Bithell, 'The past in music: introduction', 4.   **23** See Shelemay, 'Music, memory and history', 18–19.   **24** See Bithell, 'The past in music: introduction', 5.

this tableau of violent struggle, marches and laments predominate in the repertoire. Often in these tunes the memorialization can be vague or disputed in the sources. A typical case is the tune 'O'Neill's cavalcade' or 'O'Neill's riding' which was first notated by Edward Bunting.[25] O'Sullivan's commentary sidesteps the identification of the O'Neill in question, but it is often associated with Hugh O'Neill and has been described as 'a tune which can be traced back to the 1600s and possibly one of the oldest piping tunes in existence'.[26] It is parsed in the *Sources*, though, as referring to Owen Roe O'Neill, the later general of the Confederate War, possibly on the grounds of its relationship to the tune 'Owen Roe O'Neill' or 'Owen O'Neill's march' from the Pigot collection.[27] A quite separate tune of the same name appears in the Bunting manuscripts, O'Sullivan commenting that it 'is quite likely that the air is contemporaneous with him'. It is possible that in this ascription O'Sullivan was re-contextualizing the tune since the actual name recorded by Bunting was simply 'Eoghan Ruadh – Owen Roe's march', but this may be over-skeptical as it is almost certain that Bunting would not have needed to clarify which Owen Roe was in question.[28] Another Bunting tune with a more tenuous association with this period is 'O'Donnell's march', subtitled 'Marche O Neil' in the manuscripts, which seems to add weight to the suggestion in the *Sources* that this is named after Red Hugh O'Donnell.[29] Another O'Donnell march provides us with an excellent example of archaizing: the tune 'The brown little mallet', used by Alfred Perceval Graves for his pseudo-folk ballad 'O'Donnell's march', was provided with an invented history by Tadhg Crowley who claims that it was 'said to have been played by the pipers of the O'Donnell Clan on their march to the Battle of Kinsale'.[30] A clearer example of an invented memorialization is the tune 'Hugh O'Neill's lament', which by all accounts caused quite a stir on its publication in Francis O'Neill's *The music of Ireland* with O'Neill writing that it was 'another of those fine melodies from the North of Ireland contributed by Sergeant [James] O'Neill. Judging by the inquiries concerning its origin it has attracted much attention'.[31] Clearly there was excitement at the prospect of a newly-discovered lament dating from this period in Irish music, but the name is purely commemorative as Caoimhín Mac Aoidh has recently confirmed, this tune having in fact been written by James O'Neill, as admitted by Francis O'Neill in a letter to Alfred Perceval Graves.[32]

25 Bunting, *A general collection of the ancient music of Ireland*, p.17-37 at 32; Stanford, *The complete collection of Irish music*, no. 472; O'Sullivan, 'The Bunting collection of Irish folk music and songs: part v', 24–5. **26** 'Marcshlua Uí Néill (O'Neill's cavalry)', *The tartan and green: official publication of the Irish Pipe Band Association,* 16 (March, 2002), 27. **27** Fleischmann, *Sources*, ii, p. 890; Joyce, *Old Irish folk music and songs*, no. 773. **28** O'Sullivan, 'The Bunting collection of Irish folk music and songs: part v', 26; Bunting MSS, 5/67 and 34/5. **29** Bunting, *The ancient music of Ireland*, p. 80; Bunting MSS, 33(1)49, 13/71, 27/54; Fleischmann, *Sources*, ii, p. 1085. **30** John O'Daly, *The poets and poetry of Munster* (3rd ed. Dublin, 1888), p. 276; A.P. Graves & C.V. Stanford, *Songs of Erin* (London, 1901), pp 142–5; Tadhg O'Crowley, *Crowley's collection of music for the highland or Irish bagpipes, book 1* (Cork, n.d.), p. 48. See also Carl Hardebecke, *Ceol na nGaedhal* (Dublin, 1937), p. 28. **31** O'Neill, *O'Neill's music of Ireland*, no. 68; Francis O'Neill, *Irish folk music: a fascinating hobby* (Chicago, 1910; repr. Wakefield, 1973), p. 72. **32** Caoimhín Mac Aoidh, *The scribe: the life and works of James O'Neill*

Two of the most interesting tunes associated with the Flight of the Earls are the slow airs 'Caoineadh Uí Néill' and 'Caoineadh Uí Dhomhnaill' which appear to be independent of any song but have the scale and grandeur associated with the so-called 'big songs' of the *sean-nós* tradition. They are discussed together here as they share a common source, and their significance arises from the apparent contradictions between their history and provenance (as traceable) and the more popular perception of their origins. Because both tunes have been quite frequently included on recent commercial recordings the popular construction of their narrative has been achieved and accentuated through the discourse on the tunes in the notes to these releases.[33] The earliest sources for these tunes are recordings made of the Sliabh Luachra fiddle players Pádraig O'Keeffe and Denis Murphy, with O'Keeffe being the primary source – Murphy almost certainly learned these from O'Keeffe who himself learnt them from his grandmother.[34] O'Keeffe's recording of 'Caoineadh Uí Néill', made during Alan Lomax's recording tours in Ireland in the 1950s, has never been issued commercially.[35] The version recorded by Murphy differs only slightly (the opening phrase is played with F naturals in place of F sharps) and was recorded by Ciarán Mac Mathúna.[36] Both made several recordings of the second air: O'Keeffe's were recorded by Séamus Ennis in 1948 and again for the BBC in 1952; Murphy's were made by Mac Mathúna and probably by Lomax, again in the 1950s or 1960s.[37] It is somewhat surprising given the excellence of both of the airs that no earlier printed sources are found for either tune. Likewise, they have generated very little commentary with the exception of a recent short article by Terry Moylan on 'Caoineadh Uí Dhomhnaill' which confirms the absence of notated versions prior to the tunes' recording.[38] There are several other recent printed notations of this air, but remarkably, none exists of 'Caoineadh Uí Néill'.[39] Notes to O'Keeffe's recording state that 'both may be named after the two Ulster families who led the Irish forces at their downfall at the Battle of Kinsale'; other commentary on the tunes concurs, with one note claiming that 'Caoineadh Uí Néill' is 'one of the oldest surviving airs in the Irish tradition written in honour of the great Irish chieftain O'Neill'.[40] Likewise, the O'Donnell lament 'grieves for those slaughtered at Kinsale' and is 'named after Red Hugh O'Donnell, whose departure into exile after the battle of Kinsale, 1601 heralded the demise of the clan system in Ireland'.[41] If these are indeed seventeenth-century laments,

(Manorhamilton Co. Leitrim, 2006) p. 115. **33** There are eight commercial recordings of 'Caoineadh Uí Néill' available, and about twenty of 'Caoineadh Uí Dhomhnaill'. **34** Alan Ward, 'Music from Sliabh Luachra', *Traditional Music*, 5 (1976), 20, 23. **35** *IRL-Dtm*: 179-ITMA-Reel, Breandán Breathnach Reel-to-Reel 196, track A3. **36** Denis Murphy, *Music from Sliabh Luachra* (RTE CD 183, n.d.), 5. No date or location for the recording is given. **37** *Sliabh Luachra fiddle master Pádraig O'Keeffe* (RTE CD 174, 1993), 14; Pádraig O'Keeffe et al., *Kerry fiddles* (Topic TSCD 309, 1977), track 5; Murphy, *Music from Sliabh Luachra*, 5; Various, *Traditional music of Ireland: the older traditions of Connemara and Clare*, 1 (Folkways FW 8781, 1963), B3, as 'The queen of O'Donnell'. **38** Terry Moylan, 'Airs and graces: caoineadh Uí Dhónaill [*sic*]', *An Píobaire*, 4:41 (2007), 18–19. **39** See for example Tomás Ó Canainn, *Traditional music in Ireland* (London, 1978), p. 36. **40** Notes to *Sliabh Luachra fiddle master Pádraig O'Keeffe* (RTE CD 174, 1993); notes to Aoife Granville, *Sráid Eoin shuffle* (Aoife Granville AG001, 2006). **41** Various, *The Seville*

their survival for three hundred years unnoticed would be quite remarkable; and although their perceived ancientness can be interpreted as invented or constructed, it nonetheless remains meaningful for musicians today. One of the most valued items of repertoire relating to the mid-seventeenth century is the piping piece 'Mairseál Alasdruim' which memorializes Alasdair MacColla or Alasdar Mac Domhnaill, killed at the battle of Cnoc na nDos in 1647.[42] The tune itself was first notated only in the nineteenth century, but it is thought that the opening march of the piece is originally from the period and that the other sections are later additions, although the slow air or lament may have been composed after the battle.[43] Flood's contention that the 'Irish war-pipers who accompanied the funeral played a specially-composed death-march over all that remained of the brave soldier' may be fanciful, but it is echoed in more recent commentary on the piece which still retains its commemorative potency.[44] Similarly, the memory of the Williamite wars is powerfully maintained in a larger body of tunes and songs including 'The Wild Geese'[45] and 'The battle of Aughrim'. The latter title refers to a number of tunes: it occurs first in Walker, where he described it as a dramatic piece of music, 'a wild air of their own days called *Cath Eachroma*, or *Battle of Aughrim*, which serves as a kind of prologue to *The Cries*', and it formed part of a piping piece played by the blind piper Martin Reilly at the Feis Ceoil in 1901 in which 'the blare of trumpets, battle onslaught, and wailing of women were imitated'.[46]

In summary, the propagation of such historical associations imbues these tunes with added meaning, relevance, and perhaps emotional and affective weight. In their conveyance of history they exemplify how a 'traditional art will connect a people and a culture through time' and re-emphasize how traditional music is grounded in 'a system of remembering'.[47] The subject of this remembrancing is predominantly the matrix of musicians who have enriched the tradition, but place and event overlap here as a marker of identity, for the process of remembering forms an essential part of how traditional musicians establish and reinforce their identity. The tunes' setting in the seventeenth century may also give them a quality of difference or otherness – these are not run-of-the-mill dance tunes for entertainment but music which is more exotic and unusual, and hence they are

Suite: Kinsale to La Coruna (Tara CD 3030, 1992); notes to Kathleen Loughnane, *Harping on* (CD, Kathleen Loughnane, [no number], 2002). **42** Breandán Breathnach, 'Mairseál Alasdruim', in Seán Potts, Terry Moylan & Liam McNulty (eds): *The man and his music* (Dublin, 1996), p. 17; Gearóid Ó hAllmhuráin, 'Music: early modern music', in James S. Donnelly (ed.), *Encyclopedia of Irish history and culture*, 2 vols (Detroit, 2004), i, p. 453. **43** T. Crofton Croker, *Researches in the south of Ireland* (London, 1824), no. 1: for a comprehensive list of sources, see Breathnach, 'Mairseál Alasdruim'; Donnelly, 'Warpipes', iii, 20; Gearóid Ó hAllmhuráin, *A pocket history of Irish traditional music* (Dublin, 1998), p. 28; Fleischmann, *Sources*, ii, p. 1152. **44** Flood, *History*, p.195; notes to Anne-Marie O'Farrell, *The jig's up* (CD, Anne-Marie O'Farrell, [no number], 1996); Chieftains, *Bonaparte's retreat* (Claddagh CC 20, 1976). **45** John & William Neal, *A collection of the most celebrated Irish tunes* (Dublin, 1724), p. 25. **46** Walker, *Historical memoirs of the Irish bards*, p. 125; O'Neill, *Waifs and strays of Gaelic melody*, p. 25. **47** Sally Sommers Smith, 'Interpretations and translations of Irish traditional music', in Maria Tymoczko & Colin Ireland (eds), *Language and tradition in Ireland: continuities and displacements* (Amherst, MA, 2003), 101–17.

accorded a special value within the tradition. This is not the case with the majority of the 'remnants' in Table 3:1 above, which lack this function of remembrancing and hence are undistinguished within the canon.

CONCLUSION

The perception of Ireland as being particularly rich in music, and celebrated internationally for it, persists today as it did in the seventeenth century.[48] This is particularly true for Irish traditional music, a modern and confident subcultural sound said to reflect the successes of the Celtic Tiger economy. In many ways, the music of seventeenth-century Ireland is quite distant from this tradition and the discontinuity in the narrative of this musical tradition in Ireland is quite clear. Yet it still has left an imprint on the modern tradition, both actual and symbolic; and in the continuous process of recycling that is a characteristic of any musical tradition, the music of the seventeenth century will remain as a potential source for the future construction and re-imagination of Irish traditional music.

---

48 See for example MacLysaght, *Irish life*, pp 22, 317.

'Irish harpers are excellent, and their solemn music is much liked of strangers': the Irish harp in non-Irish contexts in the seventeenth century

JOHN CUNNINGHAM

The seventeenth century represents an important stage in the history of the Irish harp. In the late sixteenth and early seventeenth centuries the instrument became increasingly popular – even fashionable – among wealthy English settlers in Ireland, a trend that quickly spread to many aristocratic and wealthy households in England and which is reflected in Fynes Moryson's comment (1617) cited in the title to this chapter.[1] Several prominent courtiers owned harps: for example Sir Michael Hickes (1543–1612), Robert Cecil (1563–1612), Archbishop William Laud (1573–1645), and Robert Carr (1585/6?–1645).[2] Six harpers held official posts in the Royal Music at the English court during the first half of the seventeenth century, at least four of whom are known to have played the Irish type of instrument.[3] Once the Irish harp was embraced by colonial culture it was a logical progression for the instrument to be used in the performance of contemporary non-Irish music; indeed, for much of the first half of the century the Irish harp functioned simultaneously in the spheres of Irish and English music. Evidence of the role of the Irish harp in English consort music is meagre, and has been neglected by harp historians. Nevertheless, the development of the 'harp consort' in England (and to a lesser extent on the Continent) can be directly related to the increased popularity of the Irish harp in the first half of the seventeenth century. Contrariwise, by 1660 the popularity of the Irish harp in England was in decline, a decline that appears to be linked to the demise of the harp consort. Thus, in order to evaluate the Irish harp in non-Irish contexts in the seventeenth century this chapter will briefly examine the development and decline of the harp consort. In addition, the reception history of the Irish harp in England and on the Continent will be explored in light of the various cultural policies pursued by the later Tudor and early Stuart monarchs.

The use of the Irish harp in English consort music is perhaps the clearest expression of the popularity of the instrument in early Stuart England; however, its participation in English musical culture inevitably had consequences for the

---

1 Quoted in Caesar Litton Falkiner, *Illustrations of Irish history and topography, mainly of the seventeenth century* (London, 1904), p. 312. 2 Lynn Hulse, 'Sir Michael Hickes (1543–1612): a study in musical patronage', *ML*, 66 (1985), 220–7. Richard Charteris, 'Jacobean musicians at Hatfield House, 1605–1613', *RMA Research Chronicle*, 12 (1974), 115–36; Hulse, 'Musical patronage'; *GB-Lpro*, PROB 1/40, p. 7; *The Loseley manuscripts*, ed. Alfred Kempe (London, 1836), p. 407. 3 Cormack MacDermott, Daniel Cahill, Philip Squire, Lewis Evans (Irish harp); Malcombe Goate (Scottish harp?); Jean le Flelle (triple harp?).

harp, and for traditional performance practices. The incorporation of extra (chromatic) notes to facilitate modulation on the Irish harp is perhaps the clearest representation of the break with traditional methods of harping.[4] Chromatic Irish harps were a natural consequence of the traditionally diatonic instrument intermingling with non-Irish musical cultures, musical cultures that required the ability to modulate. The evidence for chromatic Irish harps in the seventeenth century, slight but compelling, is well known and needs only brief recapitulation here. The Dalway harp fragments (now lacking the soundbox), housed in the National Museum of Ireland, Dublin, date to 1621 and contain pins for forty-five strings, with an extra row of seven strings in the middle of the harp's range. Michael Billinge and Bonnie Shaljean have convincingly argued that the Dalway harp was at least partially chromatic (rather than diatonic throughout a six-octave range).[5] Moreover, in 1581 the Florentine Vincenzo Galilei (1520–91) described a possible double Irish harp that had between fifty-four and sixty strings; the tuning system which he described is partially chromatic.[6] Almost four decades later in Germany, Michael Praetorius (1571–1621) briefly described an 'Irlendisch Harff', which he noted had forty-three strings: again, the tuning given suggests a chromatic harp.[7] There are also descriptions of large (and presumably partially chromatic) Irish harps by the late seventeenth-century Cambridge professor and writer on music James Talbot (1664–1708),[8] and the tantalising reference to Nicholas Dall Pierse (*c*.1561–1653) who was reputed to have completed the harp 'with more wires than ever before his time were used'.[9] The musical evidence (below) certainly seems to confirm that chromatic Irish harps were used quite regularly in early seventeenth-century England.

The transposition of the harp into English musical culture also appears to have had an impact on playing techniques. Traditionally the Irish harp was played with long fingernails and produced a melting sound that 'was rich and resonant, with something of both bells and guitar'.[10] In the words of Francis Bacon (1561–1626), 'no instrument hath the sound so melting and prolonged, as the Irish harp'.[11] Indeed, modern reconstructions of the wire-strung Irish harp show that its sound was quite powerful, similar in its resonance to a small chamber organ.[12] Some Irish harpers moved away from the traditional fingernail style in the early seventeenth century. In his *Zoilomastix*, begun in the late 1620s, the contemporary Irish Catholic historian Philip O'Sullivan Beare (*c*.1590–1660)

---

4 Throughout this chapter 'chromatic' is intended to mean the ability to modulate.   **5** Billinge & Shaljean, 'Dalway'.   **6** Vincenzo Galilei, *Dialogo della musica antica e della moderna* (Florence, 1581; repr. Monuments of music and music literature in facsimile, second series, no. 20, New York, 1968), p. 143; Billinge & Shaljean, 'Dalway', 180–1.   **7** Michael Praetorius, *Syntagmatis musici tomus secundus* (Wolfenbuttel, 1618–19), ch. 32; Billinge & Shaljean, 'Dalway', 181–2.   **8** Joan Rimmer, 'James Talbot's manuscript (Christ Church library Music MS 1187): vi. Harps', *GSJ*, 16 (1963), 63–72; Billinge & Shaljean, 'Dalway', 182.   **9** John Pierse, 'Nicholas Dall Pierse of Co. Kerry, harper', *Journal of the Kerry Historical and Archaeological Society*, 6 (1973), 40–75 at 40.   **10** Joan Rimmer, 'The morphology of the Irish harp', *GSJ*, 17 (1964), 39–49 at 41.   **11** Bacon, *Sylva sylvarum*, p. 62.   **12** Representative examples of wire-strung Irish harps can be heard on *Cláirseach na hÉireann: the harp of Ireland* (Siobhán Armstrong: CD, Maya MCD0401, 2004); and *Queen of harps* (Ann Heymann: CD, Temple Records COMD2057, 1994).

noted that some 'strike the harp with the tips of their fingers'.[13] The decline of the fingernail tradition has been linked to the decline in social status of the harpers in Irish society: as harpers were socially demoted they were forced to seek employment other than through music, which would presumably have entailed some kind of manual labour not conducive to keeping long fingernails.[14] However, some of the professional Irish harpers at the English court in the early seventeenth century also appear to have adopted the fingertip style; for these harpers we must seek other explanations for the decline in the fingernail tradition. First, the Irish harpers employed at the English court were participating in a somewhat hybrid musical tradition, rather than a strictly Irish one; although this is not to suggest that they did not perform Irish music (even on occasion) nor that they were not versed in its techniques or traditions. Nevertheless, the performance of non-Irish music would not necessarily have entailed the abandonment of the fingernail style, although the fingertip style would have allowed more freedom to dampen strings to avoid discords created by the sustained sound of the harp. Indeed, on the Continent where (gut-strung) double and triple harps were frequently used in operas and other entertainments (as solo instruments and for continuo realization) contemporary harpers generally preferred the fingertip style. More significant perhaps is that the majority of the court musicians at this time would have been proficient on more than one instrument. The Irish harper Philip Squire was also employed to instruct the young Lewis Evans 'a child of great dexterity in music, to play on the Irish harp and other instruments'.[15] This suggests that both Squire and Evans were proficient on more than one instrument and were unlikely to have participated in the fingernail tradition. Indeed, these Irish harpers were unlikely to have been Irish: Squire was probably English and Evans appears to have been Welsh. Thus, several of the proponents of the Irish harp at court were perhaps themselves evidence of a somewhat diluted musical tradition. Nevertheless, it is also possible that some harpers used appendages to imitate the fingernail style. In *Rerum Scoticarum historia* (1582), George Buchanan (1506–82) noted that on the Western Scottish islands they 'employ harps of a peculiar kind, some of which are strung with brass, and some with catgut. In playing they strike the wires either with a quill, or with their nails, suffered to grow long for the purpose'.[16] These breaks with traditional Irish harping were in many ways fundamentally connected to the use of the Irish harp as an ensemble instrument in the harp consort. The instrumentation of harp consorts is unlikely to have been standardized, although it was essentially an Anglo-Irish genre – an 'Irish harp consort' – as the common ingredients appear to have been an Irish harp and a bass viol. (In the seventeenth century the bass viol was generally considered to be the English instrument *par excellence*.) Indeed, Bacon's oft-cited passage from *Sylva sylvarum* supports this musical union

13 Quoted in Carolan, 'O'Sullivan Beare', 56.   14 For example, Billinge & Shaljean, 'Dalway', 184–5.
15 *RECM*, viii, p. 78.   16 Quoted in Robert Bruce Armstrong, *The Irish and highland harps* (Edinburgh, 1904; repr. ed. Seóirse Bodley, Shannon, 1969), p. 140. Armstrong questioned this interpretation.

(which can also be read in terms of political metaphor): 'some consorts of instruments are sweeter than others (a thing not sufficiently yet observed) as the Irish harp and bass viol agree well'.[17] A symbolic expression of this cultural crossover can be observed on the forepillar of the Dalway harp, which is inscribed with the arms of England surmounting the arms of Sir John FitzEdmond Fitzgerald.

Remarkably few harp consort parts have survived, even by seventeenth-century standards. Historical accident is unlikely to account for the entire dearth of harp sources; rather, it is likely that harp parts were generally improvized, realized from treble and bass string parts, or adapted from existing keyboard parts. Notwithstanding the oral harp tradition, this essentially extemporized (or adaptive) approach to harping probably had its roots in the Irish harps of the period, which were not standardized: harps varied in size, and therefore in range and modulation abilities. In addition, the Irish harp was a particularly specialized (even arcane) instrument, which would have presented problems for composers wishing to write *obbligato* harp parts for consort ensembles.

The most complete evidence of the harp consort comes from the thirty pieces composed in the 1630s by William Lawes (1602–45) for 'the harp, bass viol, violin and theorbo'.[18] However, there are no obvious precedents for Lawes's use of the harp in a mixed consort. Peter Holman first suggested that the harp consort developed from the substitution of the harp for a keyboard instrument in the accompaniment of divisions.[19] The esoteric scoring of Lawes's ensemble suggests that the form originated and developed primarily at the English court, since few patrons outside the court could have employed such an ensemble. However, one of those few patrons was Robert Cecil, first earl of Salisbury, who, *inter alios*, employed the court musicians Cormac MacDermott, Nicholas Lanier and John Coprario.[20] MacDermott was an Irish harper, probably originally from Co. Roscommon.[21] He is first heard of transporting letters to Ireland on Cecil's behalf in 1602.[22] O'Sullivan Beare claimed that MacDermott 'refreshed with his harp the spirits of Queen Elizabeth and of James, king of England'.[23] MacDermott received an official court appointment in October 1605 'in consideration of his service in the art of music';[24] however, there is no evidence to suggest that he ever held a post in the Royal Music prior to this.[25] Thus, there were clear musical ties between the Jacobean court and Cecil's household. Moreover, Cecil owned several virginals and organs, a bass violin, several lutes, a chest of viols, and an Irish harp.[26] There is no evidence that Cecil's harp was played as part of an ensemble; however, it is tempting to imagine a nascent form of harp consort

---

17 Bacon, *Sylva sylvarum*, p. 72. **18** For a detailed discussion of the development of the genre and Lawes's collection (including complete critical edition) see John Cunningham, 'Music for the privy chamber: studies in the consort music of William Lawes (1602–45)', 2 vols (PhD, University of Leeds, 2007), chs 6–7. At the time of writing, an edition by Jane Achtman for PRB Publications is forthcoming. **19** Holman, 'Harp', esp. 191–2. **20** See Hulse, 'Musical patronage'. **21** Donnelly, 'An Irish harper and composer'; Holman, 'Harp'. **22** Holman, 'Harp', 188–90. **23** Quoted in Carolan, 'O'Sullivan Beare', 56. **24** *RECM*, iv, p. 12. **25** As suggested in Donnelly, 'An Irish harper and composer', 40. **26** See Charteris, 'Jacobean musicians at Hatfield House'; Hulse, 'Musical patronage'.

being performed under Cecil's auspices. Nevertheless, the main development of the harp consort is likely to have taken place at court. There was a long tradition of harpers at the English court, but prior to the appointment of MacDermott there had not been an official court harper since the death of William More in 1565. MacDermott was the first of a series of (sighted and mostly literate) Irish harpers to be employed at the English court that performed and composed contemporary 'art' music. This represented a significant break with the harpers of the previous century, who belonged to the minstrel tradition. MacDermott seems to be a key figure in the early development of the harp consort; indeed, Lawes based one of his harp consort pavans on a theme by MacDermott, perhaps hinting at his influence (see Ex. 4:1).[27] The harp consort probably developed gradually in the first decades of the century by the addition of improvized treble, bass, or continuo lines to a harp used to accompany divisions on the bass viol. Perhaps the most tantalizing evidence for the development of the genre comes from a letter from Sir Gerald Herbert to Sir Dudley Carleton, dated 24 May 1619:

> After supper they [the French ambassador and attendants, being entertained by the duke of Lennox] were carried to the queen's privy chamber, where French singing was by the queen's musicians; after in the queen's bed chamber they heard the Irish harp, a viol, and Mr [Nicholas] Lanier, excellently singing and playing on the lute.[28]

Whether Herbert's letter describes an ensemble or a series of individual performers is difficult to ascertain. The description of Lanier 'excellently singing and playing on the lute' suggests that he was doing so alone, not in consort. However, it is tempting to imagine Lanier providing a continuo on the lute to bass viol divisions by Alfonso Ferrabosco II, accompanied by Philip Squire – who replaced MacDermott in the Royal Music in 1618 – on the Irish harp.

By the early 1620s harp consorts also appear to have existed at the Danish court of Christian IV (1577–1648). Indeed, the Irish harp was quite popular at the Danish court in the early part of the century, which is unsurprising given the strong cultural links between the Danish and English courts at the time. Between late 1601 and early 1602 John Dowland was commissioned to return to England from Denmark to recruit some musicians and purchase instruments. Dowland engaged two musicians: the dancing master Heinrik Sandon and the (presumably Irish) harper Carolus Oralii, which appears to be a form of 'Charles O'Reilly'. An entry in the Danish court records dated 24 September 1602 suggests that Sandon and Oralii were not entirely satisfactory:

---

27 See Holman, 'Harp', 192–3; Cunningham, 'Music for the privy chamber', pp 217–18. **28** *RECM*, viii, p. 80.

As we desire that the English harpist and the dancer be discharged because their time is up, we likewise beg of you that you discharge them and please then [*sic*] by granting them the allowance which Dulant [i.e. Dowland] of England has promised and pledged, still you will have to keep the harp because we paid for it.[29]

Another Irish harper, 'Darby Scott' (Diarmait Albanach), was employed at the Danish court from 1621 until his death in 1634. Scott may have been one of the Scott family mentioned by the Drogheda-born harpist Echlin O'Kane in 1779: 'The oldest performers by profession, of note, were four brothers of the name Scot, who lived in the province of Munster, about two hundred years ago – They founded their best harp music'.[30] Reinholdt Thim's painting 'Christian IV of Denmark's musicians, 1622' represents what appears to be a harp consort: a bass viol, an Irish harp (note the curved forepillar, which Thim has initialled), a lute and a transverse flute (Illustration 4.1). The Irish harp – presumably played by Scott – is a large instrument that could easily have had fifty or sixty strings, suggesting that it was chromatic. Holman suggested that the bass viol player was Thomas Simpson or William Brade, and that the lutenist was John Stanley or Brade's son, Christian; all were members of the British community of musicians in Denmark at the time.[31] (The flautist remains unidentified; indeed, his presence in the painting throws some doubt on whether Thim was representing an actual consort group or whether he was conveying the variety of instruments available at the court.) The form of harp consort developed at the Danish court (if indeed it is one) may have been derived from the Elizabethan mixed consort, with the flute used as the treble instrument. Alternatively, a violin may have been omitted from the painting and the flute could have played the alto part (many pictures of mixed consorts have at least one instrument missing).[32] A third harper, Edward Adam, is known to have been employed at the Danish court from 1641 to 1643. Adam was apparently a Scottish harper, and was previously employed at the Brandenburg court. He presumably also played the Irish harp, although this is not specified in the court records. A harp consort may even have reached Poland by the summer of 1617: on 22 June a passport was issued to George Vincent, a servant to the prince of Poland. Vincent had come to London to acquire some 'certain necessaries'[33] and initially recruited a group of eight musicians (reduced to five by 24 August)[34] including the bass viol player (and composer of two published collections) William Corkine, and a 'Donatus O'Chaine'. Seán Donnelly has suggested that O'Chaine was 'a part latinization of [an Irish harper]

---

29 Quoted in Diana Poulton, *John Dowland* (London, 1972; 2nd ed., 1982), p. 58.   **30** Campbell, 'An account', 146.   **31** Angul Hammerich, *Musiken ved Christian den fjerdes hof* (Copenhagen, 1892); Angul Hammerich, 'Musical relations between England and Denmark in the seventeenth century', *SIMG*, 13 (1911–12), 114–19; Holman, 'Harp', 192.   **32** See for example the engraving of a mixed consort (lacking lute and flute) by Simon de Passe, reproduced in Holman, *Four and twenty fiddlers*, p. 137.   **33** *Acts of the privy council*, Aug. 1616–Dec. 1617, p. 267.   **34** *CSPD*, 1611–18, p. 564.

"Donnchadh Ó Catháin"'.[35] Indeed, another otherwise unknown Irish harper (and 'gentleman'), John Eustace, was in the service of the prince of Portugal in Brussels by 1630.[36] Despite these intriguing references, the Irish harp consort is unlikely to have spread widely on the Continent, except perhaps where there were expatriate British communities among whom there was an exponent of the Irish harp.

The harp consorts of the first decades of the century probably developed from largely improvized ensembles performing divisions to the adaptation of written-out consort music in which the harp would be substituted for the keyboard, most likely in some form of continuo role. For example, the organ accompaniments for Coprario's pieces for two bass viols and organ or in his fantasia-suites (for one and two violins, bass viol and organ) could have been quite easily adapted for the harp. Evidence for the use of the Irish harp as a continuo instrument is found in Martin Peerson's *Motets or grave chamber music* (London, 1630). *Motets* ('fit for voices and viols') is the only musical source from seventeenth-century England to specify an 'Irish harp', which is listed with virginals, bass-lute and bandora as an alternative 'for want of organs' in the performance of an optional continuo part. The organ part in Peerson's publication is a Tr-B score (a *basso seguente* and a treble part usually taken from the uppermost vocal or instrumental part), with some continuo figures (this is the first occurrence of a figured bass in an English published collection). The organ part is not essential in any of the pieces, and chords were clearly intended to be realized if used in performance. Peerson's assortment of optional continuo instruments probably represents the contemporary popularity of the listed instruments, or perhaps the instruments available to the patron of the book. Indeed, *Motets* was dedicated to the memory of Peerson's patron, the poet Fulke Greville (d. 1628). Greville was a friend of Francis Bacon and had (probably superficially cordial) connections to Cecil: in December 1607 'a portative instrument ... was brought from the right worshipful Sir Fulke Greville his house at Austin Friars unto Salisbury House and there tuned for his Honour's [Cecil's] use'.[37] It is suggestive that Peerson listed the Irish harp with other known continuo instruments, and in relation to the realization of a continuo part. Further, it establishes an example of the substitution of the Irish harp for the chamber organ in the accompaniment of chamber music; moreover, a chromatic Irish harp would have been needed to perform even the Tr-B accompaniment given by Peerson. Only one other publication of the period specifies pieces for a harp (although the type is not given), and reinforces the suggestion that the harp was used as a continuo instrument in seventeenth-century England. Christopher Simpson's *A compendium of practical music in five parts* (London, 1667; 2nd ed. 1678) includes ten pieces titled 'Lessons by sundry authors for the treble, bass-viol, and harp'. The first and last of these pieces are given in score, which would suggest that the harpist was either meant to simply

35 Donnelly, 'A Cork musician', 21, n. 43.   36 *CSPD*, 1630, p. 207 (7 Mar.), p. 163 (12 Jan. 1630), p. 168 (18 Jan. 1630).   37 Charteris, 'Jacobean musicians at Hatfield House', 119.

Illustration 4.1. Reinholdt Thim, 'Christian IV of Denmark's musicians, 1622',
Musikhistorisk Museum, Copenhagen.

double the string parts or to realize a part based on the treble and bass outline.[38] However, the intervening eight pieces are laid out with the treble on one page and the bass on the opposite (inverted) page. Thus, when it came to the performance of these pieces the harpist could only sight-read one of the lines, presumably the (unfigured) bass. Contrariwise, there may have been a harp part that was not printed but circulated in manuscript, as was the case for the organ parts for Matthew Locke's *Little consort* and Henry Purcell's trio sonatas.[39]

It is not until the elaborate Inns of Court masque *The triumph of peace* of 1634 (most of the music for which was composed by Lawes and Simon Ives) that we get the first documentary evidence of a harp consort. The ensemble called the 'symphony', which performed the symphonies and vocal music accompaniments, consisted of a harp, a violin, and several lutes and viols.[40] Most of the symphonies, choruses and songs have survived in one of Lawes's autograph scorebooks (*GB-Ob,* MS Mus.Sch.B.2). The symphonies are simple binary dances that served to introduce the songs and to cover the stage noises; they are in Tr-B format, suggesting that the harp was used (with the lutes) to realize a continuo. The songs are declamatory continuo songs typical of Jacobean and Caroline masques. Most of the members of the 'Symphony' were royal musicians. Jean le Flelle, one of Queen Henrietta Maria's harpers, was initially listed as playing the harp in the group, but was replaced before the first performance by the otherwise unknown Thomas Bedowes.[41] The 'Symphony' roughly coincides with a reference to a possibly similar ensemble in Henrietta Maria's household: 'the consort of Mons. le Flelle'.[42] However, there is only one document relating to le Flelle's consort, and nothing to suggest that it was a regular group similar to 'Coprario's Music' in the main household.[43] Indeed, le Flelle's consort most likely related to the queen's masque *The temple of love* (1635).[44] Similar mixed consorts appear to have been used in masques prior to the 1630s: in *The masque of flowers* (1614), for example, the first antimasque includes the (distorted) mixed consort of 'a bobtail, a blind harper and his boy, a bass violin, a tenor cornet, a sackbut'.[45] Two harpers also appeared in *The Irish masque at court* (1613) (discussed below).

William Lawes's appointment to the private music of Charles I (a group known variously as the Lutes, Viols and Voices) in April 1635 probably heralded what turned out to be the final stage in the development of the harp consort. Lawes's court post made an Irish harp available to him as a regular compositional

---

38 Transcribed in Cunningham, 'Music for the privy chamber', pp 653–7.   **39** See Peter Holman, '"Evenly, softly, and sweetly acchording to all": the organ accompaniment of English consort music', in Ashbee & Holman, *Jenkins*, pp 353–82, esp. 372.   **40** See also Peter Walls, *Music in the English courtly masque, 1604–1640* (Oxford, 1996), pp 172–5 & passim.   **41** Murray Lefkowitz, 'The Longleat papers of Bulstrode Whitelocke: new light on Shirley's "Triumph of peace"', *Journal of the American Musicological Society*, 18 (1965), 42–60.   **42** *RECM*, iii, p. 83.   **43** 'Coprario's Music' appears to have been formed *c.*1622 and was still in existence in 1635. Holman discusses the group in detail in *Four and twenty fiddlers*, pp 213–16.   **44** Holman, 'Harp', 198.   **45** *A book of masques in honour of Allardyce Nicoll*, ed. T.J.B Spencer & Stanley Wells (Cambridge, 1967), 164, lines 189–90. See also Walls, *Masque*, 81–3.

Example 4.1. Lawes, Harp consort: Pavan in G major based on a theme by Cormack MacDermott.

resource. He may have been familiar with some form of harp consort prior to his appointment, but was probably not in regular contact with a harp. Indeed, the instrumentation of Lawes's harp consort probably became fixed only after 1635. Many of the first twenty or so of his harp consort dances probably originated prior to Lawes's appointment in two-part (Tr-B) versions which could be easily arranged for whatever instruments were available.[46] Harp parts survive for the first twenty pieces, all of which are in a Tr-B format with some extra melodic detail given in the treble part. Thus, in these pieces the harp again appears in a continuo-type role, largely derived from extemporized practices. However, full-voiced (autograph) harp parts have also survived for the last five pieces of the collection. These last five pieces are likely to be later incarnations than the first twenty-five, and appear to have been composed specifically for the ensemble (Ex. 4.1); in these pieces Lawes is likely to have been composing for a particular Irish harp. Nevertheless, there has been some debate as to whether Lawes composed for the wire-strung Irish harp or the gut-strung triple-harp. The argument for the triple-harp is unconvincing and supported neither by the archival documentary evidence nor by the musical evidence.

When Murray Lefkowitz published the first in-depth survey of the collection, he concluded that Lawes composed for the gut-strung triple-harp.[47] This view was largely accepted by many subsequent scholars and performers including Joan Rimmer and Cheryl Ann Fulton; indeed, Rimmer boldly asserted that 'Close examination shows that [Lawes's harp consorts] are playable *only* on a triple or double harp'.[48] There matters largely rested until Holman approached the issue in 1987.[49] Holman convincingly showed that the weight of evidence, from archival and musical sources, actually suggested that the Irish harp was the more likely candidate for original performances of Lawes's consorts. The arguments for the triple-harp have not been set down in any detail; those that have been are largely based on a superficial reading of the sources combined with a poor understanding of the complex structure of the musical establishment of the early Stuart court.[50]

If the three harp sources for Lawes's collection (*GB-Och,* Mus. MS 5; *GB-Ob,* MSS Mus.Sch.B.3 and D.229) are collated and taken literally, a harp of at least sixty-four strings (including twenty unison strings) would be needed to perform all thirty pieces at one sitting, without having to retune between pieces in different keys. *Prima facie,* the triple-harp would appear to be the logical choice; certainly, an Irish harp capable of such a range would be impractical. However,

46 See Cunningham, 'Music for the privy chamber', pp 252–63.   47 Murray Lefkowitz, *William Lawes* (London, 1960), pp 88–105.   48 Rimmer, 'James Talbot's manuscript', 69; Cheryl Ann Fulton, '"For the harpe, base violl, violin and theorbo": the consorts of William Lawes (1602–1645)', *The American Harp Journal,* 10:2 (1985), 15–20.   49 Holman, 'Harp'; Layton Ring, 'A preliminary inquiry into the continuo parts of William Lawes for organ, harp and theorbo' (MA, University of Nottingham, 1972) also argues for the use of the Irish harp. Ring included comparative performances of some of the harp consorts with Irish and triple harps as part of a 1985 lecture he delivered at a joint meeting of the Viola da Gamba and Lute Societies of Great Britain, an account of which by John Catch can be found in *The Viola da Gamba Society Newsletter,* 52 (1986), 5–8.   50 For example Fulton, '"For the harpe, base violl, violin and theorbo"'.

whether an Irish or triple harp was used some retuning seems likely. Evidence from the sources suggest that a harp of at least thirty-eight strings, with a range of *D* to *d'''*, is required.[51] Seven of these strings would be retuneable between the four keys used in the harp consorts (G major, G minor, D major, D minor). The harp further requires a wholly chromatic mid-range (from *f* to *a'*); the lower range is diatonic, and the upper range is partly chromatic. If these ranges are collated the result is a harp of at least thirty-eight strings, seven of which are retuneable.[52] An Irish harp of this range is entirely feasible; indeed, it closely resembles that of the Dalway harp as suggested by Billinge and Shaljean.

Example 4.2. Range of 'Lawes's harp'.

Support for the triple-harp argument has largely been marshalled from circumstantial evidence relating to Jean le Flelle. Based on the 1635 document (cited above) it has been held by some that Lawes composed his harp consorts for the consort group headed by le Flelle.[53] However, this ignores several key factors. Although le Flelle was initially engaged as a 'musician in ordinary' to Charles I from 1629, the documentary evidence suggests that he was primarily associated with Queen Henrietta Maria's household;[54] however, there is no evidence that le Flelle came to England in the retinue of Henrietta Maria in 1625.[55] During this period, the king and queen each had their own households within the royal palaces, with their own servants and musicians. The Royal Music in the main (king's) household was further sub-divided into three sections: the wind bands, the violin band and the Lutes, Viols and Voices. As far as we can tell, there was a strong demarcation between the various sections of the Royal Music. It is highly unlikely that Lawes would have composed for le Flelle's consort, given that both men were retained in separate musical establishments. Moreover, Lawes had access to two harpers (Evans and Squire) in the Lutes, Viols and Voices, both of whom played the Irish harp. Indeed, between 1603 and 1642 le Flelle is the only court harper associated with the triple-harp (based on Marin Mersenne's

---

51 The requirements of 'Lawes's harp' are discussed in detail in John Cunningham, '"Some consorts of instruments are sweeter than others": further light on the harp of William Lawes's harp consorts', *GSJ*, 61 (2008), 147–76. 52 This assumes no retuning within keys; if this were allowed the pitches *f'–f♯''* would also be retuneable. 53 Most recently: Fulton, 'Harp', p. 907. 54 See Holman, 'Harp'; *RECM*, iii & viii. 55 Fulton, '"For the harpe, base violl, violin and theorbo"', 15–16; Fulton, 'Harp'.

comments that 'Flesle' played the triple harp 'en perfection').[56] However, Inigo Jones's sketches for *The temple of love* masque showing le Flelle playing a small single-row harp suggest that he may have played other harps.[57] Thus, we cannot assume that le Flelle would necessarily have played a triple harp in a consort under his direction. Ironically, perhaps the best evidence for the use of the Irish harp for Lawes's consorts comes from one of its most persistent critics. In 1983 Fulton recorded several of the harp consorts using a gut-strung triple-harp.[58] Although there is some fine playing, one only needs to listen to this recording to appreciate that the triple-harp is quite simply acoustically unsuitable for the task.[59]

The revival of the Irish harp at the English court in the early seventeenth century, with the appointment of Cormack MacDermott in 1605, should be understood in the context of the contemporary popularity of the instrument, a popularity that reached a climax with Lawes's use of an *obbligato* Irish harp in the English consort music tradition. However, on another level, the popularity of the harp is also underlain by an ideological position held by the later Tudors and early Stuarts: the attempted cultural assimilation of Ireland. Cultural assimilation was part of an ideological position that viewed Ireland not as an alien country to be conquered (as it had been in the reign of Elizabeth I), but as a part of the realm of Great Britain to be subdued. In the Jacobean period this policy emphasized James I's image of himself as the head of a Great Britain: the self-styled *rex pacificus*, the apex of a hierarchical and patriarchal society. As Sir John Davies (1569–1626), appointed attorney general for Ireland in 1606, recorded in his treatise of 1612:

we may conceive an hope, that the next generation [of Irish], will in tongue and heart, and every way else, become English; so as there will be no difference or distinction, but the Irish Sea betwixt us.[60]

And:

So as we may well conceive a hope, that Ireland (which heretofore might properly be called the Land of Ire, because the Irascible power was predominant there, for the space of 400 years together) will from henceforth prove a Land of Peace and Concorde.[61]

---

56 Marin Mersenne, *Harmonie universelle*, iii: *Traité des instruments a chordes* (Paris, 1636–7), p. 170.
57 See Holman, 'Harp', 198; the sketches are reproduced at 197.   58 *William Lawes: consort music for the harpe, bass viol, violin and theorbo* (Cheryl Ann Fulton *et al.*, LP, Focus Records 843, 1983. Deleted)
59 This issue is discussed in detail in John Cunningham, 'A tale of two harps: issues arising from recordings of William Lawes's harp consorts', *Early Music Performer*, 21 (2007), 13–24.   60 Sir John Davies, *A discoverie of the true causes why Ireland was never entirely subdued* (London, 1612), p. 272.
61 Ibid., p. 284.

Indeed, in a 1603 speech to the House of Lords James I had expressed a similar ideological interpretation of colonial expansion:

For even as little brooks lose their names by their running and fall into great rivers, and the very name and memory of the great rivers swallowed up in the ocean: so by the conjunction of divers little kingdoms in one, are all these private differences and questions swallowed up.[62]

One aspect of this erosion of cultural differences was the appropriation of the Irish harp, the instrument traditionally associated with the Irish bard and, more importantly, the symbol of Ireland since at least the thirteenth century.[63] Through a range of iconographical sources, Barra Boydell has provided evidence that the harp, although not specifically an Irish harp, was from the Middle Ages seen as a symbolic representation of Ireland. The growth in popularity of the Irish harp among the English upper and ruling classes in the late sixteenth and early seventeenth centuries coincided with the more accurate representation of the instrument in various iconographical sources. These iconographical representations are of significance to organology, but they also represent the gradual formation of a readily identifiable symbol: the (Irish) harp as a national signifier of Ireland. Indeed, in the late sixteenth century Vincenzo Galilei noted that the harp was 'the special emblem of the realm [i.e. Ireland], where it is depicted and sculptured on public buildings and on coins'.[64] Boydell further showed how the harp that became the symbolic representation of Ireland from Tudor times was actually based not on a realistic Irish harp, but rather on an English or Continental harp. It seems that this symbolic inaccuracy was due to Irish money being minted in London: 'Thus, the first widespread use of the harp as the symbol of Ireland depicted the instrument ... according to the preconceptions of outsiders'.[65] In the early Stuart period the Irish harp was depicted with slightly more accuracy on the coinage, a fact that Boydell attributes to the harp being fashionable among the English nobility, and to the patronage of Irish harpists at the Stuart court. It is perhaps no coincidence that the harp was symbolically assimilated into the royal coat of arms upon James I's accession in 1603, an event that roughly coincided with the surrender of the earl of Tyrone and the end of the Irish rebellion. The Irish bard was seen as epitomizing the oppositional 'otherness' of the native Irish (and, by the early seventeenth century, the 'Old Irish'), but whose status (if not symbolic power) was significantly eroded after 1601, even more so after the Flight of the Earls in 1607. Particularly in the reign of Elizabeth I, the Irish bards were viewed with great disdain in some political circles. However, by the time James I acceded to the throne attitudes towards harpers were changing. In the succinct words of Alan Fletcher:

62 *The political works of James I*, ed. Charles McIlwain (Cambridge, MA, 1918), p. 273.   63 See Boydell, 'Iconography'.   64 Galilei, *Dialogo*, quoted in Boydell, 'Iconography', p. 132.   65 Boydell, 'Iconography', p. 133.

Before the seventeenth century – for convenience one might say before the Battle of Kinsale [1601] – the English attitude towards harping had been deeply ambivalent. On the one hand, Irish harpers were seen as utterly reprobate while they served native Gaelic interests, but on the other, if once domesticated and brought within the pale of English civility, they might be highly desirable additions to households where, as well as making music, they might stand as living proof to the world of the accommodations that enlightened colonialism was happy to make. By [Richard] Boyle [first earl of Cork]'s day (post-Kinsale), the image of the harper as inciter to Gaelic sedition was largely a thing of the past, but the value of the harper as cultural trophy lingered on.[66]

There is much literary evidence of the popularity of the Irish harp (and its exponents) in early Stuart England: from the last decades of the sixteenth century English commentators, unconcerned with any negative connotations, frequently cited the Irish harp for its pleasing timbre.[67] The Dublin-born scholar and translator Richard Stanihurst (1547–1618) provides one of the very few pejorative descriptions of the Irish harp. Writing in 1584, he noted that the ('often blind') harper

has no education in music … He draws forth the sound, not with any plectrum, but with hooked nails. And although in his music he observes neither metre nor mode, nor does he pay any attention to the pitch of the sounds he makes (indeed he offends the sensitive ears of the expert like the screech of a saw, as he dins on every class of guests), yet the lower classes are singularly delighted by his crude harmony.[68]

O'Sullivan Beare took Stanihurst to task in his *Zoilomastix*: 'Hardly any harper could be found (believe me, Stanihurst) more impaired in his sight than you are in your mind'.[69] However, Stanihurst did apparently come across an Irish harper that he deemed acceptable:

There lives in our own time, Crusus [Richard Cruise], the best harper in living memory. He completely recoils from that confused din which results from strings which are untuned and clashing with themselves; on the contrary, [in] his arrangement of measure and composition of sound, he maintains a musical harmony which has a wonderful effect on the ears of the listeners, so much so that you would sooner judge him to be the only harper, not simply the greatest. From this you may understand that up to now it was not the harp that was lacking to the musicians, but musicians to the harp.[70]

66 Fletcher, *Drama, performance,* pp 231–2.   **67** See Donnelly, 'The Irish harp'.   **68** *De rebus in Hibernia gestis* (Antwerp, 1584), p. 39, trans. in *The* De rebus in Hibernia gestis *of Richard Stanihurst,* ed. John Barry & Hiram Morgan (Brepols, forthcoming). I am grateful to John Barry for providing me with the Stanihurst translations prior to publication.   **69** *Zoilomastix,* quoted in Carolan, 'O'Sullivan Beare', 56.   **70** *De*

Stanihurst's descriptions can be understood as an expression of his bias towards English musical culture. The differences between the two descriptions highlight what Stanihurst saw as the essential differences between two musical cultures, and indeed between the two cultures generally. His refined ears did not object to the sound of the harp *per se*, but rather to the way in which the music was played – or perhaps to the music that was played. Once the harp assumed the characteristics of what he perceived to be English (musical) culture – 'the rules of musical harmony' etc. – then the instrument was readily appealing and accessible. Stanihurst's demarcation of two musical cultures, and his condemnation of one (the indigenous), was in part a reinforcement of his own cultural identity, a cultural identify that he partially expressed through the civility of his musical tastes.

As illustrated by the development of the harp consort, the assimilation of the Irish harp into English musical culture continued apace during the first half of the seventeenth century. The gradual introduction of chromaticism to the Irish harp (discussed above) can be read as a significant aspect of the assimilation of the harp into English colonial culture (i.e. 'civility'). Chromaticism was largely foreign to the Irish harp tradition, but in the early seventeenth century chromaticism affected even the physicality of the instrument, with the introduction of extra strings to accommodate the new notes necessary for modulation. The old sound of the harp was retained, but it was now, in a sense, subjugated to the new colonial repertoire. That the sound was unaltered, while still bowing to colonial musical demands, is a sign that Englishness – i.e. civility (in relation to Ireland) – was largely defined against the 'other'; it was necessary to retain 'inferior' traits in order to complement the newly acquired 'superior' ones.

A similar form of cultural assimilation is represented in Ben Jonson's *Irish masque at court*.[71] In the words of James Smith, the '*Irish masque* offers an idealized containment of Old English opposition. Jonson's text imagines a New English nobility, one which conforms to standard English cultural traits and speaks standard English as evidence of its incorporation within a unified Great Britain'.[72] The point that Smith is making relates to linguistic assimilation; however, one can also relate it to music. In Jonson's masque music is used as one way of articulating the 'otherness' of the four uncouth footmen who fight among themselves to decide who is to tell the King the story of how 'te imbashators' (206, line 11) lost their festive dresses whilst crossing the Irish Sea. After their squabbling, the footmen dance an antimasque to 'bagpipe and other rude music' (210, lines 121–2). After this, the aristocratic ambassadors present themselves, (supposedly) naked under Irish mantles and dance 'to a solemn music of harps'

rebus in Hibernia gestis, p. 39. For Cruise see Carolan, 'O'Sullivan Beare', 59, n. 25. **71** *Ben Jonson: the complete masques*, ed. Stephen Orgel (New Haven, CT, 1969), pp 206–12. All further references to this masque refer to this edition, and are cited parenthetically in the text by page numbers and line numbers. The masque was performed on 29 Dec. 1613, and again five days later. **72** James M. Smith, 'Effaced history: facing the colonial contexts of Ben Jonson's Irish masque at court', *English Literary History*, 65 (1998), 297–321 at 301.

(210–11, lines 125–56). Here a clear delineation is made (in typical masque fashion) between the barbaric 'others' of the antimasque and the civility of the main masquers. Initially, there would seem to be no realistic appropriation of the harp in this case; surely we can simply see the harp music as the aural re-affirmation of the Irishness of the 'imbashators', in the same way that their dialogue emphasises their nationality linguistically? In one sense, this is the case. Quite obviously, contemporaries would have recognized an aural link between the Irish harp and Irish people, which would have been reinforced visually by actually seeing the harpers and their harps (presuming that the sound did not come from off-stage). However, the masquers who played the 'imbashators' were not Irish; they were played by five English and five Scottish courtiers. Thus, the dénouement of the masque – the transformation of the ambassadors – reveals only the fictionality of the masque itself: 'for the audience the revelation that is offered by their "transformation" is only to confirm that they are what we knew they were all along, the English [and Scottish] servants of the King'.[73] At the same time, the very fact that those representing the (non-barbaric) Irish – both actually and aurally – are English (and Scottish) signifies the assimilation of the harp music, and thus the Irish harp itself, into English polity. This becomes even more significant if (as suggested by Holman) Cormack MacDermott was one of the two harpers.[74] This civilizing of the Irish harp echoes a theme expressed by Davies when reviewing his reforms of the Irish legal system: 'The strings of this Irish harp, which the civil magistrate doth finger, are all in tune (for I omit to speak of the state ecclesiastical) and make a good harmony in this common-wealth'.[75] The use of the Irish harp in the English consort music tradition can be understood in similar terms of assimilation and appropriation. As Smith put it, 'The victims on the march towards cultural unity include those who contradict, and so implicitly question, the dominance of the incorporating power'.[76] However, despite the attempted cultural assimilation of the harp, by the middle of the century its popularity was in decline, a decline that seems to be directly linked to the demise of the harp consort.

The period 1642–60 naturally had an inimical effect on certain genres of music that were either associated with the court or that were dependant on resources seldom available outside of the court. The harp consort, like the masque, was one of these genres. Isolated examples notwithstanding, both genres floundered after the disbandment of the court in 1642 largely because the environment that had led to their creation was itself defunct. An isolated example of newly-composed harp consorts (with parts composed for the harp) are to be found in MS 5, which in addition to the Lawes pieces also contains what appears to be sixteen full-voiced harp parts.[77] The pieces date to around the middle of the century and are anonymous; Lawes, Coprario, and Ives have been suggested as

---

73 David Lindley, "Embarrassing Ben: the masques for Frances Howard", *English Literary Renaissance*, 16 (1986), 343–59 at 357.   **74** Holman, 'Harp', 194.   **75** Davies, *Discoverie*, p. 284.   **76** Smith, 'Effaced history', 301–2.   **77** See Holman, 'Harp'; Cunningham, 'Music for the privy chamber', pp 265–71.

possible composers, although a firm attribution based on style is difficult as only the harp parts have survived.[78] These parts were written for ensemble performance and appear to have been composed for a harp with similar dimensions to the 'Lawes harp' presented above. However, in 1654, around the time that these consorts were copied, the diarist John Evelyn commented on the neglect suffered by the Irish harp, thoughts which he echoed in 1668.[79] Indeed, in May 1660 Samuel Pepys noted that 'the Harp must be taken out of all their flags, it being very offensive to the King'.[80] Certainly, by the time the 1678 edition of Simpson's *Compendium* was published the Irish harp had largely fallen out of favour at court. The harp was not a significant feature of English courtly musical life after the Restoration, and where it does feature it is the Italian rather than the Irish type. Lewis Evans was reappointed to the court in 1660; however, he died in October 1666, apparently in poverty;[81] arrears of pay were a common complaint among Restoration court musicians. The last official harper employed at the Stuart court was Charles Evans, who was most likely a close relation of Lewis; however, in a document detailing the purchase by the Crown of an Italian harp for fifteen pounds Charles is described as 'musician in ordinary for the Italian harp'.[82]

The cultural assimilation of the Irish harp in the early seventeenth century does not ignore the fact that the Irish harp 'agrees well' in consort. Nor does it ignore the fact that this was a period when many instruments were trying to find solutions to the modulations required in the emergent tonal system. These points notwithstanding, the assimilation reading does suggest that from the end of the sixteenth century to the mid-seventeenth century the Irish harp itself, its musical 'self' – i.e. all that was appealing for use in consort with the viol to observers such as Bacon – gradually became more heavily imbued with a burgeoning representation of Ireland (as rebellious, Catholic, 'other'). Indeed, the Ireland that the harp signified during the first half of the seventeenth century was a dependency that, although it initially enjoyed a period of relative calm, was becoming increasingly troublesome and untrustworthy, culminating in October 1641 with the outbreak of revolt and the massacre of English and Scottish protestants in Ulster. Distrust of Ireland was heightened in the mid-1640s when it became evident that Charles I was attempting to make a deal with Irish Catholics in order to secure his return to the throne; the Cromwellian conquests did little to engender sympathy. Thus, by the end of the 1640s the Irish harp was to speak with a mute rhetoric that sat uneasily with consort music patrons and audiences: a cultural rhetoric that would not allow a harp consort to survive the turbulent period of the English civil war and interregnum. In its silence the Irish harp spoke of an 'otherness' that was in the middle of the century, more than ever before, viewed with great suspicion. Nevertheless, any argument that places too

---

78 Respectively: Holman, 'Harp'; Layton Ring, 'The harp for Lawes', *EM*, 15 (1987), 589–90; Cunningham, 'Music for the privy chamber', pp 270–1.   **79** *Diary of John Evelyn*, iii, pp 92 & 518. **80** *Diary of Samuel Pepys*, i, pp 136–7.   **81** Ibid., vii, p. 414.   **82** *RECM*, i, p. 51.

much emphasis on symbolic interpretations of musical genres in order to explain their development is at best tenuous, at worst contrived. However, if we accept, as I think we must, that there was an attempt at a general programme of assimilation of the Irish (linguistically and culturally) by the ruling English classes in the late Tudor and early Stuart reigns then the idea must surely be extended to Irish music, and hence to the Irish harp. Although not all exponents of the instrument were themselves Irish, the Irish harp was, at some level, becoming a signifier of national identity (both aurally and visually). This was a cultural (and musical) identity that was largely defined in terms of its 'otherness' or 'non-Englishness', an 'otherness' that was attempted to be effaced through Anglicization in the late sixteenth and early seventeenth centuries. The cultural assimilation of the Irish harp allowed the instrument to participate simultaneously and successfully, for albeit a brief period, in the realms of both Irish and English music. However, the cultural crossover of the Irish harp could not be sustained once the cultural network of the Stuart court had been dismantled in the 1640s and 1650s. It is perhaps no coincidence that once the Irish harp ceased to be an untenable participant in the English consort tradition the instrument's need for modulation notes dissipated, and the Irish harp largely returned to its diatonic (and Irish) origins by the end of the century. Indeed, one suspects that the tantalizing reference to a manuscript copy of 'Mr Lawes Harp Consort ... in 4 parts, quarto, fairly pricked' in Henry Playford's sale catalogue of 1690 was unlikely to have contained the complex movements of the collection, with their full-voiced harp parts.[83] Ironically, if the harp parts were included they were most likely performed on an organ or harpsichord. There were significant practical reasons for the decline of the Irish harp consort, but there were symbolic complexities too: complexities that were all too great to allow the Irish harp, an instrument nominally characterized by its nationality, to continue to speak in concert with the English consort tradition.

---

83 'A curious collection of musick-books ...', *GB-Lbl*, MSS Harl. 5936, nos. 419–20, no. 117.

The earl of Cork's musicians: music and patronage in early seventeenth-century Anglo-Irish society

BARRA BOYDELL

The changing dynamics of political and cultural power in early modern Ireland are nowhere more prominently reflected than within the New English households of the early seventeenth century. Colonists, planters and adventurers who settled in Ireland during the Tudor and early Stuart periods, the 'New English' formed a group distinct from their Anglo-Irish co-linguists the 'Old English', namely those whose ancestors had come to Ireland during the medieval period and who had become largely assimilated by custom and religion, if not necessarily by language, with the native Irish population. Whether holders of high office including the lord deputies, whose position embodied the obligation to patronize music and the arts as a 'token of English civility',[1] or lesser grandees aspiring to (and often achieving) wealth, power and eminence, the New English formed a class, often tightly-knit both politically and through marriage and kinship, among whom the patronage of music was one of a number of ways of demonstrating their civility, their sense of cultural and political superiority, and their common identity. Alan Fletcher has mapped this nexus of patronage in early modern Ireland, among which one of the outstanding figures – both in terms of musical patronage and of wealth and influence – was Richard Boyle, first earl of Cork (1566–1643), whose principal seat was at Lismore, Co. Waterford.[2]

Born in Canterbury of humble origins, Richard Boyle arrived in Ireland in 1588 'penniless but ambitious'.[3] He rose through a succession of influential

This chapter first appeared in the *REED Newsletter*, 18:2 (1993) and is reprinted here in revised form by kind permission of the publishers. Details have been revised in the light of subsequent research and primary source references updated where these have subsequently become available in modern editions: in particular, Fletcher, *Sources* (2001) provides reliable and accessible transcripts of many of the manuscript sources, including many of those originally cited after Grosart (see note 2, below). In all such cases reference is made here to Fletcher in addition to the original source or to Grosart. I reiterate here my thanks to the librarian and staff of the NLI and to Peter Day and David Pearlman, librarians at Chatsworth House, Derbyshire, for their help and assistance and for permission to publish material in their care; in particular I wish to thank Alan Fletcher who most generously shared his researches with me when we were both working independently on the Boyle sources. **1** Fletcher, *Drama, performance*, p. 213 **2** The bulk of Boyle's personal papers, including his diaries (which cover most of his career) and his extensive correspondence, are held at Chatsworth House (Lismore having passed to the Devonshire family in the eighteenth century). Some of this material has been edited and published in Grosart, *Lismore* (1) and Grosart, *Lismore* (2); see also Dorothea Townsend, *The life and letters of the great earl of Cork* (London, 1904). In addition, the surviving household accounts from Lismore from 1605–9, from 1611, and from late 1626 continuously until 1645 (two years after Boyle's death in 1643) are held in the NLI alongside other miscellaneous papers (*IRL-Dnli*, MSS 6243, 6895–900). Most but not all entries relating to music are edited in Fletcher, *Sources*, pp 404–17 **3** Nicholas Canny, *The upstart earl: a study of the social and*

contacts, the purchase of lands (most notably the Munster estates of Sir Walter Raleigh which he bought in 1602 for the sum of one thousand pounds), and two advantageous marriages, eventually becoming the wealthiest English landowner of his generation.[4] The rapid increase in Boyle's financial position was matched by a no less striking climb in his social standing: knighted in 1603, he occupied a series of important posts in Irish affairs culminating in his appointment as one of the two lords justices of Ireland from 1629 to 1633, and as lord high treasurer from 1631. In 1640 he attained his longstanding ambition when his achievements were recognized at the English court by his appointment to the king's privy council.[5] The extent of Boyle's political achievements and his position within Anglo-Irish and New English society is reflected in the size of his band of up to six musicians. Commenting on the permanent group of two boys and three to five men maintained during the period 1607 to 1612 by Robert Cecil, first earl of Salisbury and one of the leading English noblemen of the time, Lynn Hulse wrote:

> Few early seventeenth-century aristocratic households maintained a group of professional musicians in full-time employment … A number of patrons could assemble a consort of singers and/or instrumentalists, but some of its members were either competent amateurs gathered from within the household or professional musicians borrowed temporarily from relatives and friends or from court.[6]

The size of Boyle's musical household thus equalled or even surpassed the norm in England, notwithstanding the geographical isolation from the English court and the very different conditions pertaining in Ireland.[7]

In order to understand the context of music in Boyle's household in Ireland it is helpful to look briefly at the social conditions among Munster planters during the early seventeenth century and at the social and cultural aspects of the life and career of Richard Boyle himself. Between the battle of Kinsale in 1603 and the outbreak of rebellion in 1641 a climate of relative peace and stability prevailed over most of Ireland. Particularly in Munster an established infrastructure of trade and communications existed against which background English settlers could enjoy a lifestyle not significantly different to that which prevailed in England itself. Historian Michael McCarthy Morrogh has commented:

> the tendency to imagine early seventeenth century [Munster] as wild, lawless and radically different from England was shared by many at that time, and some historians today. English residents in Ireland were pained by this

mental world of Richard Boyle, first earl of Cork, 1566–1643 (Cambridge, 1982), p. 5.   **4** W.H. Grattan Flood characterized Boyle as 'one of the most unscrupulous adventurers that ever came to Ireland' (*History*, p. 190).   **5** Canny, *The upstart earl*, pp 4–7.   **6** Hulse, 'Musical patronage', 25–6.   **7** As lord deputy, Sir John Perrot also maintained a band of six musicians in 1585. See Fletcher, *Sources*, p. 426.

ignorant assumption and would carefully explain the similarities and common civilisation between the two countries … these comments confirm the image of Munster as akin to a slightly raffish county on the English borders.[8]

Nicholas Canny has highlighted Boyle's acute awareness both of his being very much a parvenu among the English aristocracy and of his lack of a cultured, aristocratic upbringing.[9] Boyle made efforts to counter the first of these short-comings by forging alliances with both the English and the Irish aristocracies (both Gaelic and Old English) through the marriages of his many children. To compensate for his lack of a cultured, aristocratic background he not only took great care in the education of his sons along socially appropriate lines, but he also lavished enormous attention on his houses and estates at Lismore, Youghal and elsewhere in Ireland. The two youngest of his seven sons, Francis (b. 1623) and Robert (b. 1627), the latter of whom was to become famous as one of the leading scientists of his day who established 'Boyle's Law', were educated at Eton. There they were taught 'to play on the viol and to sing'.[10] That singing was regarded for young gentlemen as more an aid to elocution than a musical training is however implied in a letter to Boyle from Sir Henry Wotton, provost of Eton:

My good Lord, I have commended seriously and with promise of a good reward your spirity Robin to the master of our choristers here: who maketh profession (and hath in one or two before given good proof thereof) to correct the errors of voices and pronunciation.[11]

Subsequently the two boys were sent on the Grand Tour during which their tuition included dancing, again primarily as a form of exercise and as a training in deportment.[12] On his Irish estates Boyle employed the finest craftsmen, garden designers, and others, creating a fashionable, aristocratic milieu which he could show off with pride to his in-laws and connections from the English court.[13] It is against this background that we should measure Boyle's patronage of music, rather than seeing it as necessarily a reflection of his own personal tastes. In short, Boyle aspired to create in Ireland an estate modelled physically and culturally on the finest English examples of his day, an estate and household in which the patronage of music and the arts served to project an image of wealth, civility and social status.

The Lismore accounts contain only isolated references to music from the early years of the century: on 10 June 1605 nine pence was paid 'to Mistress Ann that she gave to musicians', on 20 March 1606 six pence 'for white wine and bread a

8 Michael McCarthy Morrogh, 'The English presence in early seventeenth century Munster', in Ciaran Brady & Raymond Gillespie (eds), *Natives and newcomers* (Dublin, 1986), pp 189–90.   **9** Canny, *The upstart earl*, ch. 4.   **10** Letter from Robert Carew to Boyle, Nov. 1635. Grosart, *Lismore*, (2), iii, pp 225, 243.   **11** 6 Dec. 1635. Grosart, *Lismore*, (2), iii, p. 228.   **12** Grosart, *Lismore*, (2), iii, p. 282; iv, pp 98, 100, 103, 113, 161, 170, 201, 232.   **13** McCarthy Murrogh, 'The English presence', pp 185–6; Canny, *The upstart earl*, p. 72.

Wednesday morning for the musician[s?]',[14] and at Christmas 1607 three shillings and sixpence to 'the musicians'.[15] While the above payments were all apparently made at Lismore or at Youghal, the absence of any regular payments at this period and the amounts paid which are more in line with single payments than regular suggest that they were payments to visiting musicians on single occasions rather than to musicians in Boyle's regular employ. Any musicians casually employed by Boyle would most likely have lived in Youghal. The council book of the corporation of Youghal indicates that in 1618 the post of town drummer had been held 'in long continuance of time heretofore' by a shoe maker, Cornelas Lorgan, but there are no other references to musicians regularly paid or engaged by the council. However, in August of the same year Edmond Butler 'late of King's Lynn in the county of Norfolk' was apprenticed for seven years to 'Michael Skryne, musician', suggesting that the town did support one or more professional musicians.[16] The first mention of a musician specifically in Boyle's employ occurs in his diary for 22 July 1616 when he records a payment of fifty shillings to 'Stacie my musician'.[17] As will be shown below, William Stacy [Stacie] was to remain one of Boyle's musicians until 1634.

Although music is not referred to in the context of Boyle's household over the next few years, on a number of occasions between 1614 and 1616 his diaries mention Donnell Duff O Cahill (harper to Anne of Denmark, King James I's queen) acting as a messenger delivering letters and sums of money to Boyle's brother-in-law Piers Power of Ballygarran. Donnell Duff O Cahill is again mentioned in July and August 1616 in connection with monies sent to Sir William Fenton, also a brother-in-law of Boyle, in London. Thirteen years later, in May 1629, Donnell Duff O Cahill 'the harper' was again to deliver money when Boyle was resident for a period in England.[18] Another harper is mentioned as a messenger on 21 July 1621 when Boyle gave forty shillings to 'Ned Skott my lord Chichester's harper' to deliver to Lord Chichester, lord treasurer of Ireland (lord deputy of Ireland 1605–15 and thereafter lord treasurer until his death in 1625, Chichester was the dedicatee of Thomas Bateson's second book of madrigals (1618) and may have been directly responsible for the appointment of Bateson as organist at Christ Church cathedral Dublin in 1609).[19]

As well as recalling the traditional role in Gaelic society of travelling harpers acting as messengers, these references reflect the interest in the Irish harp among

14 Chatsworth, Lismore papers, 1, item 136, fo.285v; item 160, fo. 326 (Fletcher, *Sources,* pp 404). The 1606 entry appears to refer to one musician; however the wording is ambiguous and six shillings suggests that there was more than one musician.   **15** *IRL-Dnli*, MS 6895, p. 4 (Fletcher, *Sources,* pp 404–5).   **16** Fletcher, *Sources,* pp 402–3. Michael Skryne was one of Richard Boyle's musicians from 1627 (or earlier) until 1641 when the names of the musicians are last mentioned (see below).   **17** Chatsworth, Lismore papers, 25, p. 131 (Fletcher, *Sources, p.* 406).   **18** Fletcher, *Sources,* pp 405–6. Further on Daniel Duff O Cahill see Donnelly, 'A Cork musician'; Holman 'Harp'; and ch. 4, above.   **19** Chatsworth, Lismore papers, 25, p. 279 (Fletcher, *Sources, p.* 407). 'Ned Skott' is mentioned in 1639 as 'my tenant' at a time when Boyle was resident in England. It is unclear whether or not this is the same person (Diary, 30 May; see Grosart, *Lismore,* (1), v, p. 93). On Chichester and Bateson see Boydell, *History of music,* pp 46–7.

non-Gaelic communities in the early seventeenth century, an interest which is documented not only in England but also on the Continent.[20] Although there is no evidence that Boyle maintained a harper himself on any regular basis (there are no payments to specified harpers in the available accounts), he did own an Irish harp and on at least one occasion presented one as a gift, suggesting that he appreciated the instrument as a fine object in itself: in his diary for 20 February 1620 he wrote: 'I lent my new harp to William Barry the blind harper to raise'.[21] Grattan Flood referred without source to 'William FitzRobert FitzEdmund Barry, a famous blind harper' as being a retainer of Lord Barrymore in 1615. The Barrymore family was a leading Old English Munster family with whom Boyle cultivated close contacts, most notably in marrying his eldest daughter Alice to David, Viscount Barrymore, in 1621.[22] On 10 October 1632 Boyle wrote in his diary 'My cousin William Ryan sent me a fair new Irish harp, which I sent to the lord keeper of England ... and to his lady a runlet of whiskey.'[23] This practice of giving an Irish harp as a gift was not apparently exceptional: Hulse records a similar gift by Eleanor, countess of Desmond, to Robert Cecil, earl of Salisbury, in 1597.[24] A further reference to a harp among the circle of Boyle's English acquaintances occurs in his diary for 16 October 1638 where money is sent to Sir Henry Wotton at Eton 'which with 10*s*. he gave his man that brought over his harp'.[25]

Canny documented Boyle's clear intention prior to 1618 to transfer himself back to England. However, after 1618 Boyle evidently determined to pursue his career in Ireland and to consolidate his power-base here.[26] This decision may lie behind an apparent increase in musical activity from around this date. The reference to 'Stacie my musician' noted above in 1616 may imply that Stacy was Boyle's only musician at that time, since otherwise he might be expected to have referred to him as 'one of my musicians'. However Michael Skryne, who was one of Boyle's musicians between 1627 (or earlier) and 1641, is independently recorded as a musician living in Youghal in 1615 and 1618.[27] The first evidence for an increase in musical activity is an entry in Boyle's diary on 29 June 1617 referring to eight pounds sterling 'paid Mr Brian for a chest of viols he brought me from Minehead' (Minehead ['Mynnyott'] in Somerset was the port normally used for ships sailing between Youghal and England).[28] During the period up to

20 See ch. 4, above. Harpers travelling between different households and courts, especially between Ireland and England, may also have played a role in espionage.   **21** Chatsworth, Lismore papers, 25, p. 242 (Fletcher, *Sources,* p. 407). The 'raising' of a harp referred to the gradual bringing up to tension of the strings. See Donnelly, 'The Irish harp', 57.   **22** Flood, *History,* p. 190; Canny, *The upstart earl,* pp 46–8. See also Fletcher, *Drama, performance,* p. 232.   **23** Grosart, *Lismore,* (1), iii, p. 162. Boyle also refers to the same gifts in a letter from Dublin to Captain Price dated 14 October 1632. See *Calendar of state papers relating to Ireland: Charles I (1625–1632)* (London, 1900), p. 674. A runlet is a small barrel containing approximately 15 gallons.   **24** Hulse, 'Musical patronage', 33.   **25** Grosart, *Lismore,* (1), v, p. 61. **26** Canny, *The upstart earl,* pp 66f.   **27** See note 16.   **28** Chatsworth, Lismore papers, 25, p. 167 (Fletcher, *Sources,* p. 406). A number of people named [Mr] Brian are mentioned in the diaries at this time of whom Randall Brian, apparently a merchant or shipper (c.f. Grosart, *Lismore,* (1), ii, p. 5) would appear to be the most likely candidate here.

the resumption of surviving household accounts in September 1626 there are no further direct references in Boyle's diaries to musical activity at his household. However, he mentions a payment of five pounds to his children 'for their masque' on 24 October 1620.[29]

From late 1626 regular references to household musicians occur in the accounts. At some point between the single(?) musician employed in 1616 and the resumption of surviving accounts in 1626 Boyle had established a permanent band of musicians at his household in Munster. This may have taken place around 1617, the year in which the chest of viols was bought. On 7 November 1626 the accounts record a payment to six musicians for half a year's wages[30] and from that date onwards regular half-yearly wages were paid to a group of musicians at Lismore. The following payment, on 2 May 1627, was fourteen pounds for the six musicians (a once-off payment of five shillings 'to the musicians by your lordship's direction' had been made on 1st January 1627).[31] Until the payment made on 27 October 1628 six musicians are specified.[32] The names of four of these are first referred to in Boyle's diary on 30 March 1627:

I gave to three of my musicians three English cows that I had for heriots, one to Michael Skryne, another to Ann Swete's husband Frances [Jones], the third unto Valentine [Wayman] … and I gave to John Miles 50s., that was due for old John Crokford's heriot, paid him in money'.[33]

The names of the six musicians are confirmed in a number of entries in the accounts, for example on 2 May 1629: 'Paid … to five musicians, viz. to Stacy, Knowles, Valentine, Skryne and Francis Jones for wages – £12 10s.', John Miles having previously been identified as a musician in the accounts on 14 November 1627.[34] There are various people with the name Knowles mentioned in documents, of whom William Knowles appears to be the musician. Although never specified as such, he is frequently listed along with known musicians in rent receipt lists, etc.[35] Nevertheless, an entry in Boyle's diary on 27 January 1632 mentions 'William Knowles to be brewer in gross of Lismore for five years'.[36] If this is the same person as the musician, as is probable, it would indicate that musicians were also engaged in other occupations. The only 'Valentine' more closely identified is Valentine Wayman whose name regularly occurs together with known musicians in the rent lists, especially from December 1637 to November 1641, and whose full name occurs in a payment directly associated with musicians on 5 December 1636 (see below). Valentine is also mentioned in

---

29 Chatsworth, Lismore papers, 25, p. 258 (Fletcher, *Sources*, p. 407). A later reference to a masque at Lismore occurs in the accounts for 24 Dec. 1627 (see below).   30 *IRL-Dnli*, MS 6897, fo. [12v] (Fletcher, *Sources*, p. 408).   31 *IRL-Dnli*, MS 6897, fos. [43, 21v] (Fletcher, *Sources*, pp. 408, 409).   32 *IRL-Dnli*, MS 6897, fo. [137] (Fletcher, *Sources*, pp 409–10).   33 Chatsworth, Lismore papers, 26, p. 96 (Fletcher, *Sources*, pp 408–9). Heriot: '… a render of the best live beast or dead chattel of a deceased tenant due by legal custom to the lord of whom he held' (*OED*).   34 *IRL-Dnli*, MS 6897, fos. [171], [79], [96] (Fletcher, *Sources*, pp 409–10).   35 See for example Fletcher, *Sources*, p. 417.   36 Grosart, *Lismore*, (1), iii, p. 123.

the diaries on the same date in a non-musical context: 'Lent my servant Valentine Waynman [*sic*] £10 sterling gratis, to put him into a stock of tobacco, repayable at May, 1637'.[37]

The number of regular musicians mentioned in the accounts decreases to five after May 1629, the last time that John Miles is mentioned.[38] For the next number of years five musicians are specified and on 30 June 1630 Boyle recorded in his diary: 'Paid for five cloaks for my musicians by Henry Staynes – £8'.[39] The names of four musicians are again specified in Boyle's diaries on 1 November 1632:

I gave order to Mr Waller [John Walley, steward of Lismore] to levy £10 sterling that was due to me for a heriot upon the death of widow Maunsfield and to bestow it on four of my musicians viz to Michael Skryne £5, to Stacie 40s., to Valentine 30 s., and unto Franck 30 s., in all £10.[40]

Although the half yearly wages paid on 16 May 1635 (and subsequently) specify four musicians, on 30 November 1636 there is a payment of £9 13*s*. 6*d*. to a William Page for twenty-one yards 'of broadcloth to make six cloaks for your musicians, and two suits for your lordship's footmen'.[41] Boyle himself refers to this payment in his diary on the same date, confirming six musicians and indicating that the musicians wore red livery: 'cleared all accounts with William Page, the clothier, of Kilmackee, for the red cloth to make 6 cloaks for my six musicians, and suits for my 2 footmen, and paid him £21 9s. 6d.'.[42] On 2 September 1634 William Stacy was paid 'his half year's wages a little before hand, being not due until Michaelmas next, to relieve him in his sickness'.[43] Although his name appeared regularly in conjunction with other musicians, particularly in rent lists up until November 1634, it does not reappear after that date. The inference may be that he died following this illness.

The accounts between December 1636 and April 1637 indicate the temporary additional employment of a boy singer: on 5 December 1636 Valentine Wayman was paid twenty shillings 'which he laid forth for clothes for the musician Jack'; on 20 December nine shillings was 'given to Jack the singing musician to make up his livery cloak'; and on 6 April 1637 is noted: 'Given by your lordship to the musician boy discharged 5*s*.'.[44]

Francis Jones, [William?] Knowles, Michael Skryne, and Valentine Wayman continued as the four regular musicians until November 1641, their names also often occurring together in the rent receipts in May and November of most years. The effects of the 1641 rebellion and ensuing years of unrest are reflected in the

---

37 *Ibid.,* iv, p. 214. **38** Five musicians were paid on 2 May 1629, John Miles on 29 May. *IRL-Dnli,* MS 6897, fos. [171], [175] (Fletcher, *Sources,* p. 410 for 2 May 1629) **39** Chatsworth, Lismore papers, 26, p. 220 (Fletcher, *Sources,* p. 410). **40** Chatsworth, Lismore papers, 26, p. 311 (Fletcher, *Sources,* p. 411). **41** *IRL-Dnli,* MS 6899, fo. [24v] (Fletcher, *Sources,* p. 414). **42** Fletcher, *Sources,* p. 414. Note the discrepancy between the payment as listed in the accounts and in the diary. **43** *IRL-Dnli,* MS 6898, fo. [188v] (Fletcher, *Sources,* p. 413). **44** *IRL-Dnli,* MS 6899, fos. [25v], [29v], [45v] (Fletcher, *Sources,* p. 415).

increasing irregularity of the account books of those years, with matters of immediate military concern and the defence and repair of Lismore House (now Lismore Castle) taking over from regular payments to all but the most essential staff. It is therefore not wholly unexpected to find no further mention of the musicians after November 1641, the one exception being a payment on 20 December 1641 'to one John Downing for a trumpet 20s.'[45] The many other military expenses at this time suggest the context of this trumpet.

The gradual reduction in the number of regular musicians employed at Lismore broadly reflects Boyle's often lengthy periods of absence. Boyle spent six years from April 1628 until December 1634 in England and Dublin, only briefly visiting Lismore in the summer of 1631, and the last payment to six musicians was noted above as occurring at the beginning of May 1629, one year into this period of absence. Boyle stayed at Lismore for Christmas 1634, after which he returned to his Dublin house from late January 1635 to July 1636. The apparent reduction to four regular musicians after the November 1634 payment thus coincides with this continued stay in Dublin. From July 1636 he spent his first period of prolonged residency at Lismore for a number of years and it was during this period that the liveries specifying six musicians, possibly including two temporary appointments, were made in November 1636 and that 'Jack the singing musician' was temporarily employed at Christmas 1636.

The wages paid to the musicians employed by Boyle remained at five pounds annually (paid in two moieties) throughout the entire period under review. This falls broadly in the middle of the range of wages for other household servants at Lismore (with whom the musicians' payments were often grouped).[46] For example, a groom was paid a total of £3 10s. per annum around 1630, Strongman Page (Lord Buttevant's servant) five pounds in 1641, the park keeper five pounds in 1620 (he later received six pounds), while the head gardener earned £6 13s. 4d. in 1641 (reflecting the considerable energy and cost expended by Boyle in creating a garden of the first rank).[47] 'Four or five pounds a year' was suggested by one contemporary English writer as being a normal wage for musicians.[48] An annual wage of five pounds (whether in English or Irish currency, the latter being worth slightly less) would also seem to bear comparison with other musicians in Ireland around this period: some decades earlier three of lord deputy Sir John Perrot's six musicians in 1585 had received the same amount (one hundred shillings),[49] while John Brooks received four Irish pounds a year as Dublin city

45 *IRL-Dnli*, MS 6900, fo. [18] (Fletcher, *Sources*, p. 417).   46 For example *IRL-Dnli*, MS 6899, fo. [25v], 5 Dec. 1636 (Fletcher, *Sources*, p. 415): 'Paid to Ferdnando Hayworth [personal servant?], to four musicians, to John Foster [a groom], and to Thorpe the brewer for their several wages due at Michaelmas 1636 – £16 10s.'   47 See e.g. *IRL-Dnli*, MS 6897, fos. [208], [236] (groom, 12 Dec. 1629; 16 May 1630, both payments listed together with musicians); MS 6243, fo. [137]; MS 6900, fo. [13v] (Strongman Page, 13 Mar., 24 Nov. 1641. Strongman Page was recommended as a vicar choral at Lismore in 1639. See below, note 71); MS 6977, fo. [234], MS 6243, fo. [112v] (keeper, 3 May 1630, 22 Oct. 1640); MS 6243, fos. [145v], [161] (gardener, 26 Apr., 30 July 1641). However, a new coachman was engaged on 11 July 1637 at an annual wage of eight pounds (Grosart, *Lismore*, (1), v, p. 20).   48 Hulse, 'Musical patronage', 28. 49 Fletcher, *Sources*, p. 426. The three other musicians were paid somewhat more.

trumpeter (in addition to thirty shillings for his livery and two pounds for 'keeping the clock') in 1609–10 and 1611–12.[50] In 1636 the Dublin city musicians' stipend increased from ten pounds Irish to ten pounds English, a sum which included their livery costs, their keeping 'a good singing boy from time to time' and their relatively onerous duty to 'keep their constant waits three times a week from Michaelmas until Shrovetide yearly', duties and expenses which were doubtless more demanding than those of Boyle's musicians.[51] Boyle's musicians regularly recur in the rent receipt lists twice a year, where they normally pay between fifteen and twenty-two shillings each as 'half year's rent for a mess', indicating that they received meals in the house. Francis Jones's rent in May 1640 specifies 'for a house and garden'.[52] That the musicians (and other servants) were not solely dependant on their wages is indicated by the gift in 1627 quoted above to several musicians of cows received by Boyle as heriots and possibly by the fact that grazing rights were specified in 1620 in the payment of the park keeper who, as noted above, received approximately the same annual wage as the musicians.[53] Sympathy was extended to musicians (and to other regular servants) in times of illness, as in 1634 when William Stacy was paid his half yearly wages two months early (see above). Musicians and their wives also feature in a number of miscellaneous contexts in connection with the household: in 1635 Michael Skryne's wife Ann was paid for washing and for mending linen and William Knowles was paid to accompany 'Goodwife Burrage' to Youghal; Francis Jones was one of the witnesses to a land lease signed in 1636.[54]

The regular listing of the names of known musicians in both the half-yearly rent receipts and the wage payments at Lismore, irrespective of whether or not Boyle was in residence, suggests that Boyle did not bring his musicians with him when he spent lengthy periods living away from Lismore. Furthermore, the fact noted above that the musicians rented houses and gardens on a regular basis, kept cattle, and were involved as servants in duties unconnected with music implies that they were employed not so much as full-time musicians but as servants of the household who could provide music if and when the need arose. The relative paucity of accounts relating to the purchase and repair of instruments, strings, etc., further suggests that they may not have been called upon to play all that much.

Apart from occasional references to visits of actors, of puppet players, and of 'rope dancers',[55] the only specific occasions mentioned on which the musicians at Lismore would have played are a masque in which his children took part in October 1620 (see above) and another masque at Christmas 1627 for which

---

50 Ibid., pp 311, 314.   **51** Ibid., p. 330.   **52** *IRL-Dnli*, MS 6243, fo. [78].   **53** 'North [the new park keeper] … is to have £5 a year, the grazing of four cows and two horses in my park', Diary, 5 Jan. 1620 (Grosart, *Lismore*, (1), i, p. 238).   **54** Assuming these to be the musicians of the same names. *IRL-Dnli*, MS 6898, fos. [223v], [240], [235v] (2 Mar., 2 June, 4 May 1635); Chatsworth, Lismore papers, 18, item 143.   **55** *IRL-Dnli*, MS 6897, fos. [11], [80] (29 Oct.–4 Nov. 1626; 18 Nov. 1627); MS 6898, fo. [248v] (16 July 1635); MS 6899, fo. [108] (30 Mar. 1638) (Fletcher, *Sources*, pp 408, 409, 413, 416).

Boyle's fifteen-year-old eldest son Richard, Viscount Dungarvan, was paid three pounds 'to help ... with necessaries for his part of the masque'.[56] It is likely that at least some of the music performed in masques at Lismore would have been composed or arranged by Boyle's musicians. Noting that the twenty-one-year-old Viscount Dungarvan later took part in a 'royal masque' with Charles I in London in 1634 Fletcher comments that:

> The Lismore masques had less resources at their disposal than the royal ones and would doubtless by comparison have seemed provincial, but ... more pertinent is the fact that masques were fashionable for the Boyle household to be putting on; Viscount Dungarvan was being prepared from childhood for his court début, and joining the ranks of those aristocratic English children for whom masking was an approved pastime.[57]

No sheet music or other indication of what was played by Boyle's musicians has come to light. There is a single undated sheet with the words of a 'new song' at the end of which is written in a different hand 'To the tune let us go to Virginia / Lads and there we shall be merry'. This scurrilously anti-Catholic ballad contains references to the count of Gondomar (Spanish ambassador to the court of James I), to parliament and to the duke of Buckingham: it would appear to relate to the events of March/April 1624 when Buckingham supported parliament in its refusal to support the Spanish match negotiated by King James between the prince of Wales and the daughter of Philip IV of Spain.[58] It has already been noted that two of Boyle's sons were taught the viol and to sing while at Eton; the musicians' duties at Lismore are likely also to have included teaching the lute, viol or other instruments to the members of the family.[59]

The purchase of a chest of viols from England in 1619 has been noted, but further evidence as to what instruments Boyle's musicians played is limited to a single payment in the accounts, on 5 December 1626, 'for strings for the viols and lute bought by Francis Jones. 5*s*.'.[60] Prior to a planned visit to Ireland by Viscount Dungarvan's English parents-in-law, Lord and Lady Clifford, Boyle wrote to Dungarvan on 21 July 1634: 'I will promise my Lady [Clifford] frequent and good sermons, and music in my own chapel'.[61] A series of payments during 1626 and 1627 record the building of an organ in the chapel at Lismore,

---

56 *IRL-Dnli*, MS 6897, fo. [86v] (24 Dec. 1627). David Price has commented in this context that 'there was not only a considerable appetite among courtiers for the music and poetry of entertainments but ... this delight was transmitted to various country households and often imitated there as soon as conveniently possible' ('Gilbert Talbot, seventh earl of Shrewsbury: an Elizabethan courtier and his music', *ML*, 57 (1976), 146–7). **57** Fletcher, *Drama, performance*, p. 229. On Dungarvan's acting in the royal masque see ibid., p. 412. **58** Chatsworth, Lismore papers, 14, item 323. The ballad has nine stanzas beginning 'Heigho I'll tell you news / the pope is stark a-dandy / His head is shorn his arse is down / Oh that's as good as can be' and a refrain 'With a heigh down derry / heigh down derry / Gondomar is an ass in grain / And therefore she be merry'. I am grateful to Raymond Gillespie for identifying the context of this ballad. **59** In relation to the earl of Salisbury's musicians' teaching duties see Hulse, 'Musical patronage', 31. **60** *IRL-Dnli*, MS 6897, fo. [17] (Fletcher, *Sources*, p. 408). **61** Chatsworth, Boyle letter book ii, fo. 40.

providing the earliest evidence to date for an organ in a private household in Ireland. On 7 November 1626 twenty-two pounds was paid 'to James Rose for the wind instrument in the chapel', suggesting a small chamber-sized organ.[62] Payments for materials and work in connection with what is variously referred to as the 'wind instrument', 'organ work', and 'organs' were made to John Foxe, a joiner, on 18 November 1626 and subsequently to 'the Dutch joiner'.[63] There are payments in February 1630 of three shillings and sixpence 'for some repair of the wind instrument' and on 20 June 1638 of ten shillings 'for the mending of the organs that are in the chapel of Lismore house'.[64]

The names of organists at Lismore in the 1630s are referred to in Boyle's diaries. On 20 December 1636 he mentions 'my organist Thomas Webb' being made a vicar choral of Lismore cathedral and three years later, on 4 June 1639, he wrote: 'I sent [my cousin dean] my presentation for Frances Baven to be presented to the vicarage of Colligan, fallen void by the death of Thomas Vining, my last precentor, and organist in my chapel.'[65] It is not clear if a distinction should be made between the organists of the chapel of Lismore House and of the cathedral, which Boyle started to rebuild in 1633. A college of five vicars choral had been founded at the cathedral in the thirteenth century and it is known that there was a daily choral service in 1615.[66] The five vicars choral are mentioned in Boyle's papers on a number of occasions, sometimes by name, and it is likely that they also sang in Lismore House, for example in the context of the 'music in my own chapel' mentioned by Boyle in his letter to Dungarvan in 1634 (see above). In his diary for 25 August 1626 Boyle first refers to an unspecified number of vicars choral in connection with the church at his model town of Tallow ['Tallagh'], Co. Waterford.[67] On 6 December 1630 his chaplain William Snell 'made request unto me to be made dean of Rascarbry [Rosscarbery, Co. Cork], and parson of Christchurch in Cork, he promised me to resign his chantership of Waterford, and his vicar choral's place in Lismore, for Mr Stephen Jerome'.[68] It is however apparent from Boyle's diaries that William Snell remained a vicar choral until December 1636:

I paid Mr William Snell ... £20, for which he resigned his vicar choral's place in the cathedral church of Lismore for my organist Thomas Webb, who is made a vicar choral by the dean in his place. And Webb is to repay me my £20 sterling.[69]

---

62 *IRL-Dnli*, MS 6897, fo. [12v] (Fletcher, *Sources*, p. 408). This James Rose is not otherwise recorded as an organ builder. The earl of Salisbury paid twenty-four pounds for a 'portative wind instrument' bought from the English organ maker Thomas Dallam in 1608. See Hulse, 'Musical patronage', 31. 63 *IRL-Dnli*, MS 6897, fos. [13v], [15] (18, 23 Nov. 1626); fos. [16–19] (2, 9, 16, 23 Dec. 1626); fo. [35] 20 Mar. 1627. The 'Dutch joiner' appears in subsequent payments, but not specifying the organ: ibid, fos. [46] (22 May 1627), [95v] (29 Feb. 1628). 64 *IRL-Dnli*, MS 6897, fo. [219v] (21–7 Feb. 1630); MS 6899, fo. [124v]. 65 Grosart, *Lismore*, (1), iv, p. 216; v, p. 94. 66 Gilbert Mayes, *Saint Carthage's cathedral Lismore: some historical notes* (typed leaflet, Lismore, 1967). Grindle, *Cathedral music* first mentions Lismore cathedral in the early nineteenth century. 67 Grosart, *Lismore*, (1), ii, p. 195. 68 Ibid., iii, p. 65. 69 Ibid., iv, p. 216.

The number of vicars choral is specified in March 1638 in the context of 'building the cathedral church and houses for the five vicars chorals of Lismore'.[70] A letter dated 25 May 1639 from Robert Naylor (Boyle's cousin and dean of Lismore) to Boyle who was then in England mentions a Mr Goodrich who held a position as vicar choral. The same letter goes on to mention that:

> We have lately had a great mortality in the town of Lismore where we have buried four vicars choral, Francis Jones his wife [i.e. the wife of Francis Jones, the musician] ... and many others. God's heavy wrath is justly fallen upon them, it being grown one of the most dissolute towns in Ireland, they have all died of pestilential fevers ... My greatest care hath been to supply our church with honest quiet vicars chorals; among the rest I have bestowed one of the places on Strongman Page (a man qualified for it, because musical) who deserves very well for his great care he hath of his little lord.[71]

On 28 May 1640 Thomas Badnedge, also writing from Lismore to Boyle in England, mentions a Mr Owens, one of the vicars choral.[72]

Beyond his immediate patronage of music within his household and at Lismore cathedral and in other churches within his domains Boyle was also engaged in the mutual network of musical and artistic patronage within the wider network of Anglo-Irish (and English) society. While in Dublin in 1606 he patronized 'my lord of Howth's musicians' (who were also engaged by the merchant tailors' guild of Dublin on occasions when the Dublin city musicians were unavailable);[73] in Cork on 11 June 1617 he paid out two shillings and sixpence 'to my lord president's musicians', a reference to Donough O'Brien, earl of Thomond, who was lord president of Munster from 1615 to 1624.[74] On 10 August 1617, also in Cork, twelve pence (one shilling) was given 'to the musician's boy at Mr Clayton's' and on 22 March 1623 two shillings and sixpence was paid out for 'musicians at Sir Randall Clayton's' (Clayton, an English planter like Boyle, was clerk of the council of Munster; he and his wife acted as foster parents to several of Boyle's daughters).[75] In October 1618 five shillings were paid to 'the musicians at Bandon' (one of Boyle's 'model towns' built after the English manner).[76] On several occasions while in London Boyle made payments to the king's musicians either as regular New Year's gifts or on the occasion of an audience with the king: on 19 May 1628, two days after having been presented 'to his Majesty, whose royal hands I had the honour to kiss, accompanied with gracious language full of comfort', Boyle records in his

---

70 Ibid., v, pp 41–2; see also p. 46 (9 Apr. 1638).   71 Chatsworth, Lismore papers, 20, item 36. Strongman Page is noted in 1641 as servant to Lord Buttevant ('his little lord'). See above, p. 88. 72 Chatsworth, Lismore papers, 21, item 17.   73 Chatsworth, Lismore papers, 2, item 20, fo. 31v (Fletcher, *Sources*, p. 404); Fletcher, *Sources*, pp 311, 312.   74 Chatsworth, Lismore papers, 8, item 55 (Fletcher, *Sources*, p. 406).   75 Chatsworth, Lismore papers, 8, item 107; 1, item 1 (Fletcher, *Sources*, pp 407, 408); Canny, *The upstart earl*, pp 100–1, 188.   76 Chatsworth, Lismore papers, 9, item 80 (Fletcher, *Sources*, p. 407).

diary that he 'gave the king's trumpeters 2 pieces ... and to other trumpeters 10s.'; New Year's payments are mentioned on 3 January 1629 ('I gave ... to the king's trumpeters 20s., to his drums 10s. ... and to the Lord's trumpeters 5s.') and on 4 January 1640 ('to his [majesty's] drums a piece').[77] In Dublin a similar pattern is repeated in regard to the lord deputy's musicians and the city musicians: on 5 June 1632 Boyle noted: 'This day the lord chancellor, the earl of Kildare [Boyle's son-in-law] and myself were royally feasted by the mayor of Dublin in their courthouse with a plentiful banquet, and then all three made freemen, and I gave the city musicians 20s. sterling'.[78] New Year's gifts to musicians in Dublin are noted on 1 January 1634 ('I gave for New Year's gifts ... to my lord deputy's trumpeters, the city musicians, the porters of the several ports [gates] of the city, and others several rewards') and on 1 January 1636 ('I gave ... to the trumpeters and drums of the lord deputy 20s.').[79]

After the death of Richard Boyle, first earl of Cork, in 1643 and the return to more peaceful times following the turmoil of the 1641 rebellion and the Cromwellian period, the picture that is suggested by the incomplete Lismore accounts (which survive from September 1662 to April 1664 and then from March 1677) is of a sharp decline in musical interest among Richard Boyle's successors. Although broadly similar in general content and detail to earlier account books, the only regular musician mentioned on a number of occasions is Lord Clifford's trumpeter who received a quarterly salary of one pound ten shillings (or a half year's salary of three pounds) on a number of occasions between December 1679 and April 1681.[80] Otherwise there are only isolated payments to pipers and drummers. While the extent of musical patronage among leading Anglo-Irish families in the later seventeenth century remains unclear, this decline in musical activities at Lismore is in line with indications from other sources. For example, the extensive and detailed inventories of the various houses belonging to the dukes of Ormonde list no musical instruments in the later seventeenth century, while a list of the servants of the earl of Ossory (eldest son of the duke of Ormonde) dated 29 September 1680 includes no musicians, although elsewhere trumpeters are mentioned.[81]

The picture concerning musical activity in Anglo-Irish landed society in the early seventeenth century which emerges from this study of the musical patronage of the first earl of Cork confirms that during the first half of the century prior to the outbreak of rebellion in 1641 a relatively stable society existed in which leading families could employ regular musicians. Nevertheless, the number of musicians employed by Boyle is probably unusual and reflects his

---

77 Grosart, *Lismore*, (1), ii, pp 264, 294; v, p. 120. A 'piece' here has the meaning of a silver coin. 78 Chatsworth, Lismore papers, 26, p. 296 (Fletcher, *Sources*, p. 411). 79 Chatsworth, Lismore papers, 27, pp 1, 119 (Fletcher, *Sources*, pp 412, 413–14). 80 *IRL-Dnli*, MS 6902, fos. [85] (1 Dec. 1679), [95] 25 Mar. 1680, [118] 30 Aug. 1680, [152] 21 Apr. 1681. 81 Trumpeters: *IRL-Dnli*, MS 11,047:75 (1680); MS 11,047:28 & 39 (1678). Ormonde inventories of the later seventeenth century comprise the following: *IRL-Dnli*, MSS 2521–2, 2525, 2527–9, 2553 (also includes eighteenth century), 2554–5.

exceptional wealth and influence. With the cultural and economic emphasis of Anglo-Irish families and that of the major urban centres focussed towards England it must be assumed in the absence of more concrete evidence that the music played by these musicians would largely have reflected practices in England. In this respect the lord deputy's court at Dublin castle would have exerted a significant influence as a centre for the introduction of English cultural fashions. In particular Sir Thomas Wentworth (later earl of Strafford), lord deputy between 1633 and 1641 and with whom Boyle was engaged in a protracted power struggle, sought to make Dublin into a leading cultural centre modelled on London.[82] However, Anglo-Irish musical life would surely have been to some extent influenced by native Irish music, in particular by the music of the Irish harpers: Richard Boyle's dealings with harpers and his owning an Irish harp indicates that he was open to local cultural influences, while the corresponding presence of Irish harpers at the English royal court is discussed elsewhere in this volume.[83]

Boyle's death in 1643 coincided with a period of profound change in Irish society. The Cromwellian period in mid-century appears to have marked a watershed, not only in the accepted sense of Anglo-Irish relations and in the patterns of land ownership and society, but also in the patterns of private musical patronage.

---

82 On Wentworth's artistic patronage see Fletcher, *Drama, performance,* pp 242–4, 261–5.   **83** See ch. 4.

An early seventeenth-century library from Ulster: books on music in the collection of Lord Edward Conway (1602–55)

BARRA BOYDELL & MÁIRE EGAN-BUFFET

A manuscript volume in the Public Library of Armagh, otherwise known as the Archbishop Robinson library, contains a catalogue of the library of Edward, second Lord Viscount Conway, one of the major English landowners in early modern Ulster.[1] Born in 1594, Edward Conway inherited the lands of Killultagh, stretching from Lisburn to Lough Neagh, from his father who had been granted them by James I in 1609 after they had been seized from a branch of the O'Neill family.[2] Although he spent most of his active life in charge of the king's troops in parts of England and Ireland, Conway's primary interests lay elsewhere: a contemporary commented that he reserved 'so much time for his books and study that he was well versed in all parts of leaning'.[3] Described as being of great personal charm and a noted epicure, he corresponded with leading intellectuals of his day and was one of the foremost book collectors of his age, his agents travelling to Germany, France and Italy to seek out books for his library.[4] The presence in the catalogue of the signature of George Rawdon (who managed Conway's Ulster estates)[5] confirms that the library to which it refers was located in Ulster, most probably at Conway's principal residence in Lisnagarvey. Although it had clearly been compiled over a number of years, some volumes listed in the catalogue are dated as late as 1639. Since Conway's estate lay in ruins following the 1641 rebellion, during which his house at Lisnagarvey was at least partially ruined, the catalogue in its present state must have been completed between 1639 and 1641.[6]

---

1 *IRL(N)-Ar, Tituli catalogi sequentis in theologia,* cited hereafter as Armagh Conway MS. 2 Or possibly in 1611. See J.F. Burns, 'Lisburn's castle and cathedral', *Lisburn Historical Society,* 5 (1984), www.lisburn.com/books/historical_society/volume 5, accessed 5 Mar. 2008. 3 Edward Hyde, 1st earl of Clarendon, *History of the rebellion,* ed. W.D. Macray, 6 vols (Oxford, 1888), ii, § 83, cited after Ian Roy, 'The libraries of Edward, 2nd Viscount Conway and others: an inventory and valuation of 1643', *Bulletin of the Institute of Historical Research* (1968), 35–46 at 44. 4 *The Conway letters: the correspondence of Anne, Viscountess Conway, Henry More, and their friends, 1642–1684,* ed. Sarah Hutton (rev. ed., Oxford, 1992), pp 7–8; Fletcher, *Drama, performance,* p 241; Roy, 'The libraries of Edward', 44. Notwithstanding the above comments on his literary and intellectual interests, Charles R. Mayes ('The early Stuarts and the Irish peerage', *The English Historical Review,* 73 (1958), 227–51 at 237) cites him as 'bordering on illiteracy, [King] James often saying, in joke, that his beloved favourite [Buckingham] had furnished him with a secretary [Conway] who could neither read nor write'. 5 Armagh Conway MS, fo. 9r. 6 The nature or extent of damage to Conway's estates is unclear: Richard Bagwell, *Ireland under the Stuarts,* vol. 3 (London, 1916), pp 309–10 (cited in *The Conway letters,* p. 172n) stated that the library 'had been burned by the rebels at Brookhill, which belonged to Sir George Rawdon'. Burns, 'Lisburn's castle and

The presence within Conway's library catalogue of a substantial number of titles of musical interest is of particular significance due to the relative paucity of primary sources relating to music in early seventeenth-century Ireland. Alan Fletcher's study of the patronage of drama and performance, including music, has established a wider context for the patronage of music and the arts among the New English aristocracy in early seventeenth-century Ireland.[7] The extensive evidence outlined elsewhere in this volume for music within the household of Richard Boyle, first earl of Cork, may reflect not only the relatively peaceful and settled environment in Munster, but also the exceptional wealth and circumstances of the earl of Cork within Anglo-Irish society. Given that Ulster had only recently been planted and that resistance against the English settlers there was strongest one might not expect to find the same degree of musical activity in Ulster. And yet, as Alan Fletcher comments:

> Unappealing as early seventeenth-century Ulster may generally have seemed to prospective performers, its inhabitants were not so entirely preoccupied with their planting as to lose all sense of the value of drama and the performing arts. Indeed, perhaps it is to be expected that, precisely because the province was restless with plantation activity, the need to show off smart households, wherever possible, would have been even more urgent than in relatively quieter areas of the country.[8]

Fletcher also notes that the first recorded performance (or rather, aborted performance since it had to be called off at the last moment) of a Shakespeare play in Ireland, *Much ado about nothing,* took place not in Dublin but in the recently-founded Ulster town of Coleraine in May 1628.[9] Fletcher has also uncovered evidence that in 1633 Lord Edward Conway brought over four musicians from England who remained in Ulster when he returned for a period to England two years later.[10] It is within this environment, perhaps culturally more active than might at first be imagined, that Conway's library was located. The music books listed in the catalogue of its contents constitute the primary focus of this chapter.

The Armagh catalogue of Conway's library is divided into approximately eighty different subject areas that cover the full gamut, ranging from theology, through the natural philosophies and mathematics, to literature (both classical and contemporary, in a number of European languages), history, biography and travel. The section devoted to music (fos. 141–4) comprises a significant collection of treatises and other musical volumes: in all forty-five books are listed on four folios. They are categorized by size (13 folio volumes, 15 quarto, 15 octavo, and one each of duodecimo and sextodecimo). Forty-one of the forty-five musical

cathedral' states that 'the most valuable part of his [second Viscount Conway's] estate lay in ruins as a result of the 1641 rebellion'.   **7** Fletcher, *Drama, performance*, especially pp 206–60.   **8** Ibid., p. 240.   **9** Ibid., p. 238.   **10** Ibid., especially pp 240–1.

items on fos. 141–4 have been identified (see appendix 1); four further items remain unidentified (see appendix 2); and three further books of musical interest are included at the end of the volume (fo. 532r) under the heading *Rare et incerte materiae scriptores* ('Rare and miscellaneous writings', see appendix 3).

This is clearly a catalogue of a library belonging to an avid bibliophile whose collection of books contains as comprehensive a range of subjects as possible, rather than a collection devoted to a limited number of subject areas. Lord Conway's library provides interesting evidence for the dissemination of treatises on music that are representative both of established classics of renaissance learning and of more recently published authors including Marin Mersenne (d. 1648).[11] It also emphasizes the considerable extent to which the wealthy and educated landed classes in early seventeenth-century Ireland were up-to-date with current European intellectual and cultural interests.

THE MUSIC BOOKS

The focus of Conway's music collection is clearly not on editions of music: we find only three, or possibly, four volumes of vocal music:

- a collection of madrigals by Carlo Gesualdo, dated 1616 (Armagh Conway MS,[12] fo. 142, no. 9; appendix 1, no. 17).[13]
- a collection of Lassus chansons published by Le Roy et Ballard in 1586 which constitutes the third, revised and extended edition of his *Meslanges,* first published in 1570 (Armagh Conway MS, fo. 142, no. 6; appendix 1, no. 20).[14]
- An anonymous collection of love songs and 'airs de cour' entitled *La fleur ou eslite de toutes les chansons amouresuses et airs de court,* Rouen, 1602 (Armagh Conway MS, fo. 144; appendix 2, no. 44).[15]
- and, finally, a collection featuring the *Canzonetta nuouva* by the poet Paolo Britti (Armagh Conway MS, fo. 144; appendix 1, no. 4), published in Terne in 1631. This collection of canzonette may not contain music since Britti was primarily a poet.[16]

---

11 On contemporary music theory, see Thomas Christensen (ed.), *The Cambridge history of western music theory* (Cambridge, 2002), in particular the contributions of Cristle Collins Judd (p. 364), Gregory Barnett (p. 407), Peter Schubert (p. 503), and Albert Cohen (p. 534). **12** See note 1 above. **13** This would appear to be the fourth edition (1616) of Gesualdo's *Madrigali libro secundo,* published misleadingly under the title *Madrigali libro primo.* See *NG II,* ix, 785. See also *RISM Einzeldrücke vor 1800, A/I/3,* (1972), G1742; *Addenda corrigenda, A/I/12,* (1992), GG1742. **14** *RISM Einzeldrücke, A/I/5,* (1975), L967. **15** This anonymous volume is discussed in more detail below, p. 101 and note 32. **16** Cf. *Dizionario enciclopedico della letteratura Italiana* (Rome, 1996), p. 480. The *Catalogue of seventeenth-century Italian books in the British library* (2 vols, London, 1986), p. 151, lists twelve editions of Britti's *Canzonetta nouva,* none of which is either dated 1631 or published in Terne.

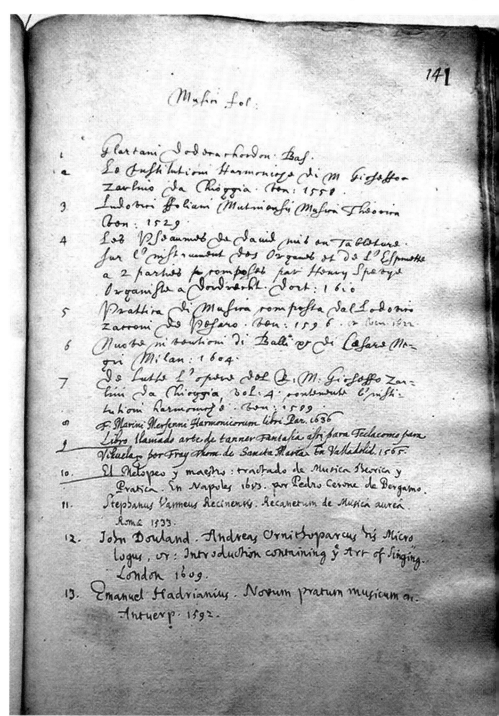

Illustration 6.1. Armagh Conway MS, fo. 141. Armagh Public Library.

Music also features in treatises relating specifically to tablatures. These include:

- a volume of *bicinia* on the psalms in organ and harpsichord tablature by H. Speuye, published in Dordrecht in 1620 (Armagh Conway MS, fo. 141, no. 4; appendix 1, no. 35).[17]
- Thomas de Santa Maria's *Libro llamando*. This is a Spanish edition that shows how to improvize fantasias on vocal music for three parts or more. It contains tablature for vihuela and other instruments (Armagh Conway MS, fo. 141, no. 9; appendix 1, no. 34).[18]
- Emanuel Hadrianius (Adriaenssen), *Novum pratum musicum* (1592) (Armagh Conway MS, fo. 141, no. 13; appendix 1, no. 19). This is concerned with French lute tablature and features instructions printed in Latin on methods of intabulating polyphonic music. Adriaenssen was noted for his intabulation tables. He was a front rank teacher and the founder of the Antwerp lute school.[19]
- Adrian Le Roy's instruction book on lute tablature in an English translation published in London by James Rowbothome in 1574 that claims to 'set all music of 8 divers tunes' (Armagh Conway MS, fo. 142, no. 3; appendix 1, no. 21).[20]

Conway's catalogue features theoretical treatises written in Latin, English, Italian, French and Spanish. These include:

- Latin: Henricus Glareanus, *Dodecachordon* (1547) (Armagh Conway MS, fo. 141, no. 1; appendix 1, no. 18).
- Italian: Gioseffo Zarlino, *Le institutioni harmoniche* (1558) and *De tutte l'opere ...* (1589) (Armagh Conway MS, fo. 141, nos 2 and 7; appendix 1, nos 40 and 41).
- Spanish: Pietro Cerone, *El melopeo y maestro* (1613) (Armagh Conway MS, fo. 141, no. 10; appendix 1, no. 11). Although Cerone was an Italian theorist, he wrote in Spanish to curry favour with the Spanish nobility in Naples.[21]
- French: [Adrian Le Roy], *Traicté de musique* (1602) (Armagh Conway MS, fo. 142, no. 4; appendix 1, no. 22).[22]

---

17 Note the French title: *Les pseaumes de David mis en tableture* and the date, 1620. Alan Curtis, 'Speuy', *NG II*, xxiv, p. 177 only mentions the 1610 Dutch edition of this music and a French edition, now lost, entitled *Certains pseaumes de David* (1621).   **18** Thomas de Santa Maria. Cf. F. Lesure, *Répertoire international de sources musicales écrits imprimés concernant la musique* (Munich, 1971), B/VI/1–2 (hereafter *RISM Écrits*), pp 752–3.   **19** Cf. Godelieve Spiessens, 'Adriaenssen' *NG II*, i, pp 167–8.   **20** Cf. *RISM Écrits*, p. 500. For a modern critical edition see: Jean Jacquot, Pierre-Yves Sordes & Jean-Michel Vaccaro (eds), *Oeuvres d'Adrian Le Roy: les instructions pour le luth (1574)*, 2 vols (Paris, 1977).   **21** Cf. Barton Hudson, 'Cerone' *NG II*, v, p. 380.   **22** Adrian Le Roy was responsible for the first edition of 1583. Cf. Adrian Le Roy, *Traicté de musique,* facsimile ed. and trans. Máire Egan-Buffet, Institute of Mediaeval Music: Musicological Studies 66 (Ottawa, 1996). Le Roy's name does not feature in the three subsequent editions (1602, 1616 and 1617), in which no substantial modifications are found. Cf. *RISM Écrits*, p. 986. For a further, more recent facsimile of the first edition ed. Olivier Trachier, see *Fac-similés Jean-Marc Fuzeau: Méthodes et traités, série 9 (Renaissance)*, 4 vols (Courlay, 2005), iv, pp 213–49.

• English: Thomas Campion, *A new way of makinge foure partes in counter-poynt* [1613] (Armagh Conway MS, fo. 143, no. 1; appendix 1, no. 7).[23]

The range of important theorists represented is quite impressive: P. Cerone, G. Doni, L. Fogliano, H. Glareanus, V. Lusitano, M. Mersenne, A. Ornithoparcus, P. Pontio, S. Vanneus, L. Zacconi and G. Zarlino are all included. Nonetheless, there are notable omissions – P. Aron, N. Vicentino, S. Heyden, F. Gaffurius and Thomas Morley to name but a few.

Treatises relating specifically to the art of singing include:

• John Dowland's English translation dated 1609 of Ornithoparcus' 1517 edition of the *Micrologus* (Armagh Conway MS, fo. 141, no. 12; appendix 1, no. 14).

• Andreas Ornithoparcus' *De arte cantandi [canendi]* (Armagh Conway MS, fo. 142, no. 1; appendix 1, no. 29). This new title was given to the *Micrologus* when published in Cologne in 1533.[24]

• William Barley's, *The pathway to musicke … whereunto is annexed a treatise of descant and certaine tables which doth teach how to remove any song higher or lower from one key to another* (1596) (Armagh Conway MS, fo. 142, no. 13; appendix 1, no. 1).[25]

• Thomas Campion's *A new way of makinge foure partes in counterpoynt … with a briefe method teaching to sing* [*c*.1613]. Note the shortened title in Conway's catalogue (Armagh Conway MS, fo. 143, no. 1; appendix 1, no. 7).[26]

• William Bathe's *A briefe introduction to the skil of songe* [*c*.1596] (Armagh Conway MS, fo. 143, no. 8; appendix 1, no. 2).

• Juan Martinez' *Arte de cante llano* (1554) (Armagh Conway MS, fo. 143, no. 12; appendix 1, no. 25); this Spanish treatise, first published in 1532, is an introduction to plainsong.[27]

In addition to a 1594 edition of Heinrich Faber [Fabri]'s *Compendium musicae* (Armagh Conway MS, fo. 143, no. 14; appendix 1, no. 15) first published in Brunswick in 1548 and described as 'a text-book for beginners in music [and] the most popular music treatise in Lutheran schools during the sixteenth and

23 Campion's treatise is edited by Christopher R. Wilson in *Music theory in Britain, 1500–1700: critical editions* (Aldershot, 2003). See also: Herissone, *Music theory*. **24** Cf. Klaus Wolfgang Niemoller, 'Ornithoparchus', *NG II,* xviii, pp 726–47. **25** Although Barley is thought to have been an accomplished musician, he is not thought to have been the author of this treatise. Note that it is not attributed to Barley in Conway's catalogue. Cf. *RISM Écrits,* p. 118; see also Barry Cooper, 'Englische Musiktheorie im 17. und 18. Jahrhundert', in *Geschichte der Musiktheorie, 9: Entstehung nationaler Traditionen: Frankreich, England.* (Darmstadt, 1986), p. 158; Miriam Miller & Jeremy L. Smith, 'William Barley', *NG II,* ii, p. 736; G.D. Johnson, 'William Barley, "Publisher and seller of bookes" 1591–1614', *The Library,* 11 (1989), 10–49; Jessie Ann Owens, 'Concepts of pitch in English music theory *c*.1560–1640', in Cristle Collins Judd (ed.), *Tonal structures in early music* (New York, 1998), pp 183–246 at 234. **26** Cf. *RISM Écrits,* p. 200. **27** F.J. Leon Tello, 'Martinez', *NG II,* xv, p. 918.

seventeenth centuries',[28] the catalogue includes two other editions of this treatise by composers Laurentius Stiphelius (1614) and Melchior Vulpius (1617) (Armagh Conway MS, fo. 143, nos 2 and 7 respectively; appendix 1, nos 36 and 38). The Conway collection evinces a preference for secular music. We have seen this in the books relating to tablature and in the music books identified above. It is also evident in books pertaining to dance. Caesare Negri's *Nuove inventioni di balli ... conveneuoli à tutti i cavalieri, et dame, per ogni sorte di ballo, balletto, et brando d'Italia, di Spagna et di Franca. Con figure bellissime in rame, et regole della musica, et intavolutara, quali si richieggono al suono, et al canto* (1604) (Armagh Conway MS, fo. 141, no. 6; appendix 1, no. 28), describes dances from Italy, Spain and France and supplies music in tablature.[29] It was first published in 1602 as *Le gratie d'amore*. Fabritio Caroso's two treatises, *Il ballarino ... s'insegnano diverse sorti di balli et balletti si all'iso d'Italia, come à quello di Francia, et Spagna. Ornato di molte figure et con l'intavolatura di liuto* (1581) and *Raccolta di varii balli in occorrenze di nozze, et festini da nobili cavalieri e dame di diverse nationi ... con aggiunta del basso e soprano della musica e intavolatura di liuta à ciascun ballo* (1630), are directed at weddings and feasts of the nobility (Armagh Conway MS, fo. 142, nos 8 and 7 respectively; appendix 1, nos 8 and 9, respectively).[30] The more complete versions of their titles given above indicate that the treatises also contain lute tablatures.

Before proceeding to the anonymous items featured in appendix 2 below, a brief word on the one treatise with an Irish connection (Armagh Conway MS, fo. 143, no. 8; appendix 1, no. 2). The author is William Bathe who was born in Dublin in 1564, the son of a judge and the grandnephew of the earl of Kildare. He studied in Oxford, was ordained a priest in Padua in 1599 and died in Madrid in 1614. His *Brief introduction*, published *c*.1586, was a revision of an earlier treatise of 1584, now lost. Bathe is credited with being the first to propose the movable *doh* system as a substitute for the earlier solmization system based on the three hexachords.[31]

An author has yet to be identified for four of the forty-five music-related entries in Conway's catalogue (Armagh Conway MS, fos. 141–4; appendix 2, nos 42–5). Only one of them, a collection of love songs and 'airs de cour' entitled *La fleur ou eslite de toutes les chansons amouresuses et airs de court*, Rouen, 1602 (Armagh Conway MS fo. 144; appendix 2, no. 44) disregards music theory. A possible composer of this music might be P. Guédron who was based in Normandy until he went to Paris in 1619. He published his first book of *Airs de court* for four and five parts in Paris in the same year, 1602.[32]

There is an interesting comparison to be made between the catalogue entry for the 1529 book on tablature – *Livre pour apprendre a faire & ordonner toutes*

---

28 Clement A. Miller, 'Faber, Heinrich', *NG II*, viii, p. 488. In some editions entitled *Compendiolum musicae*; cf. facsimile of Leipzig, 1551 edition, ed. Olivier Trachier (Baden-Baden, 2005). **29** Cf. *RISM Écrits*, p. 611. **30** Cf. ibid., p. 207. **31** Cf. *RISM Écrits*, p. 122; Rainbow, 'Bathe'; Owens, 'Concepts of pitch'. **32** Cf. G. Durosoir, 'Guédron', *NG II*, x, pp 496–7.

tablatures hors le discant (Armagh Conway MS, fo. 142, no. 11; appendix 2, no. 42) – and the complete title provided in *RISM* in the subsection entitled *Anonymes*:[33] *Livre plaisant et tres utile pour apprendre a faire et ordonner toutes tabulatures hors le discant dont et par lesquelles l'on peut facilement et legierement aprendre a jouer sur les manichordion, luc et flutes.* Antwerpen, G. Vosterman, 12 Oct. 1529. Many of the titles in the catalogue are similarly abbreviated. Although *RISM Écrits* has identified Antwerp as the place of publication and G. Vosterman as the editor, the author remains anonymous.

There are two remaining anonymous manuals (Armagh Conway MS, fo. 142, nos 2 and 10; appendix 2, nos 43 and 45): one, an *Introduction to musicke how to learne to sing,* is probably from England; the other, *Instruction pour apprendre a aisement chanter toute Musique* (1577), is from Caen. These bring to eight the total number of entries devoted to the art of singing in Conway's catalogue.[34]

In conclusion, a brief word on three music-related items found elsewhere in the catalogue (see appendix 3: *Rarae et incertae materiae scriptores*). Thoinot Arbeau's well-known *Orchesographie* (Armagh Conway MS fo. 532r; appendix 3, no. 1) is an important addition to the other treatises in Conway's catalogue devoted to the dance. The only problem is the date 1597: modern bibliographical sources refer to a 1596 edition.[35] This may simply have been a scribal error on the part of Conway's copyist. The anonymous *Instruction de bien danser* (1488) (Armagh Conway MS, fo. 532r; appendix 3, no. 2) is probably a collection of melodies for the basse dance with instructions. Its date raises an interesting line of enquiry. Howard Mayer Brown and Philippe Vendrix identified this or a similar work from Paris as belonging to Michel de Toulouse.[36] The title they give, *L'art et l'instruction de bien dancer,* appears to be an expanded version of that found in Conway's catalogue and the date they suggest is 1490, not 1488. Stanley Boorman postulates the date 1496, having noted that 1488 was added by hand on the extant copy of the book.[37] Could it be that Boorman had consulted the very book that was in Conway's collection?

Finally, Christophoro di Messisbugo (d. 1548) wrote a cookery book, first published in 1549, which is known to musicologists for its description of the wedding banquet in 1529 of Ercole, son of Alfonso I of Ferrara, to Princess Renée, daughter of Louis XII of France, a description which also refers to the music played on the occasion.[38] Conway's catalogue lists a 1617 edition of Messisbugo's book (Armagh Conway MS fo. 534r; appendix 3, no. 3).

---

33 *RISM Écrits,* p. 956. Cf. Howard Mayer Brown & Philippe Vendrix, '*Ut musica poesis*: music and poetry in France', Appendix I, no. 4, *Early Music History,* 13 (Cambridge, 1994), p. 50.   **34** Barry Cooper refers to Thomas Davidson's 'Introduction to musick' (1662) in *Englische Musiktheorie,* p. 169. There is no reference to the Caen publication by Lesure in *RISM,* by Wilhelm Seidel in 'Französische Musiktheorie im 17. und 18. Jahrhundert' in *Geschichte der Musiktheorie,* Band 9, nor in Brown & Vendrix, '*Ut musica poesis*', p. 50.   **35** Cf. Julia Sutton, 'Arbeau', *NG II,* i, pp 841–3; *RISM Écrits,* pp 92–3.   **36** Brown & Vendrix: '*Ut musica poesis*', Appendix 1:1; cf. *RISM Écrits,* p. 918.   **37** Cf. Stanley Boorman, 'Michel de Toulouse' *NG II,* xvi, pp 595–6.   **38** Cristoforo di Messisbugo, *Banchetti compositioni di vivande, et apparecchio generale* (Ferrara, 1549); see José Maria Llorens, 'Estudio de los instrumentos musicales que

In addition to his library in Ulster, Lord Conway also possessed a substantial library in London. The relationship between the music contents of the two libraries is examined here. A volume now in the Public Record Office in Kew contains an inventory and valuation of libraries that were seized by the Puritan parliament in London in 1643 from Royalist and Catholic households. Amongst these is 'An inventory of the books of the Lord Conway delinquent' listing the books sequestered from Conway's London residences at the Charterhouse and the Tower.[39] Conway's was outstandingly the largest library seized: out of a total of over 7,300 titles listed in the inventory and belonging to twenty-six different collections, no less than 4,700, i.e. nearly two-thirds of the total and valued at over two hundred pounds, belonged to Conway. By contrast, the average library listed here contained around 280 titles and was valued at about thirty-six pounds.[40]

Although the number of volumes in the Armagh catalogue broadly corresponds with that of Conway's London library, only a proportion of the music titles listed in Armagh can be positively identified in the London list. This is partially attributable to the fact that, while the Armagh catalogue usually lists books in detail by title, author, place and date of publication, the London inventory was clearly compiled in relative haste, each book being listed in a more abbreviated form, most often without the author's name. It is nevertheless evident that not all books listed in Ulster in *c*.1639–41 reappear in the London catalogue of 1643, while on the other hand the London collection included music volumes not present in the Armagh list. On the evidence of the music books, therefore, Conway's Ulster (Lisnagarvey) and London libraries appear to have been substantially independent collections, although a portion of the former was either transferred to London between 1641 and 1643 or existed there in duplicate copies. A number of examples will serve to illustrate these relationships.

Like Armagh Conway MS, the London inventory lists books by format. Subjects are not differentiated and books are listed in an apparently random order within each format. Armagh Conway MS includes thirteen music titles of folio format, one of which (Zacconi's *Prattica di Musica*) is represented by two copies, the second being a later edition (Venice, 1622) signalled by a subsequent insertion in the catalogue.[41] Only five of these thirteen folio music volumes can be identified in the London inventory: the two copies of Zacconi's treatise are listed separately, in each case simply as 'Prattica de musica It[alian]';[42] Mersenne's *Harmonicorum libri* (catalogued in Armagh Conway MS as 'F. Marini Mersenni

aparecen descritos en la relación de dos festives celebrados el año 1529 en la corte de Ferrara, *Anuario Musical*, 25 (1970), 3–26.　**39** *True catalogue of all the papists and delinquents bookes seized by vertue of severall ordinances of parlement in anno 1643 by the committee for sequestracons setting at Cambden howse London*, GB-Lpro, S.P. 20/7, pp 141–229. See also Roy, 'The libraries of Edward', 35–46 and table. **40** Roy, 'The libraries of Edward', 41, 43.　**41** Armagh Conway MS, fo. 141r.　**42** *GB-Lpro*, S.P. 20/7, pp 149, 154.

Harmonicorum libri. Par[is] 1636') is listed as 'Mersenni harmon.';[43] Adriaenssen's *Novum pratum musicum* (catalogued in Armagh Conway MS as 'Emanuel Hadrianius. Novum pratum musicum etc. Antuerp [*sic*] 1592') is listed as 'Novum pratum musicum It[alian]';[44] while Cerone's *El melopeo* (catalogued in Armagh Conway MS as 'El melopeo y maestro: tractado de musica theorica y pratica. En Napoles 1613. per Pedro Cerone de Bergamo') can possibly be equated with the entry 'De la musica Sp[anish]' in the London inventory.[45] Thus, at least eight of the thirteen folio music books listed in the Armagh catalogue are either absent or cannot be identified in the London list.

Under the quarto books, the unattributed *Traicte de musicque* associated with Adrian Le Roy,[46] a volume of Gesualdo's madrigals,[47] Pietro Pontio Parmegiano's *Ragionamento di musica* (Parma, 1588),[48] Giovanni Battista Doni's *Compendio del trattato de' generi e de' modi della musica* (Rome, 1635)[49] and possibly Luigi Dentice's *Duo dialoggi della Musica* (Rome, 1553)[50] are common to both collections; but Conway's London library also included music volumes not present in the Armagh catalogue. The following entries in the London list do not correspond with any of the remaining ten quarto titles listed in the Conway catalogue: 'Gnarth Quayts harmony',[51] 'Bellum musica',[52] and 'Mizaldi harmonia'.[53] The London inventory does however include an unspecific quarto entry 'Several treatises' which could account for one or more of the outstanding Armagh titles.[54] Blanket entries such as this, and entries listing individual lots of 'books scarce worth valuing', recur under all book sizes in the London inventory. Calvisius's *Melopoeia sive melodiae condendae ratio,* which appears in Armagh Conway MS in an edition dated 1602, may correspond to an entry 'Calvin harmonia et in acta' in the London list of octavo books.[55] None of the other smaller format music books in the Armagh Conway MS have yet been identified in the London catalogue.

The distinct yet partially overlapping contents of the two collections indicate that Lord Conway had at least two separate libraries, although some books probably accompanied him as he moved periodically between Ulster and England, and the possibility of duplication of titles between the two libraries cannot be ruled out. It was parliament's intention to sell the London library sequestered in 1643. However, this did not happen and Conway was able to purchase it back from the authorities some years later when his relationship with parliament improved.[56] Although not without interest given the possible survival

---

43 Ibid., p. 157.   **44** Ibid., p. 153.   **45** Ibid., p. 145.   **46** See note 22, above. Armagh Conway MS, fo. 142r [no.4]: 'Traicte de musicque contenant un theorique succincte pour methodiquement pratiquer la composition. Par[is] 1602'; *GB-Lpro*, 20/7, p. 173.   **47** Armagh Conway MS, fo. 142r [no.9]: 'Del prencipe di Venosa Madrigali. Venice 1616'; *GB-Lpro*, 20/7, p.195: 'Del Prencipe di Venosa Madrigali' **48** Armagh Conway MS, fo. 142r [no. 14]; *GB-Lpro*, 20/7, p. 167.   **49** Armagh Conway MS, fo. 142r [no. 15]; *GB-Lpro*, 20/7, p. 177: 'Trattado della musica'.   **50** Armagh Conway MS, fo. 142r [no. 5]; *GB-Lpro*, 20/7, p. 172 (listed simply as 'Musica It[alian]').   **51** *GB-Lpro*, SP20/7, p. 105.   **52** Ibid., p. 186 (unless this refers to Dentice's *Duo dialoggi della musica* noted above).   **53** Ibid., p. 194.   **54** Ibid., p. 158. **55** Armagh Conway MS, fo. 143r [no. 3]; *GB-Lpro*, 20/7, p. 215.   **56** Roy, 'The libraries of Edward', 44.

of the anonymous *Instruction de bien danser* (1488) noted above, the questions of what became of those books that may have remained in Ulster (if indeed they survived the rebellion of 1641) and of his reclaimed London library lie beyond the scope of this chapter.

CONCLUSION

It is evident that Conway possessed an impressive library in Ulster, a collection that included, whether by design or not, a significant number of books of musical interest. The library's subsequent fate is not known beyond the possible transference of at least part of it to London; although Conway's library may never be recovered, this possibility cannot be ruled out.[57] Evidence for the musical interests of wealthy landowners in early seventeenth-century Ireland is limited, but the existence of the Armagh catalogue provides a revealing insight into the cultural environment of someone of Conway's status and importance living in early seventeenth-century plantation Ulster. The active musical patronage undertaken by Conway in Ulster and by Boyle in Munster[58] suggests that the presence of musical books in Conway's library may possibly represent more than just the magpie interests of a compulsive bibliophile. Indeed, the presence among the otherwise mainly theoretical treatises or books of musical instruction of a handful of musical editions including Gesualdo madrigals and Lassus *chansons* does raise the possibility that some of this music might have been performed by the four musicians whom Conway is known to have brought over to Ulster from England in 1633.

APPENDIX 1: IDENTIFIED ENTRIES

These are the items for which the author has been identified.[59] Where the author's or editor's name is given within square brackets, that name is missing or miss-spelt in the catalogue but it has been possible to identify it. For example, the final entry on Armagh Conway MS, fo. 143, item 15 (appendix 1, no. 27), has the title *questions harmoniques* and the date 1633 but not the author, Marin Mersenne. The French theorist's name does however accompany his other treatise, *Harmonicorum libri* of 1636 (Armagh, Conway MS fo. 141, item 8; appendix 1, no. 26).

---

57 Other, even earlier, music collections have been successfully recovered: cf. J.A. Bernstein, 'Buyers and collectors of music publications: two sixteenth-century music libraries recovered' in J.A. Owens & A. Cummings (eds), *Music in renaissance cities and courts: studies in honor of Lewis Lockwood* (Sterling Heights, Michigan, 1977), pp 21–34. **58** See ch. 5, above. **59** Many titles have been identified in *RISM Écrits*.

1 [Barley, W.], *The pathway to musicke* 1596
2 Bathe, W., *A briefe introduction to the skil of songe* [c.1596]
3 Beurhusius, F., *Erotemata musicae lib: 2* 1591
4 [Britti, P.], *Canzonetta nuoua da Paolo Brizi.* 1631
5 Calvisius, S., *Melopoiiae* 1602
6 Camaris, J., *De graecis latinisque numeraris notis* [deleted]
7 [Campion, T.], *A new way of makinge foure partes in counterpoynt* [1613]
8 Caroso, F., *Il ballarino* 1581
9 Caroso, F., *Raccolta di varii balli* 1630
10 [Case, J.], *The praise of musicke* 1586
11 Cerone, P., *El melopeo y maestro* 1613
12 Dentice, L., *Duo dialoggi della musica* 1553
13 Doni, G. B., *Compendio del trattato de' generi ... della musica* 1635
14 Dowland, J., *Andreas Ornithoparcus his Micrologus* 1609
15 Fabri, H., *Henr. Fabri compendium musicae* 1594
16 Fogliano, L., *Musica theorica* 1529
17 [Gesualdo, C.], *Principe di Venosa madrigali* 1616
18 Glareanus, H., *Dodecachordon* [1547]
19 Hadrianus, E., *Novum pratum musicum* 1592
20 Lassus, O., *Meslanges* 1586
21 Le Roy, A., *A briefe instruction* 1574
22 [Le Roy, A.], *Traicte de musicque* 1602
23 Lusitano, V., *Introductione di canto fermo* 1558
24 Magirus, J., *Ars musica methodice legibus logicis informata* 1596
25 Martinez, J., *Arte de cante Ilano* 1554
26 Mersenne, M., *Harmonicorum libri* 1636
27 [Mersenne, M.], *Questions harmoniques* 1633
28 Negri, C., *Nuove inventioni di balli* 1604
29 Ornithoparcus, A., *De arte cantandi micrologus* 1533
30 Pontio, P., *Ragionamento di musica* 1588
31 Praetorius, C., *Erotemata musicae practica authore* 1570
32 Puteani, E., *Errici Puteani modulata pallas* 1599
33 Reinhardo A., *Musica* 1604
34 Santa Maria, T., *Libro llama[n]do arte de tanner fantasia* 1565
35 Speuye, H., *Les pseaumes de David mis en tableture* 1620
36 Stiphelius, L. (after Fabri, see no. 15), *Compendium musicum Latino-germanicum* 1614
37 Vanneus, S. J., *Recanetum de musica aurea* 1533
38 Vulpius, M. (after Fabri, see no. 15), *Musicae compendium latin-germanicum* 1617
39 Zacconi, *Prattica di musica* 1596 and 1622
40 Zarlino, G. *Le institutioni* 1558
41 Zarlino, G., *De tutte l'opere, vol: 4. contenente l'institutioni* 1589

APPENDIX 2: ANONYMOUS ENTRIES NOT IDENTIFIED

42 Anon., *Livre pour apprendre a faire & ordonner toutes tablatures hors le discant* [Antwerp, G. Vosterman, 1529]

43 Anon., *An introduction to musicke how to learne to sing*

44 Anon., *La fleur ... de toutes les chansons amouresuses et airs de court* Rouen, 1602

45 Anon., *Instruction pour apprendre a aisement chanter toute musique* Caen, 1577

APPENDIX 3: 'RARAE ET INCERTAE MATERIAE SCRIPTORES':
MUSIC-RELATED ITEMS FOUND ELSEWHERE IN THE CATALOGUE

1 fo. 532r: Arbeau, T. *Orchesographie, metode et teorie &c pour apprendre a dancer, battre la tambour &. À Langres 1597.*

2 fo. 532r: [Michel de Toulouse?], *Instruction de bien dancer. À Paris 1488.*

3 fo.534r: Messisbugo, C. da, *Libro nuovo nel qual s'insegna' modo d'ordinar banchetti &c per Christophoro di Messisbugo Venezia 1617.*

Birchensha's 'Mathematical way of composure'

CHRISTOPHER D.S. FIELD

FROM A PUPIL'S DIARY

With this entry in his diary for Monday 13 January 1662, Samuel Pepys introduces us to John Birchensha, composer, viol player, theoretician and teacher:

> Mr Berchenshaw (whom I have not seen a great while) came to see me, who stayed with me a great while talking of music; and I am resolved to begin to learn of him to compose and to begin tomorrow, he giving of me so great hopes that I shall soon do it.[1]

Over the next few weeks the diary provides a chronicle of how Pepys was taught composition by means of a system of rules that Birchensha had devised. In many ways he must have seemed an ideal pupil. A keen amateur musician, he played the theorbo, viol, violin and flageolet, could sing well at sight, and was on friendly terms with several prominent figures in the London musical scene, but had a shaky grasp of counterpoint and harmony, which was no doubt why the prospect of learning to compose with the aid of Birchensha's rules attracted him. The tuition duly commenced on 14 January: 'All the morning at home – Mr Berchenshaw, by appointment yesterday, coming to me – and begun composition of music.' Next morning

> Mr Berchenshaw came again; and after he had examined me and taught me something in my work, he and I went to breakfast in my chamber, upon a collar of brawn. And after we had eaten, he asked me whether we have not committed a fault in eating today, telling me that it is a fast-day, ordered by the parliament to pray for more seasonable weather ... I did not stir out of my house all day, but conned my music.[2]

One of the claims Birchensha made for his rules was that they allowed pupils to make rapid progress. True enough, within a month or so Pepys achieved a

This is a revised version of a paper read on 17 July 2004 at the Royal Northern College of Music, Manchester, during the eleventh Biennial International Conference on Baroque Music, and on 2 Apr. 2005 at the NUI Maynooth conference on Music and Culture in Seventeenth-Century Ireland. It has also benefitted from a seminar on Birchensha's writings held at All Souls College, Oxford, on 10 May 2006, at which Dr Benjamin Wardhaugh and the author were the main speakers. **1** *Diary of Samuel Pepys,* iii, pp 8–9. **2** Ibid., iii, pp 9–10.

modest ability in two-part writing, thanks to frequent lessons and regular practice, and by 24 February had completed his first song, 'Gaze not on swans'. At that stage he was invited to his teacher's house, where he was shown what was probably an elaborate chart of consonant and dissonant intervals in a wide range of keys. Pepys was unsure about the chart's practical usefulness, however, and was becoming anxious at how much his tuition was costing:

> Long with Mr Berchenshaw in the morning at my music practice, finishing my song of 'Gaze not on swans' in two parts, which pleases me well. And I did give him £5 for this month or five weeks that he hath taught me, which is a great deal of money and troubled me to part with it. Thence … over the water to Southwark to Mr Berchenshaw's house and there sat with him all the afternoon, he showing me his great card of the body of music, which he cries up for a rare thing; and I do believe it cost much pains, but is not so useful as he would have it. Then we sat down and set 'Nulla nulla sit formido', and he hath set it very finely.[3]

Two days later Pepys's lesson produced another song, to words by Sir William Davenant from *The siege of Rhodes* ('This cursed jealousy'), but on 27 February a discussion of Birchensha's rules flared up into heated argument:

> This morning came Mr Berchensha to me; and in our discourse, I finding that he cries up his rules for the most perfect (though I do grant them to be very good, and the best I believe that ever yet were made) and that I could not persuade him to grant wherein they were somewhat lame, we fell to angry words, so that in a pet he flung out of my chamber and I never stopped him, being intended to have put him off today whether this had happened or no, because I think I have all the rules that he hath to give, and so there remains nothing but practice now to do me good – and it is not for me to continue with him at £5 per mensem. So I settled to put all his rules in fair order in a book, which was my work all the morning till dinner.[4]

Unfortunately the book in which Pepys set out Birchensha's rules of composition 'in fair order' has not survived, nor any of the exercises he composed under Birchensha's tuition.[5] Clearly he valued what he had learnt, despite the ill-humoured way in which the lessons terminated, and it gave him much pleasure to take out his lute on 14 March and try over two of the songs on which he had worked. Two years later, as he strolled in St James's Park with Captain Silas Taylor and the physician William Hoare (both of them amateur composers), the

---

3 Ibid., iii, pp 34–5; see also pp 15–16, 19–21, 24, 26–8, 32. A setting of 'Nulla nulla sit formido' for bass voice and guitar in *GB-Cmc*, MS Pepys 2591 is in the hand of Cesare Morelli, Pepys' domestic musician between 1675 and 1682, and cannot be regarded as reliable evidence of Birchensha's teaching in 1662.
4 Ibid., iii, pp 36–7.   **5** There is no trace of this material in the *Catalogue of the Pepys Library at Magdalene College, Cambridge* 4:1, ed. John Stevens (Cambridge, 1989).

conversation turned to the subject 'of music and particularly of Mr Berchenshaw's way, which Taylor magnifies mightily, and perhaps but what it deserves'; and in October 1665 we find him 'talking till midnight' with Thomas Hill on the subject of 'Berchenshaw's music rules, which I did to his great satisfaction inform him in'.[6] From time to time he continued to try his hand at composition, following Birchensha's precepts. While waiting for his barber one Sunday morning, he records, he invented 'a duo of counterpoint; and I think it will do very well, it being by Mr Berchensha's rule'.[7]

A 'JUDICIOUS AND EXTRAORDINARILY SKILFUL MUSICIAN'

If Birchensha is remembered at all nowadays, it is usually as Pepys's teacher or because of the impression his ideas made on the mathematicians, natural philosophers and *virtuosi* of the Royal Society, some of whom may have gone so far as to see in him a British Mersenne or Kircher in the making. Henry Oldenburg, the Society's first secretary, helped to spread his fame. Writing to Marcello Malpighi in 1673, Oldenburg mentioned that 'a certain Englishman here, very well versed in both theoretical and practical music, whose name is Mr Birchenshaw', was anxious to obtain a copy of Pietro Mengoli's *Speculationi di musica* (Bologna, 1670); and in a review of this same book a few months later we find him deferring to

> the judgment of the great masters of music, especially to the judicious and extraordinarily skilful musician Mr John Birchensha; who, it is still hoped, if he be competently encouraged and assisted, will in due time publish to the world a complete system of music.[8]

Isaac Newton in Cambridge and Martin Lister in York both received accounts from Oldenburg of how 'that famous and extraordinary musician, Mr Birchinshaw' demonstrated his 'complete scale of music' to the Royal Society on 10 February 1676.[9] Though not a fellow himself, Birchensha submitted papers, letters and synopses to the Society's scrutiny, was invited to participate in acoustical experiments, and presented occasional concerts which fellows and their friends attended.

---

6 *Diary of Samuel Pepys*, iii, p. 46; v, pp 174–5; vi, pp 282–3. 7 Ibid., vi, pp 266, 320, 324; vii, pp 2, 53, 74–5, 96, 257, 362. John Hayls' portrait (1666, National Portrait Gallery, London) shows Pepys proudly holding a manuscript of his song 'Beauty, retire' – another setting of lines from *The siege of Rhodes* – which he composed on 6 Dec. 1665; for a reproduction in colour, see *The illustrated Pepys*, ed. Robert Latham (London, 1978), facing p. 104. GB-Cmc, MS Pepys 2803 contains a version of 'Beauty, retire' in Morelli's hand (fos. 111v–112v; facsimile in *Diary of Samuel Pepys*, vi, facing p. 320) which, though related to the incipit in the portrait, is plainly a later reworking. 8 *The correspondence of Henry Oldenburg*, ed. A. Rupert Hall & Marie Boas Hall (London, 1975), x, pp 6–9; *Philosophical transactions*, 8:100 (9 Feb. 1674), 7000. The letter to Malpighi is written in Latin ('est hic Anglus quidam, in musica tum theoretica tum practica apprime versatus, qui Dominus Birchenshaw appellatur'). 9 *The correspondence of Henry Oldenburg* (London, 1986), xii, p. 334; *The correspondence of Isaac Newton*,

To musicians in Restoration London, on the other hand, Birchensha must have seemed something of an enigma. It is true that no less a master than Matthew Locke recommended him to the young Oxford graduate Thomas Salmon as a composition teacher, 'assuring him I knew of no man fitter for that purpose; it being in a manner his whole business'.[10] Nevertheless one gets the impression that Birchensha and Locke moved on different planes. Here was a composer and teacher who boasted that the mysteries of the composer's craft could be reduced to 'a few, easy, certain, and perfect rules (never yet invented or published by any man) which may be understood, and made practice of, in a few weeks, or months at the farthest, by any reasonable capacity'[11] yet whose own works were not, it seems, particularly esteemed or widely performed.[12] He believed that studying the mathematical foundations of harmony 'raiseth our minds and contemplation (in music) to those things which are philosophical: and stirreth them up from those things which are only sensible, to those which are intellectual and divine';[13] but his insistence that any rational theory of harmonic intervals should be based on Pythagorean principles was at odds with how seventeenth-century instruments were actually tuned, and with most theoretical opinion since Zarlino. Though 'a professed violist',[14] he was never a court musician, nor does he appear to have been attached to any particular household – unlike Christopher Simpson, the most influential English music teacher of the period – but chose instead the life of an independent gentleman and 'philomath'.

As a theorist Birchensha first attracted attention with *Templum musicum*, his translation of Book 20 of Johann Heinrich Alsted's *Encyclopædia* (in the expanded version of 1630), which appeared in 1664.[15] His great aim was to publish a treatise on the philosophical, mathematical and practical aspects of music, entitled *Syntagma musicæ*. At one stage he promised that subscribers would receive their bound copies of this by Lady Day 1675;[16] but the work never appeared and seems to have vanished without trace.

The difficulty of tracking down theoretical and didactic texts from Birchensha's pen has long been an obstacle to fair and objective appraisal of his worth.

---

ed. H.W. Turnbull, 7 vols (Cambridge, 1959–77), i, p. 420.   **10** Matthew Locke, *Observations upon a late book, entituled, an essay to the advancement of music, &c. written by Thomas Salmon, M.A.* (London, 1672), p. 3.   **11** 'An extract of a letter written to the Royal Society by Mr. Birshenshaw, concerning music. Apr. 26. 1664', RS, Letter Book Original, i, pp 143–8 at 147.   **12** For a concise list of his works, see Christopher D.S. Field, 'John Birchensha', *NG II*, iii, pp 603–5.   **13** 'A compendious discourse of the principles of the practical & mathematical parts of music. Also, directions how to make any kind of tune, or air, without the help of the voice, or any other musical instrument. Written by John Birchensha, for the use of the Honorable Robert Boyle, Esq.':RS, Boyle Papers, xli, fos. 2–21 at fo. 7r.   **14** Locke, *Observations upon a late book*, p. 34.   **15** *Templum musicum: or the musical synopsis, of the learned and famous Johannes-Henricus-Alstedius, being a compendium of the rudiments both of the mathematical and practical part of musick: of which subject not any book is extant in our English tongue. Faithfully translated out of Latin by John Birchensha. Philomath* (London, 1664; facs. New York, 1968).   **16** This undertaking was given in an 'Animadversion' and appeal for subscribers, published in 1672. The only known copy of this printed sheet, bearing Birchensha's signature and seal, is in *GB-Lbl*, Add. MS 4388 (fo. 69). An edited version also appeared in *Philosophical transactions*, 7:90 (20 Jan. 1673), 5153–4.

Syntagma musicæ is lost; we have no exemplar of his 'complete scale of music'; and, despite numerous contemporary allusions, virtually all that was known until recently of his 'Rules of composition' came from a single source. In the past few years, however, further manuscripts have come to light – thanks in part to investigations into the archives of the Royal Society by Penelope Gouk, Leta Miller and Albert Cohen[17] – which have opened the way to a reappraisal of his competence and individuality as a teacher and theorist. A critical edition of Birchensha's writings on music, including texts of his 'Rules of composition' and 'Directions how to make any kind of tune, or air', is currently in preparation.[18] Before examining Birchensha's compositional teaching and its significance, however, it is appropriate to look afresh at what is known or can be surmised about his Irish background.

BIRCHENSHA AND IRELAND

The first writer of modern times to provide John Birchensha with an Anglo-Irish pedigree seems to have been Grattan Flood, who declared that he was a 'son of Sir Ralph Birkenshaw, comptroller of the musters and cheques'.[19] Unfortunately Flood did not give the source of his information and no documentary confirmation of its accuracy has yet been found. Nevertheless it does seem a plausible possibility that John's parents were Sir Ralph Birchensha and his wife Elizabeth. By 1592, when Ralph Birchensha was brutally sentenced by a garrison court in Flushing to have his ears cut off, he had five small children, one of whom was presumably Adam who in 1618 received a promise from James I of an annuity of £50 after his father's death; his mother Elizabeth was promised £100.[20] Ralph Birchensha was sent to Dublin by the English government in 1598 as controller general of the musters. This was a post of considerable importance and responsibility, involving frequent communication with Sir Robert Cecil and other ministers.[21] When the lord deputy of Ireland, Charles Blount, eighth Baron Mountjoy, defeated the earl of Tyrone's rebellion in 1601, Ralph dedicated an encomium in verse to him.[22] He appears to have been knighted sometime between February 1616 and August 1618, and died on 8 December 1622.[23] If

17 Penelope M. Gouk, 'Music in the natural philosophy of the early Royal Society' (PhD thesis, University of London, 1982); Leta Miller & Albert Cohen, *Music in the Royal Society of London, 1660–1806* (Detroit, 1987).   18 *John Birchensha: writings on music*, ed. Christopher Field & Benjamin Wardhaugh (Aldershot, in preparation).   19 Flood, *History*, p. 214.   20 *List and analysis of state papers. Foreign series: Elizabeth I*, ed. Richard Bruce Wernham (London, 1984), iv, p. 109; *Calendar of the state papers, relating to Ireland* (hereafter *CSPRI*), *of the reign of James I. 1615–25*, ed. C.W. Russell & J.P. Prendergast (London, 1880), pp 192, 398.   21 *CSPRI, Elizabeth, 1598–9*, ed. E.G. Atkinson (London, 1895), pp 223, 445, 448, 479; *CSPRI, Elizabeth, 1599–1600* (1899), pp 125, 149, 255, 427, 495; *CSPRI, James I, 1603–6*, eds. C.W. Russell & J.P. Prendergast (London, 1872), pp 580–3; *CSPRI, James I, 1606–8* (1874), pp 96–7, 443; *CSPRI, James I, 1608–10* (1874), pp 151–2, 191, 303; *CSPRI, James I, 1615–25* (1880), pp 116–17.   22 *A discourse occasioned upon the late defeat, given to the arch-rebels, Tyrone and Odonnell, by the right honourable the Lord Mountjoy, lord deputie of Ireland, the. 24. of December, 1601. being Christmas Eave ... by Raph Byrchensha esquire, controller generall of the musters in Ireland* (London, 1602).   23 *CSPRI,*

Ralph and Elizabeth were indeed his parents, John was probably born during the first decade of the seventeenth century. On the basis of his knowledge of Latin, philosophy and mathematics, it is tempting to conjecture that he went on to study at Trinity College, Dublin. No entrance register for the college exists for the period 1593–1637, but it is known that another of Ralph's sons – Adam, perhaps – was admitted in 1605 to the privileged status of fellow commoner and presented the college with a goblet.[24]

A note by the Oxford antiquary Anthony Wood sheds a ray of light on John's early years in Ireland:[25]

Birchensaw (John), descended of a good family, lived when young with the earl of Kildare in the city of Dublin, drove thence when the rebellion broke out in 1641, settled in London, instructed gentlemen on the viol and composed things of several parts. He was a gentle man and lived several years after King Charles 2 was restored to his kingdoms. He hath published plain rules and directions for composing in parts – in one sheet.

This is the chief evidence we have for believing that Birchensha served George Fitzgerald, sixteenth earl of Kildare (1612–60) in some capacity. A lot of the information in Wood's notes on musicians came from Benjamin Rogers, who from 1664 to 1686 was organist of Magdalen College, Oxford. Since Rogers had himself spent three years in Ireland – as organist of Christ Church cathedral, Dublin and as a vicar choral at Cloyne cathedral – before returning to England at the time of the 1641 uprising, it may well have been he who told Wood about Kildare's patronage.[26]

Birchensha's role in the Kildare establishment remains unclear.[27] Wood's use of the word 'young' might suggest apprenticeship as a boy musician. On the other hand if he was a son of Sir Ralph, he is more likely to have joined the household as a music master to the earl and countess or as a tutor to their children. Either way, it is unlikely that he would have been engaged before 1630 at the earliest. In 1629 wardship of the 17-year-old earl had been transferred from the dowager duchess of Lennox to Richard Boyle, first earl of Cork. In that same year Kildare

James I, 1615–25, pp 206, 309–10; *CSPRI, Charles I, 1625–32*, ed. R.P. Mahaffy (London, 1900), p. 200; Bernard Burke, *The general armory of England, Scotland, Ireland and Wales* [London, 1884], p. 145. Sir Ralph's heraldic shield is recorded as 'argent semée of estoiles and a pegasus passant gules', whereas John's wax seal on the 'Animadversion' for *Syntagma musicæ* (see note 16) shows a shield which, while its field could probably be described as 'semée of estoiles', has as its principal charge a bend, not a pegasus. **24** *Alumni Dublinenses: a register of the students, graduates, professors, and provosts of Trinity College, in the University of Dublin*, ed. G.D. Burtchaell & T.U. Sadleir (London, 1924), pp vii–ix, 67. **25** *GB-Ob*, MS Wood D 19 (4), fo. 19. This note was evidently the source for a similar passage in Sir John Hawkins's *A general history of the science and practice of music*, 5 vols (London, 1776), iv, p. 447. When Hawkins was collecting material for the *General history* it would have been among Wood's papers deposited in the Ashmolean Museum. **26** Shaw, *Succession of organists*, p. 410; Spink, *Restoration*, p. 321; Boydell, *History of music*, pp 56–7. **27** Searches through the letter-book of the earl of Kildare for 1628–37 (*IRL(N)-Bpro*, MS D.3078/3/1/5; transcript in *IRL-Mrjp*) and the published diary and letters of the earl of Cork have failed to uncover any references to Birchensha.

matriculated at Christ Church, Oxford, where Cork's son Lord Dunvargan was also studying. The following summer he married Joan Boyle, Cork's 19-year-old daughter, in Dublin.[28] Arrangements were made to rebuild the Fitzgeralds' castle at Maynooth as their home, and restore its chapel, at Cork's expense – an act of largess ill repaid by the prodigal Kildare. On All Saints' day 1632 Cork's chaplain preached in the chapel ('the first sermon made by a Protestant minister in any man's memory herein'). The house itself, with its wainscoted chambers, was ready for occupation by September 1634 and instructions were given for carving and painting the arms of Fitzgerald and Boyle which can still be seen above the gateway.[29] Joan Boyle, the countess, would have been accustomed in Lismore and Dublin to fairly sophisticated music-making, including consort music for viols, for (as Barra Boydell has shown) Cork kept an impressive musical establishment.[30] While it is unlikely that Kildare ever attempted musical patronage on such a scale, Birchensha's ability on the viol would doubtless have been considered a desirable accomplishment.

The Irish rebellion of 1641 put an end to this period of peace and stability. In January 1642 insurgents ransacked Maynooth castle. Birchensha fled to England, as Wood relates, perhaps accompanying Lady Kildare and her five children who arrived in London early in February.[31] At some point he settled in Southwark, just across the Thames from the city of London, and in 1651 was named by Playford in a list of metropolitan teachers 'for the voice or viol'.[32] Although there is no evidence that he ever returned to Ireland, he may not have lost touch entirely with his former patrons. Lady Kildare (who died in 1656) probably spent a good deal of time during the 1640s and early 1650s at Stalbridge, the Boyle family's house in Dorset, as did her youngest brother Robert Boyle, the natural philosopher; and it was to Robert Boyle that Birchensha was later to inscribe the manuscript of his 'Compendious discourse of the principles of the practical and mathematical parts of music', together with his 'Directions how to make any kind of tune, or air'.[33]

THE 'MELOPOETICAL OR COMPOSITIVE PART' OF MUSIC

Birchensha claimed in 1664 that he had devoted 'more then twenty years labour and study' to research into 'the mathematical and practical part of music'.[34] From this it may be deduced that he began his speculative work in earnest soon after moving to England in 1642. By the beginning of 1662, when Pepys became his pupil, his rules of composition must already have been at a fairly advanced stage of development.

---

28 Jane Ohlmeyer, 'George Fitzgerald, sixteenth earl of Kildare', *ODNB*, xix, pp 793–4. **29** Grosart, *Lismore* (1), iii, pp 48, 134–5, 152, 162, 164–5, 190, 207–8; iv, pp 6, 23, 37, 42–5, 81, 191. **30** Boydell, 'Earl of Cork' (see ch. 5, above); Fletcher, *Sources*, pp 404–17. **31** See the countess of Kildare's letter of 8 Feb. 1642 to her father, in Grosart, *Lismore* (2), iv, pp 267–9. **32** *A musicall banquet* (London, 1651), sig. A4. **33** See note 13. **34** 'An extract of a letter', p. 143.

Two years after teaching Pepys, Birchensha dedicated his Alsted translation, *Templum musicum*, to Pepys's cousin and patron the earl of Sandwich, a fellow of the Royal Society and amateur musician; it was entered at Stationers' Hall on 5 February 1664.[35] Birchensha's preface to this book is virtually a manifesto – the earliest of several – for his system of instruction. He writes of 'Rules' that

> may be yet further, and are already, in part, contrived (drawn from the mathematical principles of music), by which musical consonants and dissonants (artificially applied and disposed, according to the nature of their proportions...) may afford, in two, three, four, five, six, seven or more parts, as good music, that is, as agreeable, artificial, and formal, as can be composed by the help of any instrument.

In other words, the rules are still undergoing development and refinement. Arguing that 'it is a more noble way to work by rules and precepts in any art', he asserts that 'by such a way of operation the composer shall work more certainly, firmly, readily, and with more facility then by any other way', because 'if music be an art, then it may be contracted and collected into certain rules which may discover all those mysteries that are contained in that science, by which a man may become an excellent musician, and expert, both in the theorical and practical parts thereof'. We are told that a number of pupils have already benefitted from these advances: 'To the completing of such forcible rules I have contributed my mite, whose certainty and reality has been experienced by divers, and may likewise be further known unto others, if they please or desire to understand them'. Birchensha declares that progress can be achieved surprisingly quickly. Aspects that normally 'require the study and expense of many years, might be performed without any difficulty in a few weeks, or months at the farthest. And that this way is found out and effected in a great measure, I say, many persons of worth and quality are able experimentally to testify'.[36]

In April 1664, following a suggestion from Silas Taylor to Sir Robert Moray, a committee of the Royal Society was formed to hear Birchensha's views on music. Its eminent members included Viscount Brouncker, Sir Robert Moray, the earl of Sandwich, the Hon. Robert Boyle and Dr John Pell. At the committee's request Birchensha wrote a letter, dated 26 April, which was read at a meeting of the Society the following day. Afterwards Birchensha was 'called in, and thanked for his respect to the Society', and given an assurance that the committee would consider 'ways to encourage and promote his design and study'.[37] In his letter, Birchensha elaborated on what he had written in the *Templum musicum* preface. He argued that

35 *A transcript of the registers of the Worshipful Company of Stationers from 1640–1708*, ed. G.E.B. Eyre & C.R. Rivington, 3 vols (London, 1913–14), ii, p. 337.   36 *Templum musicum*, sig. A7v–A8r; *John Birchensha: writings*, ch. 1.   37 RS, Journal Book Original, ii, pp 71–4.

as for the practical part of music, which hath respect to composition, it is so obscure, that few do understand it, but do grope at their work, as men in the dark … It is so difficult, that many after the expense of most of their lifetime in laborious practice, do not attain to such a reasonable measure of perfection in this art, as to compose tolerably well and commendably. It is so irregular, that (a few ordinary observations excepted) there is no certain rule to compose by. And herein this art is more unhappy than any other art in the world: for grammar, logic, and all other sciences are drawn into rule. The want of this hath made many composers to consult their instruments almost in all things they do, as to find out the consecution of sounds in single airs, and of consonants and dissonants in the composing of many parts: which although it is not without its proper use, is but a low and mechanic[al] way. But to compose by a rule, is a more noble, artificial, and commendable way, by which the composer may work with more ease, certainty, and celerity.

Here, for the first time, we find Birchensha distinguishing between two sets of rules: those for inventing the melodic line of an air, and those for composing in two or more parts. He promises that

As to the melopoetical or compositive part [of music], I shall discover a few, easy, certain, and perfect rules (never yet invented or published by any man) which may be understood, and made practice of, in a few weeks, or months at the farthest, by any reasonable capacity; and which shall contain all things, that appertain to the making of excellent and good air in any part or kind of music; and all things, which belong to the consecution of sounds in a single part, and of consonants, and dissonants in many parts: the taking of cadences, and all ways of syncope; the way of taking of discords by binding or pass; the nature of counterpoint simple or compounded; the laws of ornate and florid discant; the elegant art of fuguing, in a few or great body of parts; the making of canons without, or upon a plain song; and whatsoever else may be done by this art, for the advantage of air and harmony. By which rules not only those who skilfully can sing or play on some instrument may learn to compose, but also those who can neither sing nor play: I say, that by my said rules such may both make good air and compose two, three, four or more parts artificially.

In support of the success of his system he again offers the testimony and work of 'divers persons of worth and quality, who already have experienced these things in a great measure, and can testify the same, whose compositions shall be produced, and be exposed to the judgments of any, who desire to hear them.'[38]

This last passage suggests that part of the purpose behind Birchensha's concerts in London in 1664 may have been to let fellows of the Royal Society hear examples of music composed by pupils using his rules. The concerts – one

---

38 RS, Letter Book Original, i, pp 143–8; *John Birchensha: writings*, ch. 2.

of which was attended by John Evelyn on 3 August, and another by Brouncker, Moray, Taylor and Pepys a week later – would also have helped to bring Birchensha and his ideas to wider public notice. They seem to have taken place in a room near the junction of Threadneedle Street and Cornhill and been held on Wednesday afternoons so that members of the Royal Society could go on to them after their meetings at Gresham College. Pepys, who attended at Taylor's suggestion and whose compositions were evidently not included, confessed that he 'found no pleasure at all' in the programme of instrumental music that he heard, but Evelyn's critique was more favourable: 'to London: this day was a consort of excellent musicians especially one Mr Berkenshaw, that rare artist who invented a mathematical way of composure very extraordinary: true as to the exact rules of art, but without much harmony.'[39]

BIRCHENSHA'S PUPILS

Birchensha seems to have drawn his pupils largely from the ranks of 'persons of worth and quality'. Presumably it was only the well-off who could afford a course of private instruction from him. At a time when many of the king's musicians were expected to subsist on five pounds a month or less, the five pounds that Pepys paid for his six weeks of lessons was indeed 'a great deal of money'. There is no evidence that Birchensha ever tried out his system on children or young ladies, though he may have done so; and it was perhaps only after manuscripts of his rules began to pass from hand to hand that professional musicians such as Francis Withey, Philip Becket and William Corbett had the opportunity to study and adapt them.[40]

Not everyone who received a copy of Birchensha's rules should be assumed to have been his pupil. A distinction needs to be made between those to whom he gave texts in the hope that they would promote his cause, and those who were persuaded to subscribe to a course of lessons. In the former category we should almost certainly place William, second Viscount Brouncker (1620–84), the annotator of Descartes's *Compendium musicæ* and first president of the Royal Society, who owned a manuscript of the rules of composition, and also the Hon. Robert Boyle (1627–91), who received the only known copy of the 'Directions how to make any kind of tune, or air'.[41] Brouncker and Boyle had both been born

39 *Diary of John Evelyn*, iii, p. 377; *Diary of Samuel Pepys*, v, p. 238. The Royal Society meetings on 3 and 10 Aug. both included experiments with a monochord; Birchensha took part in the latter by special invitation.   **40** Withey copied Birchensha's rules into his commonplace book (*GB-Och*, MS Mus. 337), and Corbett acquired an autograph manuscript of them (*B-Br*, MS II 4168): these sources are discussed below. Becket advertised in the press on 1 Dec. 1681 offering to teach 'Composition in music in Mr Birchinshaw's method, having enlarg'd it, giving more liberty': see Michael Tilmouth, 'A calendar of references to music in newspapers published in London and the provinces (1660–1719)', *RMA Research Chronicle*, 1 (1961), 5.   **41** Brouncker's manuscript is lost, but Silas Taylor copied out parts of it for his own use into *GB-Lbl*, Add. MS 4910. Boyle's copy of the 'Directions' is in RS, Boyle Papers, 41, fos.

in Ireland, the former at Castlelyons, the latter at Lismore; Brouncker's father had been vice-chamberlain to Charles II when he was prince of Wales, while Boyle was the youngest son of the first earl of Cork and brother-in-law of Birchensha's former patron the earl of Kildare. Significantly, they were also both members of the Royal Society committee formed on 20 April 1664 to examine Birchensha's proposals.

Four pupils can however be identified with some confidence: Silas Taylor *alias* Domvill (1624–78), Samuel Pepys (1633–1703), George Villiers, second duke of Buckingham (1628–87), and Thomas Salmon (1647–1706). Of these four, Taylor had already achieved some recognition as a composer before encountering Birchensha's teaching, as the publication in 1655 of two suites by him shows.[42] Taylor's 'Collection of rules in music' (*GB-Lbl*, Add. MS 4910, fos. 39–61) reveals an eclectic taste in music theory: besides 'Mr Birchensha's six rules of composition', there are extracts from Simpson's *Compendium*, a scale devised and presented to Taylor by 'Mr Allison of the Covent-Garden' in 1668, and instructions for playing from thoroughbass which he got from Matthew Locke and probably antedate the publication of *Melothesia* (1673). In August 1659 Taylor moved to London as captain of a troop of horse and commissioner for the Westminster militia,[43] and it was probably soon afterwards that he met Birchensha. He quickly became an enthusiast for Birchensha's system which (as Pepys remarked in 1664) he 'magnifies mightily'. From 1661 onwards Taylor's duties, including a voyage to Virginia in 1663–4, limited the time he could spend in London; nevertheless he kept up an interest in the Royal Society. Though never a fellow, he took part in discussions and committees, had papers published, donated scientific specimens, and even pledged money towards the Society's proposed new college.[44] It was his suggestion that led to Birchensha being invited to lay his ideas before the Society in April 1664.[45]

It may have been Taylor who introduced Pepys to Birchensha. The diarist describes a convivial evening spent in a Westminster coffee-house early in 1660 with 'Captain Taylor', Matthew Locke and 'Mr Pursell'.[46] Although he criticized aspects of Birchensha's rules, Pepys was not unsympathetic to his teacher's musical philosophy. In 1667, for example, we find him musing that 'it is only the

20r–21v.   **42** John Playford, *Court-Ayres: or, pavins, almains, corants, and sarabands of two parts* (London, 1655), nos. 199–201 and 216–18. Taylor later composed vocal duets (see *Diary of Samuel Pepys*, vi, pp 80–1) and anthems (*GB-Cu*, Ely MSS 1, 4, 28; *GB-Y*, MSS M.1 (S) (the Gostling partbooks); see also Aubrey, *Brief lives*, ii, pp 254–6; *Diary of Samuel Pepys*, ix, p. 251.   **43** Anthony Wood, *Athenæ Oxonienses*, ed. Philip Bliss, 4 vols (London, 1813–20), iii, col. 1176; Aubrey, *Brief lives*, ii, pp 254–6. **44** Thomas Birch, *The history of the Royal Society of London*, 4 vols (London, 1756–7), i, pp 183–4, 266, 270, 272, 280–1, 293, 310, 346, 383, 447–8, 452, 456–7, 460, 483; ii, pp 115, 262; iii, p. 323; Michael Hunter, 'The social basis and changing fortunes of an early scientific institution: an analysis of the membership of the Royal Society, 1660–85', *Notes and Records of the Royal Society of London*, 31 (1976), 9–114 at 12–13.   **45** RS, Journal Book Original, ii, pp 71–2 (20 Apr. 1664): 'Sir Robert Moray suggested, that Capt. Taylor had mentioned to him, a gentleman, who did pretend to discover some musical errors, generally committed, by all modern masters of music … and desired to be heard by some members of this society, versed in music'.   **46** *Diary of Samuel Pepys*, i, p. 63.

want of an ingenious man that is master in music' which hinders the art from being brought 'to a certainty and ease in composition'.[47] Pepys was elected to the Royal Society in 1665, and went on to be its president in 1684–5.

The evidence for counting the duke of Buckingham among Birchensha's pupils is a letter written by Robert Hooke, the Royal Society's curator of experiments, to Robert Boyle in Oxford just before one of a series of acoustical experiments that took place at Gresham College in July and August 1664, in which Birchensha took part. Hooke remarked:

> There is a gentleman here in town, that has a better way of teaching music than what Kircher causelessly enough vaunted his *ars combinatoria* to be, whereby he has presently taught the duke of Buckingham to compose very well, though he knows nothing of the practic[al] part of music.[48]

There can be little doubt that the unnamed gentleman teacher was Birchensha. That Buckingham dabbled in composition is borne out by a story recounted by Anthony Hamilton, the Irish Jacobite. While visiting London in 1662–4, the Comte de Gramont (Hamilton's brother-in-law) saw how Buckingham exercised his charms on Frances Stuart, a celebrated beauty at Charles II's court. Gramont's memoirs tell of 'la belle Stuart's' passion for music, describe the duke as a pleasant singer, and reveal that he composed *vaudevilles* – a term applied to lighter types of courtly song – for her delight.[49] According to Pepys, Buckingham's household musicians were 'the best in town'.[50] His plays were admired, he had a scientific laboratory in his house, he was a fellow of the Royal Society and a privy councillor, and in the early 1660s was still very wealthy. Though Dryden was to lampoon him for being 'every thing by starts, and nothing long',[51] Birchensha's reputation would have been enhanced by having so prominent a personage as a student.

The last and youngest of Birchensha's identifiable pupils was Thomas Salmon. Son of a London alderman, he read mathematics at Trinity College, Oxford, graduating in 1668. It was probably in 1669, when he was 21, that he approached Birchensha for composition lessons, on the advice of Matthew Locke. Writing in April 1672, Locke explains that 'about three years' previously Salmon had

---

47 Ibid., viii, pp 574–5.   **48** *The works of the Honourable Robert Boyle*, ed. Thomas Birch, 5 vols (London, 1744), v, pp 535–9; R.T. Gunther, *Early science in Oxford, vi: The life and work of Robert Hooke, part I* (Oxford, 1930), pp 183–5. From the context Gunther assigned the letter, which is undated, to 5 July 1664. For identification of the 'gentleman' as Birchensha, see J.C. Kassler & D.R. Oldroyd, 'Robert Hooke's Trinity College "Musick scripts", his music theory and the role of music in his cosmology', *Annals of Science*, 40 (1983), 559–95 at 594; Gouk, *Music, science and natural magic*, p. 61. Boyle was already acquainted with Birchensha, but Hooke may have forgotten this.   **49** *Mémoires du Comte de Grammont, par Monsieur le Comte Antoine Hamilton*, ed. Horace Walpole (Twickenham, 1772), p. 112: 'Elle ne laissait pas de se plaire à la musique, et d'avoir quelque goût pour le chant. Le duc de Buckingham … chantait agréablement … il faisait des vaudevilles'.   **50** *Diary of Samuel Pepys*, ix, pp 12–13.   **51** *Absalom and Achitophel* (first published in 1681), lines 545–50.

made his address to me for instruction in composition; but I, never having contrived any method that way, referred him to Mr. Simpson's *Compendium of practical musick* for the first rudiments, and to Mr. Birchensha ... for his further advance; assuring him I knew no man fitter for that purpose; it being in a manner his whole business. This advice was civilly and kindly taken, and after a short time put in execution.[52]

Having taken holy orders, Salmon moved to Meppershall in Bedfordshire as rector in 1673. Thereafter it is for his theoretical writings on music that he is chiefly remembered. If he continued to compose, his music cannot have circulated much.[53] His first treatise, *An essay to the advancement of musick* (1672), made radical proposals for simplifying notation and gave rise to a famous controversy with Locke.[54] Birchensha lent his support by writing a preface in which he commended the 'ingenious author'; Salmon, in turn, praised his teacher as 'a person who for his knowledge and industry in music deserved rather ... encouragement than envy'.[55] There was also backing for Salmon from fellows of the Royal Society, notably the mathematician John Wallis, who had taught him at Oxford.[56]

SOURCES OF BIRCHENSHA'S RULES

Birchensha intended to devote a portion of *Syntagma musicæ* to his 'Directions how to make any kind of tune' and 'Rules of composition'. In the 'Animadversion' of 1672 he announced this in characteristically hyperbolic terms:[57]

An easy way is by the said author invented for making airy tunes of all sorts by a certain rule (which most men think impossible to be done) and the composing of two, three, four, five, six, and seven parts; which by the learner may be performed in a few months; viz. in two months he may (exquisitely, and with all the elegancies of music) compose two parts; in three months, three parts; and so forwards to seven parts, (as many persons of honour and

---

52 Locke, *Observations upon a late book*, p. 3.   53 Eitner listed under Salmon's name a 'divertimento' for two violins and bass, the source being a manuscript formerly in a private collection at Marburg: see Robert Eitner, *Biographisch-bibliographisches Quellen-Lexikon*, 11 vols (2nd ed., Graz, 1959), vii, p. 401. Its present location is unknown.   54 Thomas Salmon, *An essay to the advancement of musick, by casting away the perplexity of different cliffs* [sic]*, and uniting all sorts of musick ... in one universal character* (London, 1672; facs. ed., New York, 1966). Salmon's *Essay* appeared early in Feb. 1672. It was followed by Locke's *Observations upon a late book*, dated 11 Apr.; Salmon's *A vindication of an essay to the advancement of musick, from Mr. Matthew Lock's observations* (London, 1672), dated 1 June; and Locke's *The present practice of musick vindicated* (London, 1673), dated 24 July and published with John Phillips's 'Duellum musicum' and an open letter to Salmon from John Playford (dated 26 Aug. 1672).   55 Salmon, *An essay*, sig. A3r–A5r ('The publisher to the reader', signed 'John Birchensha'); Salmon, *A vindication*, p. 32.   56 Salmon, *A vindication*, p. 1. The *Essay* was reviewed in *Philosophical transactions*, 6:80 (19 Feb. 1672), 3095.   57 See note 16; *John Birchensha: writings*, ch. 5.

worth have often experienced): which otherwise cannot be done in so many years.

A summary prepared for the Royal Society in February 1676 goes into more detail, but gives the impression that the book is still not complete.[58] It divides the 'practical part' into twenty-six chapters, with the 'directions' and 'rules' treated in chapters 16–19:

16 Of the compounding of sounds, for the making of harmony, or of the art of composition; which I have comprehended in six canons or rules: of their examples, variations, observations; general and special order; when they are to be observed and kept, and when to be altered: of the transposing of the treble into the bass; and bass into the upper part.
17 Of counterpoint, and figurate discant.
18 Directions how to compose artificially and skilfully in a few weeks; and better, than by any way yet known, a man may attain unto in many years.
19 How to make a tune without the help of an instrument; with a definition and discovery of the parts of which melodious tunes, called airs, are constituted: with directions and rules, by which good airs or tunes (of any sort or mood) may be made: which skill and art is, by most musicians, thought impossible to be attained unto.

Cognate topics listed include 'the rhetorical part of music', 'how notes are to be adapted to words', and 'directions how to play of a bass continual … on the theorbo, harpsicon etc.' The summary concludes:

Thus I shall endeavour to reduce all the parts of music to a regularity and just order, without too strict a limitation of the musician's fancy or invention; my rules for effecting these things being grounded on the principles of the philosophical and mathematical parts of music, and on the true reason of the natures of sounds, considered physically, and artificially, viz. as related to one another. And by this means I will bring the philosophical, mathematical, and practical parts of music to analogize and agree in all things which, I trust, will be a work acceptable to all prudent and ingenious lovers of musical harmony.

After delivering his paper on 10 February 1676 Birchensha 'had the thanks of the [Royal] Society given him for this respect and kindness, and was exhorted to finish his work'.[59] Nothing more is heard of *Syntagma musicæ* after that. Birchensha probably died no later than 1681. On 14 May of that year a John Birchenshaw was buried in Westminster Abbey cloisters, though it is not certain

---

58 'An account of divers particulars remarkable in my book; in which I will write of music philosophically, mathematically, and practically': RS, Classified papers, 22:1, no. 7; *John Birchensha: writings*, ch. 6.
59 RS, Journal book, v, p. 143.

that this was the musician.[60] Six months later one Philip Becket advertised in the London press, offering to teach 'any gentlemen or ladies [who] are desirous to learn composition in music in Mr Birchinshaw's method, having enlarged it, giving more liberty', with an assurance that they 'may in a short time attain unto it at a very reasonable rate'.[61] Such an advertisement for an improved version of the rules is unlikely to have appeared while Birchensha was still alive. Its proponent may have been the Philip Becket (or Beckett) who until 1678 was a violinist and cornett player at Charles II's court and who occasionally composed music for the king's band of violins.[62]

Coincidentally in about 1681 John Playford – who once called Birchensha 'no mean person in the science of music'[63] – published 'A sheet of plain rules and directions for composing music in parts, by Mr. John Birchenshaw; the price 6*d.*' It may or may not have been authorized by Birchensha, but in any case it cannot have contained much more than a summary of the rules, with little room for music examples. The sheet was advertised in the second edition of *Musick's recreation on the viol, lyra-way* (1682) and was mentioned by Anthony Wood, but no copy can now be found.[64]

Consequently we rely wholly on manuscripts for knowledge of Birchensha's rules. Those for melody-writing – the 'Directions' – are found in a single autograph source, RS, Boyle Papers, xli (fos. 20–1).[65] Birchensha included them as an appendix to his 'Compendious discourse' before presenting the manuscript to Robert Boyle. The two unpaginated leaves are headed: 'How to make any kind of tune, air, or song, without the help of the voice, or any other instrument'. The manuscript is undated, but on present evidence the most likely date for its production and presentation seems to be *c.*1664–5.

Of the rules of part-writing three sources survive, only one of which – *GB-Lbl*, Add. MS 4910 (fos. 39–61) – is at all well known.[66] The wrapper is helpfully inscribed:

A collection of rules in music from the most knowing masters in that science with Mr Birchensha's six rules of composition; and his enlargements thereon to the Right Honorable William Lord Viscount Brouncker &c: collected by me, Silas Domvill alias Taylor.

---

60 *The marriage, baptismal, and burial registers of the collegiate church or abbey of St Peter, Westminster*, ed. J.L. Chester (London, 1876), p. 202. 61 *The Loyal Protestant and True Domestick Intelligence*, 1 Dec. 1681: see note 40. 62 Andrew Ashbee & David Lasocki, *A biographical dictionary of English court musicians, 1485–1714* (Aldershot, 1998), pp 136–8; Holman, *Four and twenty fiddlers*, pp 320–1. 63 Locke, *The present practice of musick*, p. 78. 64 [J. Playford], *Musick's recreation on the viol, lyra-way* (2nd ed. London, 1682; facs. ed. Hebden Bridge, 2002), sig. A4v; *GB-Ob*, MS Wood D 19 (4), fo.19. 65 See note 13; *John Birchensha: writings*, ch. 3, will contain an edited transcription. The manuscript is also discussed in Leta Miller, 'John Birchensha and the early Royal Society: grand scales and scientific composition', *JRMA*, 115 (1990), 63–79. 66 This is the only source of the rules mentioned in Miller, 'John Birchensha', and in Herissone, *Music theory. John Birchensha: writings*, ch. 8, will contain an edited transcription.

The dozen leaves containing Birchensha's rules probably once formed part of a music notebook. As is clear from Taylor's annotations in red ink, there are two layers, one written for him by Birchensha, the other copied out by Taylor. In Birchensha's hand there are brief statements of Rules 1–3, with music examples.[67] They undoubtedly show the rules at an early stage of development: this lends support to the hypothesis that Taylor studied with Birchensha between 1659 and 1661 and that the autograph layer of this manuscript dates from that time. Later – probably in or after 1664 – Taylor extensively supplemented this original autograph layer by drawing on a lost book belonging to Lord Brouncker.[68] Taylor's manuscript is thus a complex but important and authoritative source. Its main deficiency is that the music example for the sixth ('fugue') rule lacks any explanatory text.[69] All the music examples are in two parts.

The second source – *B-Br*, MS II 4168, a bound music notebook – valuably complements Taylor's copy.[70] It is almost entirely autograph and deals with all six rules; and if it does not take the student to the dizzy height of composing in seven parts, it at least furnishes welcome examples of four-part writing. Birchensha used both ends of the book, one for the rules themselves and the other for ancillary material. The manuscript is undated and its recipient is not identified, but comparison of handwriting and content with Taylor's copy and the 'Compendious Discourse' suggest that it probably originated in the mid- to late 1660s. It later belonged to the violinist and composer William Corbett (1680–1748), who signed and inscribed it: 'William Corbett his book 1695 / Berkinshaw / Rules of composition'. Although he was obviously not the first owner, we may for convenience call it 'Corbett's copy'.

The third source, to which Robert Thompson has drawn attention, is a musical notebook of Francis Withey or Withy (*c.*1645–1727), *GB-Och*, Mus. 337.[71] A son of Thomas Tomkins's friend John Withy, Francis was a well-known musician in Restoration Oxford who became a singing man at Christ Church in 1670, worked as a music copyist, played the bass viol and violin, and composed divisions for the viol. He had the notebook bound with his new copy of Simpson's *Compendium* which he signed: 'Francis Withey / his book / October 12 1667'.

67 Rule 1, fos. 46v–47r; Rule 2, fos. 48v–49r; Rule 3, fos. 50v–51r. In each case Birchensha wrote music examples on the ruled verso pages, and explanations on the unruled recto pages. 68 Miller simply dates the manuscript '*c.*1668', Herissone 'about 1673'. Besides further material relating to Rules 1–3, Taylor copied out explanations and examples of Rules 4–5 (fos. 52v–55r), an example of Rule 6 (fo. 56r), and a 'Method for the rules' (fo. 40r). 69 Miller is not quite accurate when she writes: 'Unfortunately, although the title-page advertises Birchensha's "6 Rules", the manuscript contains only five, the sixth having apparently been lost before the document was bound and numbered in its present form" ('John Birchensha and the early Royal Society', 70). 70 There are forty-six leaves, thirty-three of which are ruled for music; the rest are unruled. About half the book remained unused. An armorial bookplate shows that before 1791 the manuscript belonged to one of the earls of Donegal – probably Arthur Chichester (1739–99), the fifth earl and first marquess, who was an avid book-collector. It was bought in 1851 by the musicologist François-Joseph Fétis; the Bibliothèque Royale acquired it in 1872. *John Birchensha: writings*, ch. 9, will contain an edited transcription. 71 Robert Thompson, '"Francis Withie of Oxon" and his commonplace book, Christ Church, Oxford, MS 337', *Chelys,* 20 (1991), 3–27.

Over a period of thirty years – between about 1668 and 1698 – he copied into it extracts from treatises ranging from Morley and Elway Bevin to Locke's *Melothesia* (1673) and the 1694 edition of Playford's *Introduction to the skill of music*. He also noted down advice gleaned from contemporaries such as Henry Hall, John Lenton and Bartholomew Isaack, and excerpts from music by Jenkins, Christopher Gibbons, Locke, Purcell, Lully, Corelli and Bassani. Withey evidently considered Birchensha's rules sufficiently valuable to devote sixteen pages to them. The material is haphazardly arranged, and the sixth ('fugue') rule is omitted, but there are extensive music examples, including some in three parts.[72] Directly or indirectly, Withey's copy must have been based on a lost autograph source.

THE 'DIRECTIONS HOW TO MAKE ANY KIND OF TUNE'

The original stimulus for the 'Directions' perhaps came from a passage in Alsted's *Encyclopædia* which Birchensha translated as follows: 'A young composer should first compose the most simple melodies, which arise not from the musical *dyads* and *triads*, but from *monads*, or a simple disposition of musical voices.'[73] Birchensha cannot have been unaware of the difficulty of digesting the technique of writing melodies into a few concise guidelines. In the animadversion for *Syntagma musicæ* he described it as a task 'which most men think impossible to be done'. Yet he insisted that the technique could be learned, and that it could be performed mentally 'without the help of the voice, or any other instrument'.

The 'Directions', whose contents have been usefully summarized by Leta Miller,[74] are divided into three parts: 'Things to be preconsidered, and resolved on'; 'What you are to observe in making a tune'; and 'Negative precepts'. In some respects they are very up-to-date. For example, it is recognized that a pupil may wish to write a gavotte, a type of dance that in the mid-1660s was only just beginning to come into vogue in England (for a 'Gavot' by Birchensha, see appendix 1). The range of key-notes said to be 'in common use' is remarkably wide: it includes E flat and F sharp, at a time when compositions in E flat major or F sharp minor were still rare.[75] One of the first things the pupil is taught to consider before composing a tune is 'In what key you will make it'. Keys are not classified as 'major' or 'minor'; instead, you must decide 'whether your song shall be flat or sharp, in the third, sixth and seventh', bearing in mind that some keys are naturally sharp in these degrees while others are flat, but that by means of signs you can force them 'to be otherwise accidentally'. But some of Birchensha's maxims seem too general – that 'you are to observe the proper movement' of your tune – or too rudimentary – that 'you must know what the

<hr>

72 *John Birchensha: writings*, ch. 10, will contain an edited transcription. Withey's notebook is unpaginated, but if the next page after p. 176 of the *Compendium* is reckoned as p. 1, the Rules occupy pp 72–90.   **73** Birchensha, *Templum musicum*, p. 62. *Voces musicales* ('musical voices') was a traditional way of referring to the notes of the hexachord.   **74** Miller, 'John Birchensha', 68–70.   **75** Christopher D.S. Field, 'Jenkins and the cosmography of harmony', in Ashbee & Holman, *Jenkins*, pp 49–60.

second part of a note is' – to be of much help to a beginner, and some of his terminology – such as the use of 'defective third' or 'false third' for a diminished fourth – itself appears defective.[76] Perhaps the 'Directions' were still at a formative stage when Birchensha made the copy for Boyle.

THE 'SIX RULES OF COMPOSITION'

Taylor's, Corbett's and Withey's copies furnish us with three separate versions of the rules of part-writing. Though Evelyn's phrase, 'a mathematical way of composure', might suggest a rigid system, the manuscripts give the impression of a set of rules that continued to evolve and be refined during the 1660s. Like John Coprario's 'Rules how to compose',[77] Birchensha's rules relied as much on musical example as on verbal precept. Recurrent patterns in his illustrations can certainly be discerned from manuscript to manuscript; but, as one would expect from any live harmony teaching, neither the examples nor the precise wording of the rules remained constant. Presumably each source reflects the instruction of an individual pupil.

Some of the differences between versions no doubt reflect Birchensha's efforts to organize his teaching in the most satisfactory way. In the first layer of Taylor's copy, for example, Rule 1 is entitled 'The rule of gradual motion both in the upper part and bass', and the examples show two parts moving by step, mainly in similar motion;[78] but in Corbett's copy it is called the 'rule of two parts ascending or descending together gradually, or by saltation' – a significant change, because it allowed consideration of voices moving by leap ('saltation') in thirds or sixths to be brought under this rule. An example of leaping thirds appears under Rule 1 in Taylor's second layer, so the change must already have occurred by the time Lord Brouncker's manuscript was written. In Taylor's copy Birchensha included 'syncope' under the 'rule of gradual motion', but in Corbett's this type of syncopation is dealt with under Rule 5 (the 'dividing rule'). It is worth noting that under Rule 1 Birchensha implicitly allows descending conjunct motion from a perfect fifth to a *semidiapente* or diminished fifth:[79] examples of this progression are found in Taylor's and Corbett's copies.

Rule 2 is the 'rule of gradual motion in the upper part, and of saltation in the bass'. By the time the first layer of Taylor's copy was written Birchensha had reduced this procedure to three basic patterns. In each case the treble moves by step, first descending, then ascending, while the bass falls a fourth or a fifth depending on whether the voices begin an octave, a third or a fifth apart. Corbett's copy shows each pattern in both a major and a minor form:

76 Cf. Miller, 'John Birchensha', 71 (examples 2a, 2b).   **77** Giovanni Coprario, *Rules how to compose: a facsimile edition of a manuscript from the library of the earl of Bridgewater*, ed. Manfred F. Bukofzer (Los Angeles, 1952); *A new way of making fowre parts in counterpoint by Thomas Campion and rules how to compose by Giovanni Coprario*, ed. Christopher R. Wilson (Aldershot, 2003).   **78** For a facsimile, see Miller, 'John Birchensha', 72, fig. 1 (first two systems).   **79** As pointed out in Herissone, *Music theory*, pp 165–6.

Example 7.1: John Birchensha, examples of Rule 2 ('When the upper part moveth gradually, and the bass by saltation'), showing movement from (a) an octave; (b) a third; (c) a fifth.

Rule 3, the 'transverse rule', deals with various kinds of contrary motion. When the first layer of Taylor's copy was written, there were two categories: 'breaking', and 'simple counterpoint'. The latter is what we would call note-against-note counterpoint, while the former involves 'breaking' or 'dividing' into crotchet movement in one of the voices, with or without the use of passing discords (as will be seen in Example 7.5). Subsequently a third category was added: 'Transverse motion by saltation'. This is systematically and exhaustively exemplified in Withey's copy, where treble and bass in turn are shown first rising, then falling, in ever-widening steps from a second to an octave, while the other voice demonstrates the various available ways of moving from a given consonance (octave, third, fifth, sixth) to another consonance.

At some point between the writing of Lord Brouncker's book and Corbett's copy the numbering of the next two rules was changed. The revision presumably reflects what experience showed was the more logical order in which to impart them. So the 'Rule of cadences or of binding discords' appears in the second layer of Taylor's copy as Rule 5, but in Corbett's and Withey's copies becomes Rule 4; conversely the 'Rule of division' is Rule 4 in Taylor, but Rule 5 in Corbett and Withey. Under the former rule, Birchensha illustrates three classes of suspended discord: 4–3, 7–6, and 2–3. Interestingly, he shows how the 'binding note' may be prolonged and the 'cadent note' (or note of resolution) shortened – a sign of French influence, perhaps:

Examples 7.2 (a), (b), (c):
John Birchensha, examples
of Rule 4 ('Binding
cadences') with delayed and
shortened 'cadent note'.

In its simplest form, as set out in Taylor's second layer, the 'rule of division' or 'dividing rule' deals with crotchet or quaver movement 'upon a holding ground or upon a moving ground' – in other words, on a cantus firmus that remains stationary or moves in semibreves.[80] Division 'is either in the upper part or bass at the will of the composer'. Birchensha shows how the dividing part may proceed by 'gradual motion', by 'saltation', or by 'both mixed'. In the first and third, the student is given practice in the use of 'passing discords' and is taught to 'lay the discord between two concords: both when the discord is the first and second part of the note' – that is to say, whether it is stressed or unstressed. By the time Corbett's copy was written, two further techniques – 'chromatic notes' and 'syncopation' – had been brought under the umbrella of the 'dividing rule'.[81] In the following example, Birchensha shows how 'chromatic notes are borne out by a third or sixth, either holding or by saltation':

Example 7.3: John Birchensha, example of dividing 'by chromatic notes'.

---

80 For a facsimile of the music examples, see Miller, 'John Birchensha', 74.   81 In Withey's copy, too, syncopation appears to come under Rule 5 ('the Division Rule').

Placing 'syncopation' under Rule 5 (rather than Rule 1) had the advantage of allowing disjunct as well as conjunct movement to be considered:

Example 7.4: John Birchensha, example of dividing 'by syncopation': (a) 'gradual', and (b) 'saltation'.

In Rule 6, the 'fugue rule', the pupil is introduced to canon and imitation. Regarding canon, Birchensha advises: 'Prick out the fugue in the following part in what key you please and at what distance you will. Then make discant to the fugue so pricked out. Then prick out that discant and so proceed as long as you please.' In imitation, on the other hand, 'you may break off the fugue when you please and bring it in again where the discant will bear it. Sometimes the movement of the fugue may be imitated, although the point be not directly followed.'[82] A music example in Taylor's copy (also used in a modified form in Corbett's copy) shows various possibilities for imitating a given subject at the third, fifth or fourth above, and at the octave, fourth, second or fifth below.

Having grasped the six rules, the student crucially has to learn how to apply them. To this end Birchensha devised a 'Method'. Three versions survive – one copied by Taylor presumably out of Lord Brouncker's book, another in Birchensha's hand in Corbett's copy, and a third which Withey apparently received from the composer John Lenton. The first is comparatively straightforward:

1   Bring in your fugue or any part of it, as the descant will allow.
2   Mark where you take any cadence [discord].
3   See where you can operate by your second or [third] rule.
4   Then work by your first rule.
5   Where any holding notes remain make use of the dividing rule.

Version 2 is more sophisticated, though its first and second steps are the same. After placing points of imitation and 'binding cadences', the pupil determines

82 *B-Br*, MS II 4168, fo. 39r.

Example 7.5: John Birchensha, examples of Rule 3 ('Transverse rule: by breaking'), 'composed into 4 parts'.

where those middle closes occur that can be approached by parallel sixths or a diminished fifth (Rule 1); where transverse counterpoint, giving the interval sequence 6–8–10 or introducing 'breaking' notes, is feasible (Rule 3); where gradual motion in the treble and saltation in the bass is appropriate (Rule 2); where ascending or descending parallel thirds may be used (Rule 1); and where transverse counterpoint giving the sequence 12–10–8 or 8–10–12 is possible (Rule 3). Division, chromatic notes, syncopation and dotted rhythms may be introduced if a suitable occasion presents itself. The 'Method' thus imposes a routine way of working and circumscribes the student's freedom of choice. In Taylor's copy he is told: 'These things observe unless designedly you will make use of any particular rule, contrary to this method'; in Corbett's he is given a check-list of occasions when it may be necessary 'to alter what you have wrought by your method' and look for an alternative solution. If need be, he must pass through the rules 'in order … over and over; until you have completed and filled up your song'. There is little here that could not be perfectly well done nowadays by a computer.

Birchensha's Rules are basically conceived in terms of two-part writing. Once they have been mastered, it is assumed that the ability to handle more complex textures will follow. In Withey's copy a number of music examples have a second treble part lightly sketched in. In Corbett's there is a section in which examples of Rules 1–4 are 'composed into four parts', a process that usually means adding middle parts to a two-part example, as in his illustration of 'transverse and breaking' motion (Rule 3) (see Example 7.5). Birchensha here uses the treble clef for inner parts in order to simplify things for the student. His advice is succinct: 'If any of those middle parts fail you then work by another rule'. Nevertheless some of these filled-out examples, despite being in the master's hand, contain what would usually be regarded as solecisms, such as consecutive octaves, or errors such as missing flats. Birchensha may have preferred on the whole to impart positive advice rather than 'negative precepts'; but such lapses contribute to an impression of fallibility.

It is instructive to compare Birchensha's rules and method with the combinatorial system of composition described in Kircher's *Musurgia universalis*.[83] Especially striking is the similarity of language used by the two theorists when advancing claims for their respective systems (see appendices 2 and 3). Each allows someone totally unskilled in music to learn, in a few weeks, a way of composing music in two, three, four, or more parts to a standard which otherwise might not be reached in years. Both men lay down a series of procedures that have to be carried out. Obviously there were fundamental differences between their approaches. Kircher's was the more mechanical way: it involved use of an 'Arca musarithmica', a chest containing tablets on which were encoded chord sequences that could be utilized for setting texts to music in a variety of rhythms and tones, and was intended to benefit Jesuit missionaries.[84] Birchensha's made pragmatic use of traditional didactic methods and was aimed primarily at the British gentleman amateur. Nevertheless it is noteworthy that in his letter to Robert Boyle of 1664 Hooke apparently refers in the same breath to Kircher's *ars combinatoria* and Birchensha's success in teaching Buckingham, who was ignorant of 'the practic[al] part of music'.[85] Perhaps it was no coincidence that Pepys later acquired an 'arca musarithmica'.[86]

---

83 Athanasius Kircher, *Musurgia universalis* (Rome, 1650).   **84** Kircher presented one to Duke August of Brunswick-Lüneburg-Wolfenbüttel; it is now in *D-W*. See Carlo Mario Chierotti, 'Comporre senza conoscere la musica: Athanasius Kircher e la *musurgia mirifica*', *Nuova rivista musicale italiana*, 28 (1994), 382–410. **85** See note 48.   **86** Now in *GB-Cmc*; see R.T. Gunther, *Early science in Cambridge* (Oxford, 1937), p. 96. *GB-Cmc* has Pepys's copy of Kircher's *Musurgia universalis*, bought on 22 Feb. 1668.

CONCLUSION

Writing in 1700 to Arthur Charlett, the master of University College, Oxford, Pepys expressed the view that more people would derive satisfaction from music and invent compositions of their own 'were the doctrine of it brought within the simplicity, perspicuity, and certainty common to all other the parts of mathematic knowledge'.[87] Such a sentiment might easily have come from Birchensha himself.

The idea that the philosophical, mathematical and practical aspects of music are interdependent lies at the heart of Birchensha's theorizing. Like Lippius and Alsted, he considered the unison to be the origin and root of all musical intervals.[88] At the beginning of Corbett's copy of the 'Rules' the pupil is presented with the sonorous body of material he or she has to work with in the shape of a 'Table to find out all consonant and dissonant intervals in an octave'.[89] In adherence to Pythagorean doctrine, the diatonic semitone is shown as smaller than the *apotome* or chromatic semitone. Progressive, in contrast, is the way intervals are expressed 'in all keys practicable by our instruments', including C sharp and A flat, with double flat and double sharp signs used where necessary.[90]

Oldenburg probably overrated Birchensha's intellect and musicianship. Others poked fun at his pretensions. In a prefatory letter to Simpson's *Compendium* Locke implicitly disparages both Birchensha's vaunted rules and the Royal Society's zeal for experiments, such as those conducted in old St Paul's in 1664:

And though perchance our new lights (of which this age has been monstrous fruitful) who can speculate how many hair's-breadths will reach from the top of Paul's steeple to the centre of a full moon, and demonstrate that the thousandth part of a minute after, there will be so many thousand more hairs necessary, by reason of the Earth's or moon's motion. Yet we poor practical men, who do because we do (as they are pleased to censure us), are content with such rules and predicaments only as are or may be useful to us ... leaving the rest to those who love to busy themselves about nothing, or to no purpose; of whom I shall make bold to deliver this truth, that I could never yet see that done by them which they pretend to be most versed in, viz. the production of air, which, in my opinion, is the soul of music.[91]

The idea that rules alone could turn a novice into a good composer in a matter of weeks invited satire. In Shadwell's *The Humorists* Mr Brisk, an 'airy, fantastic, singing, dancing coxcomb' who is in the habit of humming a 'merry and luscious'

87 Letter of 5 Nov. 1700: *Private correspondence and miscellaneous papers of Samuel Pepys*, ed. J.R. Tanner, 2 vols (London, 1926), ii, p. 109.   **88** Birchensha, *Templum musicum*, p. 16.   **89** An almost identical table also appears at the end of the 'practical part' of the 'Compendious discourse': RS, Boyle papers, 41, fo. 6r. The 'great card' that Pepys was shown in 1662 may have been similar.   **90** Ibid. The 'Compendious discourse' seems to be the earliest English treatise to use the terms 'double flat' and 'double sharp'.   **91** Simpson, *Compendium*, sig. A5v; Locke's letter is dated 1 June 1667.

courant by Birchensha, quips: 'Berkenshaw is a rare fellow, give him his due, for he can teach men to compose, that are deaf, dumb, and blind'.[92]

Arguably it took a society in which rational thought flourished, in which composers as skilful as Jenkins and Locke did not disdain to write two-part airs, and in which gentlemen who could compose songs or improvise divisions were applauded, for Birchensha's rules to acquire the celebrity they did. Before joining those historians who have dismissed him as a 'kind of musical adventurer' or 'quack-theorist',[93] however, we ought to be sure we know what he was trying to accomplish.

APPENDIX 1

Example 7.6: 'J. Birkinsha', Gavot (from a Suite *a* 2 in B flat major comprising Overture, Branle 1, Branle 2, Branle 3, Gavot, Courant, Minuet and Rondeau). *GB-Lcm*, MS 2087: [i] fos. 187v–90r; [ii] fos. 178v–81r. In the source the time-signature is reversed, indicating a quick tempo.

---

92 *The complete works of Thomas Shadwell*, ed. Montague Summers, 5 vols (London, 1927), i, pp 217–18, 221. The play was first given at Lincoln's Inn Fields in Dec. 1670.   **93** Charles Burney, *A general history of music, from the earliest ages to the present period*, 4 vols (London, 1789), iii, p. 472; Spink, *Restoration*, p. 274.

APPENDIX 2: KIRCHER'S CLAIMS FOR HIS 'ARS MUSARITHMICA'

(a) *Musurgia universalis* (Rome, 1650), ii, p. 2:
Serio iam à multis annis huic negotio incubui, nihil non intentatum relinquendo, quo artem aliquam reperirem, qua quavis etiam quantumvis musicæ imperitus, id exiguo temporis spacio et sine labore consequi posset, quo practici compositores vix multorum annorum spacio consequuntur.

[For many years now I have earnestly pondered this matter, leaving no stone unturned, in order to find a method by which anybody, however unskilled in music, would be able in a short time and without effort to achieve what practising composers scarcely achieve in many years.]

(b) *Musurgia universalis* (Rome, 1650), ii, p. 185:
Musurgia mechanica nihil aliud est, quàm certa quædam ratio à nobis inventa, qua quivis etiam amusos varia instrumentorum melotheticorum applicatione cantilenas iuxta petitum artificium componere possit.

['Mechanical composing' is simply a trusty system invented by us, by means of which anybody, even an unmusical person, may, through employing 'melothetic' devices in various ways, compose songs to the desired level of skill.]

(c) *Ars magna sciendi sive combinatoria* (Amsterdam, 1669), p. 480:

Nova musurgia, qua universali quadam ratione, & dato quolibet harmonico stylo, quispiam etiam Musicæ imperitus impositum sibi munus implere possit, per compositionem melodiarum 1. 2. 3. 4. 5. 6. 7. 8. usque ad 20 vocum.

[A new way of composing, by which universal system anybody (even if unskilled in music) may be able to fulfill a task involving the composition of melodic lines, in any given harmonic style, for one, two, three, four, five, six, seven, eight, even up to twenty voices.]

APPENDIX 3: BIRCHENSHA'S CLAIMS FOR HIS RULES OF COMPOSITION

(a) *Templum musicum* (London, 1664), sig. A7r:
I dare boldly affirm, and if occasion be offered undertake to prove it, that such rules may be yet further, and are already, in part, contrived (drawn from the mathematical principles of music), by which musical consonants and dissonants (artificially applied and disposed, according to the nature of their proportions, and by the forementioned canons) may afford, in two, three, four, five, six, seven or more parts, as good music, that is, as agreeable, artificial, and formal, as can be composed by the help of any instrument.

(b) Letter to the Royal Society, 26 April 1664:

As to the melopoetical or compositive part [of music], I shall discover a few, easy, certain, and perfect rules (never yet invented or published by any man) which may be understood, and made practice of, in a few weeks, or months at the farthest, by any reasonable capacity; ... By which rules not only those who skilfully can sing or play on some instrument may learn to compose, but also those who can neither sing nor play: I say, that by my said rules such may both make good air and compose two, three, four or more parts artificially.

(c) Animadversion for *Syntagma musicæ*, 1672:

An easy way is by the said author invented for making airy tunes of all sorts by a certain rule (which most men think impossible to be done) and the composing of two, three, four, five, six, and seven parts; which by the learner may be performed in a few months; viz. in two months he may (exquisitely, and with all the elegancies of music) compose two parts; in three months, three parts; and so forwards to seven parts, (as many persons of honour and worth have often experienced): which otherwise cannot be done in so many years.

Narcissus Marsh: ground-breaking bishop

ANDREW ROBINSON

Long before it came to be applied in general to innovative thinking, 'ground-breaking' had a precise musical meaning: in 1659 Christopher Simpson defined 'breaking the ground' as 'the dividing its notes into more diminute notes. As for instance, a semibreve may be broken into two minims, four crotchets, eight quavers, sixteen semiquavers, etc.'[1] The art of breaking a newly-composed ground occupies a special place in the history of music; it is preserved in today's chord-sequence-based musical genres. Sixteenth-century Italy popularized a number of traditional grounds such as the *Passamezzo, Ruggiero, Folia*, and *Romanesca* over which endless variations were improvized, and by the early seventeenth-century music theorists had begun making all their harmonic reckonings in the modern way: with respect to the bass rather than to the tenor. Simpson's *The division-viol* was not the first to deal with breaking and descanting on bass-lines, but it is a model of clarity among the often obscure literature of musical composition. Simpson's ground-breaking manual came out just at the time when Narcissus Marsh was learning to play the viol, and a copy of it is listed in an early catalogue of his library. We may reasonably suppose that that copy was Marsh's own, though we can not confirm this, as it has since gone missing.[2] Marsh is remembered now principally as a philanthropist who founded a public library, but he was active, far-sighted and innovative in many fields. In a sour 'character' of Marsh written about 1710 his dean, Jonathan Swift, conceded 'Doing good is his pleasure'.[3]

Marsh came to Ireland as provost of Trinity College Dublin in 1679, and remained here for the rest of his life, with one brief hiatus during the Jacobite troubles when he fled to London. He was made successively bishop of various Irish dioceses, and was primate archbishop of Armagh when he died in 1713. He was also one of the lords justices who ruled Ireland after the accession of William and Mary in 1691. He endowed the library of St Sepulchres, now better known as Marsh's library, and comfortably housed it between the archbishop's residence and St Patrick's cathedral, Dublin.[4] It was to be the most publicly accessible

1 Christopher Simpson, *The division-viol, or the art of playing ex tempore upon a ground* (London, 1659; facsimile repr. (2nd ed. 1667) London, 1955), p. 28. This book predates by decades the first occurrence of such phrases as 'ground-breaking', and 'break new ground' cited in *OED*.   2 Richard Charteris, 'Music manuscripts and books missing from Archbishop Marsh's Library, Dublin', *ML*, 59 (1980), 310–17.   3 Raymond Gillespie (ed.), *Scholar bishop: the recollections and diary of Narcissus Marsh, 1638–96* (Cork, 2003), pp 83–4. Swift's jaundiced opinion of Marsh was that 'His high station hath placed him in the way of great employments, which, without the least polishing his native rusticity, have given him a tincture of pride and ambition. But these vices would have passed concealed under his natural simplicity,

library in these islands, for the use of 'all graduates and gentlemen';[5] he was motivated to establish it in order to counter the prohibitive restrictions he found had been placed on access to the library of Trinity College – students were not allowed so much as to read a book there unless accompanied by a fellow of the college.[6] Marsh had the building designed by Sir William Robinson, loosely basing it on the Bodleian library in Oxford.[7] He took great care to stock it with both his own extensive library (with the exception of his oriental manuscripts, which he left to the Bodleian) and with another collection he bought specially for it; his first librarian also donated books of his own. Among this treasure there remains a set of rare and valuable musical books and manuscripts, many of them personal to Marsh.

Born in Wiltshire in 1638, Narcissus Marsh was bred up to scholarship. He entered Oxford university in 1654, where he excelled in 'old philosophy, mathematics and oriental languages', taking his master's degree in 1660 at the age of 21. Throughout his life he would occasionally solve problems in mathematics, as a form of recreation. While at Oxford he took lessons on the bass viol with a master, possibly the German Theodore Steffkin, and he both attended and hosted weekly 'music meetings' in which viol consort music was played. The name 'Mr Stephkins' or 'Stifkins' appears as the composer of several of the pieces in the manuscript now known as Narcissus Marsh's lyra viol book.[8] Marsh's own handwriting also appears throughout this book, first on the fly-sheets at each end (the book is written from both ends), claiming ownership of the book in the year 1666, and in the body of the book naming and spelling out the various tunings of the lyra viol, attributing pieces to various composers, and notating many of the pieces themselves.[9] His meticulous nature is seen in the neatness of his handwriting, compared to the hurried scrawl of its main contributor (possibly Steffkin), and also in the corrections he made, twice altering the perfectly acceptable spelling of 'corant' to 'corrant'.

There is something curious about the fact that eighteen of the twenty-five pieces written in Marsh's hand are left without composers' names, while thirty of the thirty-two in the other hand are duly attributed by Marsh to their various composers. The first scribe's pieces are numbered in the manuscript, and Marsh's are interspersed without numbering, which shows that he added his pieces in pre-ruled staves left blank by the first writer. The omission of attributions for most of the pieces in Marsh's hand has led the book's modern editor, Richard Rastall, to surmise that they may have been Marsh's own compositions. They are simple

if he had not endeavoured to hide them by art.'   **4** St Sepulchres remained the official residence of the archbishops of Dublin until 1806. It later became the headquarters for the Dublin Metropolitan Police and a Garda station in 1925.   **5** Muriel McCarthy, *All graduates and gentlemen* (Dublin, 1980), p. 36. **6** Gillespie (ed.), *Scholar bishop*, p. 60.   **7** Edward McParland, 'Building Marsh's library' in Muriel McCarthy & Ann Simmons (eds), *The making of Marsh's library* (Dublin, 2004), pp 41–50.   **8** *IRL-Dm*, Z.3.5.13; facsimile ed. Richard Rastall (Clanbrickan, 1978). See also Charteris, *Catalogue*, pp 118–21. **9** Muriel McCarthy, Keeper of Marsh's library, comments that the signature on the fly-sheets, in large formal italic, is quite unlike all other examples of Marsh's handwriting.

enough dance movements, using chords and double stops but without requiring knowledge of counterpoint for their composition; they could have been improvised, then polished up and written down. The ungrammatical use of six-four chords, perfectly harmonious to the ear but narrowly circumscribed in the rules of composition, points to a talented amateur as the composer of these pieces.[10]

The composers that are named in the lyra viol book, all English except for Steffkin, generally belonged to the older generation. The same is true of the composers in Marsh's consort part books, again almost exclusively English.[11] The books Marsh played from in his weekly music meetings have been preserved in his library, in excellent condition. At first sight they seem too clean to have been ever used at all; some of the pieces contain mistakes, which reinforces the suspicion that the books could not have been players' copies. No later markings are added to put matters right, which is surprising since the style of composition is such that one missing rest or wrong note-value is often enough to abort a reading outright.

Marsh's part books contain 62 pieces for three viols, 80 for four, 67 for five and 64 for six viols: 273 pieces altogether, copied by several hands, of which one is Marsh's own. The length of a piece, it would appear, is generally determined by what will fill two pages, that is, one opening of a part-book. Most of these pieces are fantazias: contrapuntal music of delicious complexity, in which each player counts his rests and then enters, alone, with a theme. No part is assigned such a menial role as 'accompaniment', but those players not stating the theme weave melodic lines around it, or count out more rests. To compound the difficulty, the parts are copied without barlines, although the music is generally measured in regular breve units. The puzzle or game aspect was perhaps a more considerable element in contrapuntal music than players liked to admit publicly, and it had been wittily exploited since the fifteenth century by composers who delighted in writing unexpected entries and rhythms, calculated to throw the reader off. It was even put to expressive effect, as when Heinrich Schütz set the words *non confundentur* to a fugal passage with the entries piled on together so closely that they threaten to merge disastrously into one another. Schütz was clearly punning on the word *confundentur*, which means 'mingled' and 'thrown into disorder' as well as 'bewildered' and 'ashamed'.[12]

---

10 Altogether 10 of the 57 pieces in the lyra-viol book commit the solecism of the 'unprepared six-four': 4 unattributed in Marsh's hand, 2 unattributed in the earlier hand, one by Taylor, 2 by Burroughs, and one by Steffkin. The brothers Silas and Sylvanus Taylor were in Marsh's Oxford viol-playing circle, and one if not both of them composed anthems and viol pieces; Burroughs has not been identified. Those composers whose names are better known – Lawes, Jenkins, Ives, Mace, Coleman and Este – all avoid the offending chord. In France at the same time the nobleman M. de Sainte-Colombe was similarly flouting the rules to produce naive but, in his case, highly virtuosic viol music. **11** See Charteris, *Catalogue* for a complete list. See also Richard Charteris, 'Consort music manuscripts in Archbishop Marsh's library, Dublin', *RMA Research Chronicle*, 13 (1976), 27–63. **12** Heinrich Schütz, SWV 268, *Symphoniæ Sacræ I* (1629), no. 12. The text is from Ps 34:5: 'and their faces were not ashamed' (AV).

This learned music was supremely suitable for the clergy, as it coincided with the contemporary style of church music and was written by the very same composers. Besides the pleasant and stimulating recreation of ensemble playing, it could be argued that ignorance of the ways and methods of the church's musical servants should be undesirable to their employers. Viol playing was traditionally cultivated by choristers, at least since the time of Byrd, and a number of church anthems were written with viol consort participation – we should hesitate to call it accompaniment – by some of the foremost viol consort composers. To vary the diet of fantazias, collections such as Marsh's typically included ensemble divisions on popular tunes, on a hexachord, or on a plainsong (these last being mainly *In nomines*) harking right back to the beginnings of counterpoint in twelfth-century discant, and some dance movements: majestic pavans, downbeat almains, stonking galliards. Marsh's set however consists almost entirely of fantazias; these number 236, with only 11 pavans, 2 almains, 3 galliards, 3 sets of variations, 7 transcriptions of vocal pieces, and 11 *In nomines*. The vocal pieces are the only non-English pieces, if we (justifiably) count Coprario, Ferrabosco II, Lupo, and Mico as English composers.

One clinching piece of evidence, noted by Richard Charteris, shows how these part books really could have been used by Marsh in his music meetings.[13] Two further manuscript books in the collection contain scores of some of the pieces in the part books, and two more contain keyboard and thoroughbass parts; and, critically, these pieces are marked with the same numbers they bear in the part-books. This cross-reference also solves the problem of the otherwise disastrous, though few, uncorrected notes and rests in the parts. One music master, armed with a score or short score and sometimes but not always playing a keyboard or lute, would preside over the consort, giving leads where necessary. This follows descriptions left by a fellow consort player, Anthony Wood, in his Oxford memoirs, and by other contemporary writers.[14]

It is hard to be sure of the dates of Marsh's musical activity: those we have are clear enough, yet somewhat contradictory. In 1690 he began to keep a diary starting with a chronology up to that year.[15] In this, having just referred to 1662 and then confusingly to 'before this in the year 1664', he wrote:

I had also before this betaken myself to the practice of music, especially of the bass viol, and after the fire of London I constantly kept a weekly consort (of instrumental music and sometimes vocal) in my chamber on Wednesday in the afternoon, and then on Thursday, as long as I lived in Oxford. This I did as an exercise, using no other, but labouring harder at my study all the rest of the week.

Yet O Lord I beseech thee to forgive me this loss of time and vain conver-sation.[16]

13 Charteris, *Catalogue*, p. 40.   14 Andrew Clark (ed.), *The life and times of Anthony Wood, antiquary, of Oxford, 1632–95*, 5 vols (Oxford, 1891–5), i, pp 204–6, 273–5.   15 Marsh's diary is printed in Gillespie (ed.), *Scholar bishop*.   16 Ibid., *Scholar bishop*, p. 20.

The fire of London in 1666 must have been an unforgettable milestone, and yet according to Wood, Marsh both attended and hosted music meetings well before that.[17] Wood's chronology is not always reliable, but he lists Marsh among those attending meetings in the house of the organist William Ellis in 1659. Wood remarks that Marsh seldom played at these meetings, as he held his own meetings in Exeter College – where he lived as a fellow from his graduation in 1658 until he was made master of St Alban Hall in 1673. He was away from Oxford for a year around 1662, when he was sent as vicar to Swindon in Wiltshire, a living he gave up when he found that its retention was conditional on his marrying a certain gentlewoman. In his diary he tells how, 'being averse to the entangling myself in the cares of the world (but indeed and chiefly my father being averse to it, without which I had done it but without him I would do nothing)' he smartly extricated himself and returned to Oxford.[18] Perhaps Marsh simply attended and hosted consort meetings less regularly before the fire of London than after it; the date of 1666 seems significant none the less, as that is also the year he acquired his lyra viol book.

The form of these meetings was usually an afternoon gathering of college men, students and graduates, a good proportion being college Fellows and therefore in holy orders, with some professional musicians including singing-men of the college chapels. Most of them were violists, though some sang their parts, and some played the organ, virginals or lute. Wood gives two lists, the first dated 1656 and the second, which includes Marsh, 1659. Violinists only appear in the second list, after the great German violinist Thomas Baltzar's arrival in England had raised that instrument's respectability.[19] The descriptions given by Wood suggest that a few of the company played at a time, while others listened:

> John Parker, one of the university musicians, would be sometimes among them; but Mr Low [an organist], a proud man, could not endure any common musician to come to the meeting, much less to play among them. Among these I must put John Haselwood an apothecary, a starched formal clisterpipe, who usually played on the bass-viol and sometimes on the counter-tenor. He was very conceited of his skill (though he had but little of it) and therefore would be ever and anon ready to take up a viol before his betters: which being observed by all, they usually called him *Handlewood*.[20]

The practice of composing and playing viol fantazias was becoming rare by the time of the Restoration,[21] and though fifteen wonderful pieces for three to

17 Clark (ed.), *Anthony Wood,* i, pp 273–5. **18** Gillespie (ed.), *Scholar bishop,* p.19. **19** Called by Wood 'the most famous artist for the violin that the world had yet produced', Thomas Baltzar (*c*.1630–63) played at one of the meetings in Ellis' house in Oxford in 1658, to the astonishment of his hearers. John Wilson, the professor of music at the university, 'did, after his humoursome way, stoop down to Baltzar's feet' to check whether he had hooves or human feet (Clark (ed.), *Anthony Wood,* i, p. 256). **20** Ibid., pp 205–6. **21** Richard Rastall, 'Benjamin Rogers (1614–98): some notes on his instrumental music', *ML,* 46:3 (1965), 237–42 at 240 describes Oxford as 'one of the few places, perhaps, where music for a whole consort of

seven viols were yet to be written by Purcell in 1680, he actually appears to have kept them secret: since Roger North, himself an amateur viol player who occasionally played chamber music with Purcell, in later years named Matthew Locke, who had died in 1677, as the last composer ever to write viol fantazias.[22] Unlike Charles I, who had studied the viol and played consorts with Coprario, King Charles II was not a lover of fantazias; he preferred the French style of music, to which he could beat time, and his distaste may explain Purcell's apparent silence.

For some of his Oxford years Marsh was chaplain to the university's chancellor, Edward Hyde, who supported and encouraged him in his studies; after court intrigue forced Hyde to flee to France in 1667, Marsh 'became acquainted with that excellent man and good patron, Dr John Fell, then dean of Christ Church and afterwards bishop of Oxford, whose memory is precious'.[23] In 1678 Fell offered him, on behalf of the lord lieutenant of Ireland, the provostship of 'Trinity College near Dublin'. Marsh embraced the offer; leaving Oxford two days after his fortieth birthday and arriving in Dublin almost three weeks later, he was invested as provost in January 1679.

As a protegé of Hyde, Marsh's religion must have been of the orthodox Church of England variety, free of puritanism;[24] but by temperament he was punctilious, and his management of both St Alban Hall, Oxford, and Trinity College, Dublin, appears to have been strict and disciplinarian. However, leading by example, he was apparently very successful in both posts. Marsh had a morbid fear of Catholicism which expressed itself in disturbing dreams,[25] and as lord justice he had the onus of enacting some of the penal laws. However his actions show that, like certain other bishops of the Church of Ireland, notably Bedell before him and Berkeley after him, he actively engaged with the Irish-speaking people and took steps which we would now call positive discrimination in order to promote their education, and not just that of the English-speaking city- and Pale-dwellers and planters. He learnt the Irish language, and even wrote a grammar of it, now lost. As provost, in the face of active discouragement from his archbishop, who wanted to stamp out the Irish language, he made it mandatory that a proportion of lectures and sermons in Trinity College be given in Irish; the latter he attended himself. He finished the job, begun by Bishop Bedell, of publishing the Old Testament in Irish; Marsh, with the help of native speakers, personally checked each verse against the Hebrew, Greek and Latin of his polyglot bible, and saw the completed book through the press.[26]

* * *

viols would not have been considered rather old-fashioned by 1668.'   **22** John Wilson (ed.), *Roger North on music; being a selection from his essays written during the years c.1695–1728* (London, 1959), p. 301. **23** Gillespie (ed.), *Scholar bishop,* p. 21.   **24** Hyde was one of the Great Tew circle during Charles I's reign, who informally framed the constitution of the Church of England that would take effect when the Restoration ended the puritan ascendancy. See Hugh Trevor-Roper, *Catholics, Anglicans and Puritans* (2nd ed. London, 1989), pp 166–230.   **25** Gillespie (ed.), *Scholar bishop,* pp 27–8.   **26** *Leabhuir na*

Nothing is known of any musical activity by Marsh after he left England, beyond the mention of unspecified musical instruments which he left to his niece in his will, and an essay he presented to the Dublin Society in 1683 *On the doctrine of sounds*. Before examining that essay it is worth looking at a paper he published shortly before coming to Dublin, an *Essay touching the (esteemed) sympathy between lute or viol strings*.[27] In this Marsh developed some remarks Descartes had made in his *Compendium of music*, a little tract written in 1618 and published posthumously in 1650.[28] One of Descartes' themes was a new method of visualizing musical concords by making equal divisions of lines, and in passing he mentioned a fact he had confirmed experimentally, namely that a lute string vibrates when a lower string of concordant pitch is sounded.

Marsh expanded this observation into a paper of some five thousand words with over twenty diagrams. Most of the material is mathematical, drawing deductions from variations in the length, tension and thickness of strings to the resulting variations in pitch. Marsh gave the general formula $\frac{T}{LxD}$ for what he called 'acuteness of sound', where T is the tension, L the length and D the diameter of a string. He expounded nine cases, halving and doubling one or more of these variables, and calculating the resulting pitch, the results being unison with the original, or one or more octaves higher or lower.

Some of Marsh's observations and deductions are in line with today's theory, others not: he has got it right about variations in the length and diameter of strings, but wrong about the tension. Surprisingly he appears unaware of Mersenne's harmonic studies even though his own collection included some of Mersenne's theological and scientific books.[29] Mersenne had experimented with ropes and wires over forty metres long, so that he could count their frequency of vibration by eye. Mersenne's law, as it is now known, is a very similar formula to Marsh's, in different terms, but Mersenne discovered what Marsh did not: that pitch is not directly proportional to the tension of a string, but to the square root of the tension. To give him his due, we should note that Marsh did not define tension at all, or relate it to other measurements. Tension is now measured as Mersenne measured it, in terms of mass: suspending a weight of a kilogram from a string puts it under what we may call one kilogram of tension. If we allow that Marsh had a different concept of tension, which, if worked out, would have been proportional to the square root of a supposed suspended weight, then his formula is correct. This is of course special pleading: it would appear that Marsh simply did not consider the measurement of tension at all, beyond noting what everyone has always known, namely that increasing the tension raises the pitch. All the experiments he described could be done on a lute or viol without disturbing it,

Seintiomna ar na ttaruing go gaidlig tre cúram & dútras an Doctúir Uiliam Bedel (London, 1685) was published at the expense of Robert Boyle.   **27** Robert Plot, *The natural history of Oxfordshire* (Oxford, 1677), pp 289–99.   **28** This was Descartes' first essay on any subject. After writing it at the age of twenty-two he corresponded at length with other mathematicians and musicologists, notably Marin Mersenne, on the topics he had raised.   **29** Mersenne published his findings in his *Harmonie universelle,* 2 vols (Paris, 1636–7).

whereas a special monochord, from whose string-end weights could be hung, would be required to establish the relationship of pitch to suspended mass. In Marsh's favour we should note that Descartes himself, supremely aware of the distinction between arithmetic and logarithmic scales, had deliberately used arithmetic values for the visual representation of exponential proportions in his *Compendium*.

Mersenne's Law uses three variables, tension, length, and mass per unit length, while Marsh uses tension, length, and diameter. The third variable, diameter, does end up in agreement between the two theorists, since the factor in Mersenne's formula is the square root of the mass per unit length. Since this mass is proportional to the cross-section area, πr^2, its square root is directly proportional to the radius, and therefore also the diameter, of the string.

In the experiments he did, and the derivation of his conclusions, Marsh would have been a potential butt of Matthew Locke's derision. Locke's theoretical writings boldly ignored rational deductions from first principles, leaning instead towards the newly emerging philosophy of empiricism.[30] He ridiculed 'our new lights (of which this age has been monstrous fruitful) who can speculate how many hair's-breadths will reach from the top of St Paul's steeple to the centre of a full moon', while 'we poor practical men, who do because we do (as they are pleased to censure us), are content with such rules and predicaments only as are or may be useful to us'.[31] In fact Marsh did at one point note in his diary 'Thy name be praised O Lord for all thy mercies, this evening I invented a way to find out the moon's distance from the centre of the Earth without the help of its parallax.'[32]

One distraction that Marsh allowed into his theory was the consideration of the force of the stroke as a factor determining pitch. His explanation of the higher pitch of a string under high tension was that the string when struck is displaced less, that is to say, into an arc of a greater circle, 'which doing brisk and smartly with a quick return, because of the little compass it fetches, 'twill beget a sound so much the more acute'.[33] This explanation depends on his supposition that sound is transmitted by the carrying of shaped arcs through the air rather than pulses of pressure interspersed with troughs of rarefaction: 'for the air being put into an arched figure and motion by the string that is touched, rolls away to the other ... it easily (by the force it received from the touched string) imprints both figure and motion into it'.[34] He did not pursue the apparent conclusion, that a small displacement from a gentle stroke should on his hypothesis produce a much higher note, by several octaves perhaps, than a more forceful stroke which displaces the string to a greater amplitude, approximating (to the naked eye) to an arc of a smaller circle.

---

30 See Matthew Locke, *Melothesia* (London, 1673). This gives rules for realizing figured bass which are so discontinuous as to suggest a bluffer's guide rather than a theoretical system.   **31** Matthew Locke, commendatory letter prefaced to Simpson, *Compendium*, sig. A5v; see also Simpson, *Compendium*, ed. Phillip J. Lord (Oxford, 1970), p. xlvii. For a fuller quotation see p.131, above.   **32** Gillespie (ed.), *Scholar bishop*, p. 36.   **33** Plot, *The natural history of Oxfordshire*, p. 290.   **34** Ibid., pp 295–6.

Marsh took Descartes to task in two instances. Descartes had asserted that 'when one of [the strings of a lute] is being plucked, the ones which are an octave or a fifth higher vibrate and sound audibly of their own accord; the strings that are lower do not do this at all'.[35] Marsh's paper dealt with the motion of a string vibrating in two halves, with a still point or node at the centre. Creating a node at the mid-point of a string gives an octave harmonic, an effect familiar to harp, guitar, and bowed-string players. Marsh reported wrapping narrow strips of paper loosely round a string at various points, and noting that a strip placed at the node remained still, while the others would 'dance and play up and down and about the string' when it was excited into motion in sympathy with a string tuned an octave higher.[36]

Marsh says: 'If the lesser of two octaves … be touched … each half of the greater … will answer it, the middle [of the lower string] standing still … though Descartes denies it'.[37] He is entitled to his victory here: all the Cartesian can answer is that the lower string does not vibrate in sympathy *at its own pitch*, but only at a harmonic; yet vibrate it certainly does, and audibly too.

Marsh's second challenge to Descartes is similar. According to Descartes, 'If we pluck one of [a lute's, or any other instrument's] strings, the force of its sound will set in vibration all the strings which are higher by any type of fifth or major third, but nothing will happen to those strings which are at the distance of a fourth or any other consonance.'[38] Marsh on the other hand asserts that 'all tuned strings whatever (whether thirds, fourths, fifths, sixths, &c.) will answer each other more or less, at the due touch of their correspondents … contrary to what Descartes asserts, that such vibrations are found only in upper thirds and fifths'.[39]

We could accuse Descartes of straying into propaganda here, rather than reporting objectively. He had taken on board Zarlino's harmonic theory and apparently wished to give it scientific backing; but, as Marsh reveals, he somewhat misrepresented the facts.[40] A string tuned at the fourth above a struck string will indeed vibrate in sympathy – in three segments, with nodes at a third and two-thirds of its length. The pitch of this quite audible overtone is a twelfth

---

35 Descartes, *Compendium of music [Compendium musicæ]*, trans. Walter Robert ([Rome], 1961), p. 16.
36 The phenomenon of nodes was discussed in another paper published by the mathematician John Wallis in 1677, the same year as Marsh's. According to Wallis this phenomenon had been known to the Oxford musicians for years. See Sigalia Dostrovsky/Murray Campbell, 'Physics of music, §2' in *NG II*, xix, p. 636.
37 Plot, *The natural history of Oxfordshire*, p. 296   38 Descartes, *Compendium of music*, p. 21.   39 Plot, *The natural history of Oxfordshire*, pp 298–9.   40 Gioseffo Zarlino, in *Le istitutioni harmoniche* (Venice, 1588), had made the long-overdue step of including the intervals of the major and minor third in the official list of consonances. This required adding the fifth and sixth harmonics (or partials, or overtones) to the list from which the consonant intervals were derived. Greek theory had recognized all upper partials as consonant with their fundamental, but medieval theory restricted the concept of 'perfect consonance' to the first four. By extending acceptability to the sixth harmonic Zarlino licenced major and minor thirds and sixths, arbitrarily drawing the line at sevenths. Major and minor triads had been in use for centuries by Zarlino's time, but up to the early sixteenth century compositions were required to reach a final cadence on unisons, octaves and perfect fifths only, with even the use of fourths strictly circumscribed – by the same rule we have noted in the context of six-four chords in Marsh's lyra viol book (see p. 137, above), a rule that survived Zarlino's extension of consonance.

higher than the responding string, that is to say two octaves above the sounded string. A string tuned a major sixth above a sounded string will also respond at the interval of a twelfth, coinciding with the major third two octaves above the sounded string. Again all we can say in Descartes' favour is that he was simply not counting response at the upper partials. Marsh did confess that these responses are only heard faintly and by those who know what they are listening for: 'the tremor or vibration in some of them being in many places at the same time ... it cannot always be discerned by the sense, but follows by a parity of reason';[41] but he and his fellow experimenters had hit on a simple yet effective method of amplifying those tiny motions of a string, by attaching paper buzzers.

The essay ends with a report of a curiosity Marsh had witnessed, namely men who could sing overtones; he supplies a speculative, but not convincing, explanation of how this might be achieved, based on opening the mouth in two places at once, making apertures of proportional size. He cites one Hooper of Oxford who did this, but adds, 'I know two other persons now living here, that can do it though their lips seem not to be set in that posture.' He continues: 'But he that excels them all, and indeed to a miracle, is one Mr Joshua Dring, a young gentleman of Hart-hall, who sings a song articulately, *ore patulo* [with open mouth], and all in octaves so very strongly, & yet without much straining, that he equals if not excels the loudest organ.' Marsh concludes by speculating that there may be some 'unequal application of the uvula to the epiglottis' involved, since the young man cannot himself explain what he does, 'only that he performs it in the lower part of his throat.'[42]

* * *

The first president of the Royal Society of London, the Irish mathematician William Brouncker, had published an English translation of Descartes' *Compendium of music* in 1653, with addenda promoting some theories of his own. In 1683 Robert Plot, Marsh's contemporary in Oxford who had published his paper on sympathetic vibration, became secretary of the Royal Society and was given the responsibility for publishing its *Philosophical transactions*. Accordingly the following year the Royal Society published *An introductory essay to the doctrine of sounds, containing some proposals for the improvement of acoustics; as it was presented to the Dublin Society Nov. 12. 1683 by the Right Reverend Father in God Narcissus lord bishop of Ferns and Leighlin*.[43]

This is a very different paper from the first. Starting by taking cues from the terminology of the flourishing science of optics, Marsh challenges the scientific world to make similar strides in a new science which he christens *acoustics*: 'Hearing may be divided into direct, refracted and reflexed, which are yet nameless unless we call them acoustics, diacoustics, catacoustics'.[44]

41 Plot, *The natural history of Oxfordshire*, pp 298–9.   **42** Ibid., p. 299.   **43** *Philosophical transactions of the Royal Society of London*, 14 (Feb. 1684), 472–88.   **44** Ibid., p. 473. Marsh spelt such words as 'acoustics' with a k ('acousticks', etc.).

Once again his discussion runs to around five thousand words, comparable to the length of this chapter. Marsh coins nine neologisms in the essay, taking words from the Greek to name his concepts, as others were to do later for things such as the telegraph and telephone. Among the words for which the *Oxford English Dictionary* quotes Marsh as the primary source are *acoustics, phonics,* and *microphone.*

His primary purpose in the essay is to propose things for others to invent, after giving a decent minimum of his own observations and deductions to set them off. In these once again he risks opprobrium from the likes of Matthew Locke by allowing theoretical speculation to lead him where empirical observation would not. Translating the observations of optics somewhat over-confidently into parallel acoustical effects, he declares for instance that a concave reflector 'echoes back the sound bigger, slower (though stronger) and also inverted' – adding, after perhaps a moment of mild consternation, 'but never according to the order of words. Nor do I think it possible for the art of man to contrive a single echo, that shall invert the sound and repeat backwards; because then the words last spoken, that is, which do last occur [...], must first be repelled; which cannot be. For where in the mean time should the first words hang and be concealed or lie dormant? Or how, after such a pause, be revived and animated again into motion? Yet in complicated or compound echoes, where many receive from one another, I know not whether something that way may not be done.'

He hits his stride in setting the agenda for future acousticians, in passages that deserve to be quoted at length:

I mean, by showing, that this [sense] of hearing, is capable of all those improvements which the sense of seeing has received from art, besides many more advantages, that the ear may enjoy, by the help of our doctrine, above the eye; all which moreover will be of as great benefit to mankind, as any thing that optics have yet discovered, if not of greater, which, with some other pre-eminencies that it has upon another score, will happily render acoustics the nobler science of the two. ...

And I do hope, that by the rules, which may happily be laid down, concerning the nature, propagation and proportion or adapting of sounds, a way may be found out, both to improve musical instruments already in use, and to invent new ones, that shall be more sweet and luscious, than any yet known. Besides that by the same means instruments may be made, that shall imitate any sound in nature, that is not articulate; be it of bird, beast, or what thing else soever. ...

As by polyscopes or multiplying glasses, one thing is represented to the eye as many, whether in the same or different shapes (for so multiplying glasses may be contrived): so by a polyphone or polyacoustic well ordered one sound may be heard as many, either of the same or a different note. Insomuch that who uses this instrument, he shall at the sound of a single viol seem to hear a whole consort, and all true harmony. ...

For, as a fine glass bubble, filled with clear water, and placed before a burning candle or lamp, does help it to dart forth its rays to a prodigious length and brightness: so an instrument may be invented, that applied to the mouth (or any sonorous body) shall send forth the voice distinctly to as prodigious a distance and loudness ... Now of what use such an instrument might be for speaking clearly and articulately at a distance, (and that without altering the tone of the voice) whether it be at sea or land (but especially at sea in tempestuous weather and in the night) is obvious to any man to conceive. ...

As instruments have been invented to help the eye, so likewise are there some, and more such there may be, for the ear.

For, as spectacles and other glasses are made to help the purblind and weak eyes, to see at any competent distance: so there are otacoustics (and better may be made) to help weak ears to hear at a reasonable distance also. Which would be as great help to the infirmity of old age, as the other invention of spectacles is, and perhaps greater; forasmuch as the hearing what is spoken is of more daily use and concern to such men, than to be able to read books or to view pictures.

As perspective-glasses[45] and telescopes help the eye to see objects at a very great distance, which otherwise would not be discernable; in like manner may a sort of otacoustics be so contrived as that they shall receive in sounds made at a very great distance also; but with so much advantage, that the ear shall be able to hear them, which otherwise would have been inaudible. ...

As microscopes or magnifying glasses, help the eye to see near objects, that by reason of their smallness were invisible before; which objects they magnify to a strange greatness: so microphones or micracoustics, that is, magnifying ear instruments may be contrived after that manner, that they shall render the most minute sound in nature distinctly audible, by magnifying it to an unconceivable loudness.

Marsh concludes his flight of fancy by putting his speculations into three formal 'problems', couched, like university examination questions, in Latin, followed by their translations and his final remarks. These are unapproachably daunting, given only the technology of the late seventeenth century:

[1.] To make the least sound (by the help of instruments) as loud as the greatest; a whisper to become as loud as the shot of a cannon;

[2.] To propagate any (the least) sound to the greatest distance ... by this means a weather-cock may be so contrived, as that with an ordinary blast of wind it shall cry (or whistle) loud enough to be heard many leagues;

and finally,

---

45 Perspective-glass meant any optical instrument, such as a magnifying glass, though after the mid-seventeenth century the term usually denoted a telescope.

[3.] That a sound may be conveyed from one extreme to the other (or from one distant place to another) so as not to be heard in the middle. By the help of this problem a man may talk to his friend at a very considerable distance, so that those in the middle space shall hear nothing of what passed betwixt them.

Marsh's acoustical problems were not, as he hoped, soluble within the physics of shaped reflectors and refracting lens-like bodies; in fact they were to remain unsolved throughout the whole eighteenth century. Steam whistles and foghorns were not developed until the mid-nineteenth century, and with the exception of early sound recording and amplification as pioneered by Edison in the 1870s, the other devices he sought were only made possible with the aid of electronics: telephone and radio.[46] His most wildly ambitious project, the 'polyphone or polyacoustic' that could automatically harmonize a melody, would have to wait three hundred years, for the invention of computerized musical instruments. It is easy for us to smile at the presumption Marsh showed, that these problems could have 'acoustic' (by contrast with 'electronic') solutions; we might also be tempted to apply to his flights of fancy the same kind of criticism that Dr Johnson made of Swift's *Gulliver's travels*: 'When once you have thought of big men and little men, it is very easy to do all the rest'. Marsh did begin by the simple expedient of transposing recent discoveries in optics into the field of acoustics; but his imagination proved wonderfully fertile in the course of making that translation, and he did come up with some ground-breaking proposals.

46 Of the three devices – telephone, radio, and sound recording – the first to be developed was, perhaps surprisingly, the telephone. The inventor Antonio Meucci set up a working telephone system in his house in the 1850s and demonstrated it in New York in 1860.

Music fit for a king: the Restoration of Charles II and the Dublin cathedral repertoire

KERRY HOUSTON

At first sight, the task of assessing repertoire at St Patrick's and Christ Church cathedrals in the seventeenth century is a daunting one – with the exception of one organ book now held in the library of Durham cathedral,[1] no seventeenth-century music manuscript sources have survived from the Dublin cathedrals. However, financial and other non-musical records assist in the challenge. It is possible to deduce the probable repertoire and, more importantly, repertoire development at St Patrick's and Christ Church from the pre-Commonwealth period to the early eighteenth century when musical texts become available and more definitive assessments can be made. This chapter surveys printed and manuscript material which are used to trace repertoire in the seventeenth century and to follow its rapid development and expansion into the early eighteenth century.

Music has been an integral part of the daily life of both Christ Church and St Patrick's cathedrals from their foundations in the eleventh and thirteenth centuries respectively. Choir schools were established at both institutions in the fifteenth century indicating the use of boys' voices in the choirs from that time, although it is likely they were utilized earlier. The daily patterns of worship in the monastic Christ Church and the secular St Patrick's were severely disrupted at the reformation. The cathedral foundation at St Patrick's was suppressed on 8 January 1547 but was restored by the charter of Philip and Mary dated 15 June 1555.[2] The cathedral status of Christ Church was also under threat, but it survived under a new charter as a cathedral of the 'new foundation'. Sacred music performed in the early years of the reformation probably followed English patterns as it did in later periods and it is likely that Dublin cathedral congregations heard the works of Tallis, Byrd and Gibbons. If there was any compositional activity by indigenous composers, no trace of it has survived. Music was sung from manuscripts and the transmission of repertoire to Dublin from England in general, and the Chapel Royal in particular, was via the many singers and organists who travelled across the Irish Sea to take up posts in the Irish capital. Likely couriers of music in the post-reformation period include John Farmer (*c*.1570–1601),[3] Thomas Bateson

1 *GB-DRc*, MS B1 (the Hosier MS).   2 H.J. Lawlor, *Fasti of St Patrick's cathedral, Dublin* (Dundalk, 1930), p. 12. Despite this interruption in cathedral status, St Patrick's most correctly falls into the category of a cathedral of the 'old foundation'.   3 Farmer was organist of Christ Church cathedral 1596–9 and he may also have been organist of St Patrick's cathedral. Shaw, *Succession of organists*, pp 408–9, 417; Boydell, *History of music*, p. 189.

ANTHEMS,
To be Sung
At the Celebration of
D I V I N E   S E R V I C E,
I N
The Cathedrall Church of the Holy
and Vndivided Trinity in
D U B L I N.

*Let the word of Christ dwell in you richly, in
all wisdom, teaching and admonishing one
another in Psalms, and Hymns, and spiri-
tuall Songs, singing with Grace in your
hearts to the Lord,* Col. 3. 16.

Printed *Anno Domini,* 1662.

Illustration 9.1. *Anthems to be sung* (Dublin, 1662), title page. Trinity College Dublin.

(*c*.1570–1630), Benjamin Rogers (1614–98) and Randall Jewett (*c*.1603–75), all of whom served as organists in the Dublin cathedrals and are known to have composed sacred music (for Bateson, Rogers and Jewett, see below).

St Patrick's and Christ Church cathedrals had recovered from the turmoil of the reformation when another challenge to their establishments materialized in the form of puritan reforms and the eventual cessation of choral services under the Commonwealth. This interregnum was short-lived, however, and the Restoration of Charles II marked the beginning of a renaissance of choral worship in both England and Ireland.

Assessment of cathedral repertoire in Dublin in the immediate pre-Commonwealth period can only be speculative. Many English cathedrals possess manuscripts dating from this period providing the surest guide to music in use at these locations. In places where no manuscripts survive, John Barnard's *The first book of selected church musick* (London, 1641) is often cited as the best guide to repertoire. Although this publication is dated 1641 on the title page and despite its dedication to Charles I it was probably not issued until after the Restoration of Charles II in 1660.[4] As such, it represents an assessment of popular repertoire in England shortly before choral services ceased. At the Restoration it served as a valuable resource at the many cathedral and collegiate establishments where pre-Commonwealth manuscripts had been lost or destroyed. Barnard's *First book of selected church musick* was purchased by Westminster Abbey and many English cathedrals including Canterbury, Gloucester, Hereford, Lichfield, Salisbury and Worcester.[5] However, there is no evidence to propose that it was purchased by either Christ Church or St Patrick's cathedrals: its repertoire does not appear to have been prominent in Dublin, suggesting that this important publication did not make its way to Ireland or influence the choice of music at the newly re-established choral foundations there. For this reason, it is not helpful in establishing repertoire in pre-Commonwealth Dublin.

Anthem word books began to be published in the post-Restoration period, but the earliest example comes from Christ Church cathedral, Dublin. *Anthems, to be sung at the celebration of divine service, in the cathedral church of the holy and undivided Trinity in Dublin* was published in Dublin in 1662 but, as with Barnard's *First book of selected church musick*, the genesis of the volume appears to lie in pre-Commonwealth times. It contains the words of 51 anthems but composers are indicated for only 28 of these; a further 17 may be identified with reasonable accuracy by investigation of settings of the texts by contemporary composers. The indication of verse and chorus sections and word repetition has assisted greatly in the identification of unattributed anthems.

The large number of unattributed anthem texts is not surprising as the earliest surviving manuscripts from the Dublin cathedrals contain many works without an indication of composer. These are likely to be descendents of the manuscripts in use at the time of the compilation of *Anthems, to be sung*. Indeed, the

4 Spink, *Restoration*, pp 75–6.   5 Ibid., p. 76.

identification of these unattributed pieces has proved to be one of the most revealing aspects of research into cathedral music in seventeenth- and eighteenth-century Ireland.[6] This 1662 word book contains an index but curiously it only records the first forty-three items. This is a key piece of evidence to suggest that the compilation of the book commenced in the pre-Commonwealth period and was put to one side at the cessation of cathedral services. A further eight anthems were subsequently added after the Restoration but were omitted from the index which had been completed earlier. An analysis of the contents of the book supports this proposition. The first forty-three anthems (hereafter referred to as the 'first part' of the book) are summarized in Table 9.1:

Table 9.1. *Anthems to be sung* (1662), first part.[7]

Composer and number of works	Date	Employment
Unknown (4)		
Batten (1)	*c*.1590–1637	London
Bull (2)	*c*.1562–1628	Chapel Royal
Byrd (4)	*c*.1542–1623	Chapel Royal
East (1)	*c*.1580–1648	Ely/Lichfield/London
Fido (1)	*c*.1570–*c*.1640	Cambridge/Dublin/Lincoln/ Hereford/Wells/Worcester
Gibbons (7)	1583–1625	Chapel Royal
Giles (2 or 3)	*c*.1558–1633	Chapel Royal
Heath (1)	*c*.1590–1668	Rochester
Hooper (1 or 2)	*c*.1553–1621	Chapel Royal
Hutchinson (3)	b. 1616	?York
Jeffreys (1)	*fl. c*.1590	
Jewett (3)	*c*.1603–1675	Chester/Dublin/London
Morley (1)	1557–1603	Chapel Royal
Mudd (1)		
Mundy (1)	*c*.1528–*c*. 1591	Chapel Royal
Peerson (1)	*c*.1572–1650	London
Ramsey (0 or 1)	*fl. c*.1610–1644	Cambridge
Rogers (2)	1614–1698	Windsor/Dublin/Oxford
Tomkins (1 or 2)	1576–1656	Chapel Royal
Ward (1)	*fl.* early-17th cent	Canterbury/London
Wilkinson (3)	*fl.* ?1575–?1612	Cambridge/?Norwich

About half of the repertoire in the book was penned by those with Chapel Royal connections, a further eight per cent from those with other links to London.

---

6 See Houston, 'Music manuscripts'; Boydell, *History of music*. 7 The geographical information in this table has been compiled from *NG II*, Boydell, *History of music* and Ralph T. Daniel & Peter le Huray, *The sources of English church music (1549–1660)* (London, 1972).

Only thirteen per cent of the anthems are associated with composers who lived in Dublin, while the remaining quarter were written by those whose main activity was outside the two capital cities. It is unlikely that any of the unidentified anthems were written by native Dublin composers since these would surely have been known to the compiler of the book. It is therefore reasonable to assume that the unidentified items have an English provenance. The bulk of this repertoire is provided by composers who died before 1640 which supports the view that the compilation of the first part of the book has its roots in pre-Commonwealth times. Of the later composers in the first part of the book, Randall Jewett's anthems were almost certainly written before he left Dublin sometime in the late 1640s or early 1650s – indeed, some of them may predate his arrival in Ireland in the late 1620s. Jewett was probably a chorister at Chester cathedral from 1612 to 1615 and has a rather complex history after that. He seems to have come to Dublin around 1628 and to have become organist of both Dublin cathedrals by 1631.[8] After a short break as organist of Chester cathedral in 1643 he was back in Dublin by the end of 1644 as organist of St Patrick's and was probably organist of Christ Church cathedral by 1646. Jewett went to London during the Interregnum, but at the Restoration St Patrick's still regarded him as their organist, noting that 'Mr Hawkshaw' would officiate during Jewett's absence. However, Jewett had obtained a minor canonry at St Paul's cathedral, London, where he remained until the fire of 1666. He was appointed organist of Winchester cathedral in 1666, and retained that position until his death in 1675.[9] Three of Jewett's anthems are present in the first part of the book with one further item in the second part.

Apart from Jewett, the only other composer active after the Restoration and represented in the first part of *Anthems, to be sung* is Benjamin Rogers. Rogers acted as organist of Christ Church cathedral, Dublin, in 1638 following Jewett's departure and was officially appointed to the post in the following year. Rogers left Christ Church in 1641 and went to be a vicar choral in Cloyne cathedral before returning to England during the Interregnum, taking the positions at St George's chapel, Windsor and Eton College. He became *informator choristarum* at Magdalen College, Oxford, in 1665.[10] Although none of Rogers's music appears in pre-Restoration sources, the inclusion of two anthems in *Anthems, to be sung* suggests that they date from his years in Dublin. Unfortunately, no musical text for these two anthems can be traced.

Thomas Bateson was appointed organist of Christ Church cathedral on 5 April 1609.[11] It is curious that his anthem *Holy, Lord God Almighty* is not included in *Anthems, to be sung*. This anthem was probably composed as an exercise for the (first) degree of Bachelor of Music which was conferred on him by Trinity College in 1612.[12] The scoring is unusual being in seven parts – two trebles, two

8 The first references to payments to him as organist are from the Christ Church cathedral accounts 1629–30. Boydell, *Music at Christ Church*, p. 82.   9 Shaw, *Succession of organists*, pp 64, 298, 410, 417–18; Gillen & Johnstone, *IMS 6*, pp 71–2.   10 Spink, *Restoration*, p. 321; Boydell, *History of music*, pp 56–7; Shaw, *Succession of organists*, pp 345, 374, 381, 410.   11 Shaw, *Succession of organists*, p. 409; Boydell, *History of music*, pp 46, 50, 189.   12 On Bateson's degree see Brian Boydell, 'Thomas Bateson

altos, two tenors and one bass. As Barra Boydell observes, this seems to have been dictated by the paucity of basses in Christ Church choir at that time.[13] Perhaps this scoring made performance problematic in later times and it had fallen from the repertoire by the time the word book was being compiled. The fact that no manuscript sources for the piece have survived in Ireland also suggests that it did not remain in the repertoire for long.

The first part of *Anthems, to be sung* is the best guide to the probable repertoire in the Dublin cathedrals in the immediate pre-commonwealth period. Interestingly, only seven of the fifty-one anthems in the whole book are included in Barnard's *First book of selected church musick*. This shows that repertoire developed in a rather different way in Dublin to other parts of the British Isles. As with Barnard's book, there is no evidence that Tomkin's *Musica Deo sacra* (London, 1668), the other significant English cathedral music publication of the time, was purchased by the Dublin cathedrals. Indeed Tomkin's music is conspicuous by its absence from the earliest surviving music manuscripts from Dublin.

An analysis of the last eight anthems (referred to hereafter as the 'second part' of the book) which are not included in the index of *Anthems to be sung* is revealing and supports the proposition that they are a later addition (Table 9.2).

Table 9.2. *Anthems to be sung* (1662), second part.

Attribution	Probable composers	Unidentified
Giles (1)	Bull (1)	2 anthems
Holmes (1)	Giles (1)	
Hosier (1)	Jewett (1)	

Only three of the anthems in the second part have attributions in the word book – one each by Giles, Holmes and Hosier. Three others are probably by Bull, Giles and Jewett. The remaining two have not yet been identified.

At least three anthems from the second part have possible connections with Restoration celebrations. Richard Hosier's *Now that the Lord hath re-advanced the crown* was written for the very triumphalist service held at St Patrick's cathedral on the 27 January 1661 when twelve bishops were consecrated in the presence of dignitaries of church, state and learning. Biographical details of Hosier are sketchy, but it is likely that the Richard Hosier who was a stipendiary in the choir of Christ Church cathedral for a few months in 1634 (he was dismissed in December 1634 for neglect of duty) is the same Richard Hosier who was in the choir of King's College, Cambridge in 1637 and was a gentleman in

and the earliest degrees in music awarded by the University of Dublin', *Hermathena*, 146 (1989), 53-60.
13 Boydell, *History of music*, pp 41, 59.

(32)

> bnd my heart faileth me, faileth me : Forfake me not o Lord my
> God, my God, be thou not far from me, from me : H ste thee to
> help me, hafte thee to help me, hafte thee to help me, hafte thee
> to help me, hafte thee to help me, o Lord God my falvation.
> *Cho.*   o Lord God my falvation, fo be it, fo be it, fo be it, fo be it.

Anth. XLIX.

I heard a Voice from Heaven!

Ver. *I Heard a Voice from Heaven!* Saying unto me, from henceforth
bleffed are the dead which die in the Lord, for they fhall reft from
their labour, and their works follow them.
Cho.   For they fhall reft from their labors: and their works follow them
Ver.   And they fung the fong of the Lamb, faying, Great and mira-
culous are thy works, great and miraculous are thy works Lord
God Almighty; Juft and true are thy wayes, juft and true are thy
wayes, thy wayes, o King of Saints.
Cho.   Great and marvailous are thy works O Lord God Almighty,
Almighty; Juft and true are thy wayes O King of Saints, thy
wayes O King of Saints.
Ver.   Glory be to the Father, and to the Son, and to the Holy Ghoft.
Cho.   As it was in the beginning, and is now, and ever fhall be, world
without end, Amen; without end Amen, world without end,
A men, A men-

Anth. L. After the Confecration.

Quum denuo exaltavit Dominus Coronam.

Treble **N**Ow that the Lord hath Readvanc't the Crown
Which thrift of Spoyl, and Frantick Zeal pull'd down:
Tenor, Now that the Lord the Miter hath reftor'd,
Which with the Crown lay in the duft abhor'd.
Trble. Praife him ye Kings, ⎱ *Chorus, All Sing.*
Tenor. Praife him ye Priefts, ⎰
Glory to Chrift our High Prieft, Higheft King,
Treble May Judah's Royall Scepter ftill fhine clear;
Tenor May Aaron's Holy Rod ftill Bloffoms bear.
Treble & Scepter and Rod rule ftill, and guide our Land;
Tenor And thefe whom God anoints, feel no rude hand;
May Love, Peace, Plenty, wait on Crown and Chair;
And may both fhare in Bleffings as in Care,
Chorus Angels look down, and Joy to fee,
Like that above, A Monarchie;
Angels look down, and Joy to fee,
Like that above, An Hierarchy.

Ezch. Hosier.

Illustration 9.2. *Anthems, to be sung* (Dublin, 1662): text of Hosier's 'Now that the Lord hath
readvanced the crown'. Trinity College Dublin.

(33)

Anth. LI.

O God that art the well-ſpring of all Peace.

Ver. *O God*, O God thaſ art the well-ſpring of all Peace,
2 Means. Make all thy gifts, make all thy gifts in CHARLES his
Raign increaſe.
England preſerve, *Scotland* proteƈt, make *Ireland* in thy ſervice
perfeƈt, Make *Ireland* in thy Service perfeƈt.

That all theſe Kingdoms under Great Brittains King, That
all theſe Kingdoms under Great Brittains King.
May ſtill be watered with the Goſpell Spring, May ſtill be
watered with the Goſpel Spring, May ſtill be watered with the
Goſpel Spring, May ſtill be watered with the Goſpel Spring,
with the Goſpel Spring.

Cho. That all theſe Kingdomes, that all theſe Kingdoms under
great Brittains King.
May ſtill be watered with the Goſpel ſpring, May ſtill be
watered with the Goſpel ſpring, May ſtill be watered with the
Goſpel ſpring.

Oh never let unhallowed breath have ſpace, to { Blight
{ Blaſt
Veri
2 Means. thoſe blooming buds of union, to blight thoſe blooming buds
of union; But let us all, but let us all with mutual love em-
brace, one Name, one King, and one Religion.

Ah let this Peace be thought the onely Gemme,
That can adorn King CHARLES his Diadem,
That can adorn King CHARLES his Diadem,
That can adorn King CHARLES his Diadem.

Cho. And let this Peace be thought the onely Gemme,
That can adorn King CHARLES his Diadem,
That can adorn King CHARLES his Diadem.
King CHARLES his Diadem. That can adorn King
CHARLES his Diadem. Halelujah, Halelujah, &c.

Ver. Halelujah, Halelujah,

Cho. A-.men.

John Holmes

I

Anth.

Illustration 9.3. *Anthems, to be sung* (Dublin, 1662): text of Holmes's 'O God that art the well-
spring of all peace'. Trinity College Dublin.

the Chapel Royal in 1641, returning to Dublin at the Restoration to take a place in the choirs of both cathedrals.[14] Barra Boydell also suggests that the Richard Hosier who was admitted a probationary minor canon at Bristol cathedral in April 1622 may be the 'Dublin Hosier.'[15] Whatever about the details of his early career, Hosier was appointed dean's vicar and master of the boys at both St Patrick's and Christ Church cathedrals at the Restoration.[16]

Now that the Lord hath readvanced the crown shows signs of being assembled in some haste and contains serious compositional weaknesses. Indeed, as Barra Boydell observes, this may be one of Hosier's first attempts at composition – possibly under considerable pressure to provide music for the text which had been penned by the dean of St Patrick's, William Fuller.[17] The text of the anthem as given in *Anthems, to be sung*, in Monck Mason's history of St Patrick's from 1819 and in the sole surviving musical text *GB-DRc*, MS B1 contain only minor variants, but curiously, the anthem word book and Monck Mason indicate treble and tenor soloists whereas *GB-DRc*, MS B1 allocates the solos to treble and bass.[18] The choice of a solo treble is noteworthy in an anthem written for such an important occasion and indicates a high level of competence in the boys so soon after the re-establishment of the choir.

Dean Fuller's text displays a great sense of celebration, and perhaps relief, at the restoration of the monarchy and episcopacy.

> Now that the Lord hath re-advanced the crown,
> Which thirst of spoil and frantic zeal threw down.
> Now that the Lord the mitre hath restored,
> Which with the crown lay in the dust abhorred.
> Praise him ye kings, praise him ye priests,
> Glory to Christ our high priest, highest king.
> May Judah's royal sceptre still shine clear,
> May Aaron's holy rod still blossoms bear;
> Sceptre and rod rule still and guide our land!
> And those whom God anoints feel no rude hand!
> May love, peace, plenty, wait on crown and chair,
> And may both share in blessings as in care.
> Angels, look down, and joy to see,
> Like that above, a monarchy.
> Angels, look down, and joy to see,
> Like that above, an hierarchy.

14 Spink, *Restoration*, p. 225; Boydell, *Music at Christ Church*, p. 69.   15 Barra Boydell, '"Now that the Lord hath readvanc'd the crown": Richard Hosier, Durham MS B.1 and early anthem repertoire at the Dublin cathedrals', *EM*, 28 (2000), 238–51 at 243.   16 Boydell, *Music at Christ Church*, pp 96, 133, 252; Boydell, *History of music*, p. 65 n. 11; Lawlor, *Fasti*, pp 216, 257.   17 Boydell, *History of music*, pp 93–5. 18 Boydell, *Music at Christ Church*, pp 195–9. See also Boydell, 'Now that the Lord', 238–51 and William Monck Mason, *The history and antiquities of the collegiate and cathedral church of St Patrick, near Dublin, from its foundation in 1190, to the year 1819* (Dublin, 1819).

This anthem is the penultimate one in the word book, supporting the view that it was a latter addition to a book compiled in pre-Commonwealth times. The final anthem, John Holmes's *O God, that art the well-spring of all peace*, may also have been used at the consecration service at St Patrick's in 1661.[19] Holmes probably wrote this anthem for the coronation of Charles I in 1625 but the text may have been revised for 1661. The words would certainly be a good bed fellow for Dean Fuller's text for Hosier's anthem:

> O God, that art the well spring of all peace,
> Make all Thy gifts in Charles his reign increase.
> England preserve, Scotland protect,
> Make all Ireland in Thy service perfect.
> That all these kingdoms under Great Britain's king
> May still be watered with the gospel spring.
> Oh never let unhallowed breath have space
> To blight those blooming buds of union
> But let us all with mutual love embrace
> One name, one king, and one religion.
> Ah, let this peace be thought the only gem
> That can adorn King Charles his diadem
> Hallelujah, Amen.

The position of *O God, that art the well spring* immediately after *Now that the Lord hath readvanced the crown* reinforces the proposition that the second part was a later addition to the word book. Another anthem from the second part of *Anthems, to be sung* has a royalist theme. *The king shall rejoice* (unattributed) is a setting of the words from Psalm 21, and this too may have been used at the celebration in St Patrick's in 1661. Of the other anthems in the second part of the book, Jewett's *I heard a voice in heaven* is the only one of his anthems to have survived in Dublin where chorus parts for alto, tenor and bass are preserved in eighteenth-century hands.[20]

Anthems, to be sung is a retrospective document, the first part outlining repertoire at the Dublin cathedrals in pre-Commonwealth times. The small representation of anthems with possible Dublin connections was composed by the English composers Jewett and Rogers who worked there for part of their lives. Most of the anthems in *Anthems, to be sung* lost their place in the repertoire in the decades immediately after the Restoration. This suggests a desire keep the repertoire up to date with the latest available compositions. The almost complete dependence on English sacred music for use in Dublin continued until the beginning of the eighteenth century.

---

19 Boydell, *History of music*, pp 67–9. **20** Two editions of *I heard a voice from heaven* have been published: ed. Maurice Bevan (Chichester, 1989); Gillen and Johnstone, *IMS* 6, pp 41–56.

Arrangements in Dublin during the post-Restoration period allowed singers and organists to hold posts in both cathedrals (and later at Trinity College and the Chapel Royal in Dublin Castle). The Chapel Royal in London was the only other ecclesiastical institution which permitted such plurality. The substantial remuneration available made the posts in Dublin very lucrative and many abandoned less well paid jobs in England to avail of the opportunities on offer in Dublin. A benefit of this increased traffic across the Irish Sea was the rapid introduction of newly composed works to Dublin. The changes in taste in the post-Restoration period were spearheaded by composers based at the Chapel Royal in London and these were quickly embraced in Dublin.

The earliest post-Restoration manuscript to have survived from Dublin is *GB-DRc*, MS B1 mentioned above. This organ book is the best indication of how repertoire was developing in the years immediately after the publication of *Anthems, to be sung*. The predominant representation of post-Restoration Chapel Royal musicians alongside local Dublin composers again shows a determined effort to keep the repertoire in Dublin up to date with developments in England. The inclusion of symphony anthems (with instrumental parts in some cases) indicates the use of strings at the Dublin cathedrals in the immediate post-Restoration period. This extravagance was normally restricted to the Chapel Royal in England and its use in Ireland indicates a healthy musical establishment. Indeed, the use of strings at Christ Church may be as a result of that cathedral fulfilling the function of a Chapel Royal in Dublin. The accounts of Christ Church cathedral include payments to string players in the period up to the death of Charles II in 1685 when the practice of using instruments also decreased at the Chapel Royal in London.[21] The proctor's accounts at St Patrick's from before the 1720s are very fragmentary, and no payments to string players can be located in them, but it may be that strings were used at St Patrick's also. By 1720 if not considerably earlier, the practice of using strings at Christ Church had, except on certain ceremonial occasions, fallen into abeyance.

Richard Hosier's music has not survived at the Dublin cathedrals, but *GB-DRc* MS B1 contains six of his anthems and Hosier has been identified as the main copyist of this book. Copying of the manuscript took place between 1660 and 1677 (the year of Hosier's death). There are only three anthems common to this manuscript and *Anthems, to be sung*, showing how quickly repertoire was developing and older works were being discarded. Hosier's *Now that the Lord* and Holmes' *O God, that art the well spring* are two of the common elements together with Orlando Gibbons' *Glorious and powerful God*.[22] It is significant that two of the three anthems in common come from the second part of the word book and therefore are later additions introduced to the repertoire after 1660 (Table 9.3).

---

21 Boydell, 'Now that the Lord', 242–4.   22 The fragment *I will magnify thee* in *GB-DRc*, MS B1 could be from anthem 33 (Peerson) or 46 (Giles) in *Anthems to be sung*.

Table 9.3. Contents of *GB-DRc* MS B1 (Hosier MS)

Composer	Anthems	Services
Anonymous	6	
John Blett (d. *c.*1666)	1	
John Blow (1649–1708)	1	
Henry Cooke (*c.*1615–72)	2	
William Child (1606–97)	2	
John Ferrabosco (1626–82)	3	
?Thomas Ford (d. 1648)	1	
Christopher Gibbons (1615–76)	2	
Orlando Gibbons (1583–1625)	1	
Richard Hinde (*fl. c.*1630)	1	
Walter Hitchcock (b. *c.*1655)	1	
John Holmes (d. 1629)	1	
Richard Hosier (d. 1677)	6	
Pelham Humfrey (1647–74)	6	
?Benjamin Isaack (1661–1709)	1	
George Jeffreys (*c.*1610–85)	1	
William Lawes (1602–45)	2	
Matthew Locke (1621 or 1622–77)	1	
John Loggins	1	
Richard Portman (d. before 29 Feb 1656)	1	
Benjamin Rogers (1614–98)	1	1
Thomas Tallis (1505–85)		1
Silas Taylor (1624–78)	1	
Thomas Tomkins (1576–1656)	2	
William Tucker (d. 1679)	3	
Thomas Wilkinson (*fl.* ?1575–?1612)	1	
Michael Wise (*c.*1648–87)	3	

The only anthems in this book which have possible compositional connections with Dublin are the six by Hosier, one by Blett[23] and one by Rogers. About seventy-five per cent of the repertoire is post-Restoration and Chapel Royal composers are particularly well represented: Pelham Humfrey (six), Michael Wise (three), Christopher Gibbons (two), John Blow (one), Mathew Locke (one) and the royalist captain Henry Cooke (two).[24] Pelham Humfrey's strong representation includes five symphony anthems and this preference for symphony anthems is reflected in the selection of anthems by other Chapel Royal composers. Both of Henry Cooke's anthems are scored with strings as are the sole representations by Blow and Locke. This Durham manuscript does not

23 John Blett (*d.* Dublin before 8 Jan. 1666) was appointed a stipendiary choirman at Christ Church in Sept. 1661 and became a vicar choral at St Patrick's in 1664. See Boydell, *History of music,* p. 89.
24 Pre-Commonwealth Chapel Royal composers are also represented: Orlando Gibbons (1), Thomas Tallis

provide the string parts for all of these anthems which suggests organ-only performances in some cases.

How did this book find its way to Durham? Brian Crosby observed that the contents show that this manuscript was not produced for use in Durham, as many of the pieces do not appear anywhere else at the cathedral. Nor do some items have concordances elsewhere. His attempts to trace the origins of the manuscript focussed on two matters: (a) the strong Chapel Royal connections; and (b) the presence of six anthems by Richard Hosier. Crosby put forward the case for Hosier as a strong candidate as copyist, an argument that Barra Boydell was able to substantiate by comparison with Hosier's handwriting in documents from Christ Church cathedral.[25] The case for the Dublin origin of the manuscript is now well established.

The presence of Hosier's *Now that the Lord hath readvanced the crown* dating from 1661 towards the beginning of *GB-DRc* MS B1 (the Hosier MS) intimates that this book began to be copied in the early years of the Restoration.[26] Hosier died in Dublin in 1677 and Ian Spink suggests that MS B1 might have found its way to Durham via John Blundeville who was a member of the choirs of the Dublin cathedrals between 1677 and 1680 before moving to York in 1681 and then to Durham in 1703.[27] Crosby notes a 'John Blundevile' leaving the Chapel Royal as a chorister on Christmas Day 1664, and it seems likely that this is the same Blundevile who came to Dublin and also turns up in the records at York and Durham.[28]

The next evidence which assists in establishing the development of repertoire at Dublin in the post-Restoration period is contained in the chapter acts of both cathedrals. The chapter acts of St Patrick's cathedral of 17 March 1698 record that Robert Hodge was paid for delivering and transcribing some anthems from England (see Table 9.4).[29] This was probably the Robert Hodge who was organist of Wells cathedral 1688–90, a lay clerk at Durham cathedral 1691–2, and who left Durham for 'Hibernia'.[30] He became the vicar choral of the prebendary of Swords at St Patrick's on 19 April 1693 and organist on 19 October 1694, retaining that post until 15 November 1698 when he was succeeded by Daniel Roseingrave.[31] Hodge retained his post as vicar choral after Roseingrave's appointment as organist and brought two choristers to St Patrick's from England on 7 February 1706.[32] A similar reference occurs in the Christ Church accounts for 2 November 1699: 'Five pounds to Mr Hodge for his service in bringing over several anthems out of England for the service of this church.'[33] It may be that this payment from Christ Church is for the same music provided for St Patrick's.[34]

(1) and Thomas Tomkins (2).   **25** Brian Crosby, 'An early restoration liturgical music manuscript', *ML*, 55 (1974), 458–64; Boydell, *Music at Christ Church*, pp 177–8.   **26** Spink, *Restoration*, pp 225–6; Boydell, *History of music*, p. 89.   **27** The names 'John Blunderfild' and 'Thomas Blunderfild' are written in the cover of *GB-DRc*, MS B1. See Brian Crosby, *A catalogue of Durham cathedral music manuscripts* (Oxford, 1986), p. 463; Lawlor, *Fasti*, pp 228, 244.   **28** For further discussion of *GB-DRc*, MS B1 see Boydell, *Music at Christ Church*, pp 88–96 and Boydell 'Now that the Lord'.   **29** *IRL-Drcb*, St Patrick's chapter acts 1678–1713 (MSS C2.1.3.5–6).   **30** Shaw, *Succession of organists*, p. 420.   **31** Lawlor, *Fasti*, pp 243, 250.   **32** Shaw, *Succession of organists*, p. 420.   **33** Boydell, *Music at Christ Church*, p. 105.   **34** Shaw, *Succession of*

Table 9.4. The repertoire brought to Dublin from England by Hodge.[35]

No.	Composer	Verse Anthems	Full Anthems	Services
1	Blow	God is our hope and strength (Thanksgiving day)		
2	[Tucker]	God is gone up on high		
3*	[Blow]	We will rejoice		
4	[Blow, Child or Purcell]	Sing unto God		
5*	[Aldrich, Blow or Purcell]	O give thanks unto the Lord		
6	[Blow]	Turn thee unto me, O Lord		
7	[W. Parsons, Tallis, Whythorne or Tucker]	Wherewith shall a young man cleanse his way		
8	Blow	I was glad when they said unto me		
9	[Hawkins]	In Jury is God known		
10	[Blow]		My God, my Lord, look upon me	
11*	[Blow]		The Lord hear thee in the day of trouble	
12*	[Purcell, Tucker or Turner]		O Lord God of host[s]	
13*	[Aldrich or Blow]		God is our hope and strength	
14				Aldrich, Blow and Child and Purcell

This appears to be new repertoire as it is not represented in either *Anthems, to be sung* or the Hosier MS. Only five of these pieces (marked with an asterisk) are contained in the earliest surviving manuscripts at St Patrick's which were complied in the late 1730s. This again demonstrates the continual revitalisation of the repertoire.[36] Blow's *I was glad when they said unto me* was written for the

organists, p. 420.   **35** Grindle, *Cathedral music*, pp 32–3. The names of possible composers suggested by Grindle are given here in square brackets.   **36** It is likely that these five works are descendants of Hodge's

opening of the choir of St Paul's cathedral on 2 December 1697, and its arrival in Ireland just a few months later shows how quickly music travelled between the two islands.[37] Service settings by Aldrich, Blow and Child appear in the earliest surviving part books at St Patrick's but none of Purcell's service music is present, even though it is known that his *Te Deum* in D was performed in St Patrick's at celebrations to mark St Cecilia's day in 1731.[38]

On 14 December 1699 it was resolved to pay Hodge's successor Daniel Roseingrave for transcribing the following pieces for use at St Patrick's: Aldrich's Service in G, Byrd's 'Full' service, Farrant's 'High' service and Wise's communion services in E and F.[39] The chapter acts of Christ Church cathedral of 15 December 1699 award 'Daniel Roseingrave three pounds as a gratuity for his writing three services and two creeds for the use of the church'.[40] As the descriptions of the music mentioned in both cathedrals is very similar, it is almost certain that it was the same music (the two 'creeds' referred to in the Christ Church acts being Wise's communion services contained in the earliest set of part books at St Patrick's). The accounts of Christ Church cathedral in 1698 record a payment of £6 7*s*. 6*d*. to 'Mr Rosingrave for writing the organ books and postage of anthems'.[41] The inclusion of an amount for postage indicates the transmission of music across the Irish Sea. Unfortunately, no details of these anthems are provided.

At first sight another chapter act from the same period is less promising:

Upon reading the certificate of Mr John Worrall, Mr Robert Hodge and Mr John Harris, vicars of the said cathedral church setting forth that they had examined … the books pricked by Mr Thomas Finell and we find that there are 83 anthems and 15 services fairly written and pricked.[42]

This minute does not yield any information about the identity of the repertoire in itself. The statement that there are eighty-three anthems indicates the extent of the repertoire which is about half the number of anthems present in the earliest surviving set of part books from St Patrick's. However, when the anthems from this set of part books written by later composers including Croft, Greene, Ralph Roseingrave and Boyce are excluded, the total of seventy-two anthems is close enough to the eighty-three mentioned in the chapter act. Therefore, the repertoire of these part books appears to be based on these eighty-three anthems together with subsequent, early eighteenth-century pieces. Similarly, when early eighteenth-century service settings are excluded, the number of services is close to that mentioned in the chapter acts (see Table 9.5).

copying.   **37** Shaw, *Succession of organists*, p. 420.   **38** Boydell, *Musical calendar*, p. 48 n. 3.
39 Shaw, *Succession of organists*, p. 421.   **40** Boydell, *Music at Christ Church*, p. 106.   **41** Ibid., p. 142.
42 *IRL-Drcb*, St Patrick's chapter acts, 1690–1719 (MS C2.1.3.7).

Table 9.5. Conjectured repertoire *c*.1700 at St Patrick's cathedral.

Composer	Anthems	Services
Aldrich (1648–1710)	8	2
Batten (1591–1637)	1	
Bishop (1665–1737)	1	
Blow (1649–1708)	16	2
Byrd (1543–1623)	1	
Child (1606–97)	1	3
Clarke (1674–1707)	3	
Creighton (1636 or 1637–1734)	1	
Farrant (?*c*.1529–80)	2	1
Gibbons (1583–1625)	1	1
Godfrey (?-?1689)	2	
Goldwin (*c*.1667–1719)	1	
Hall (1656–1707)	3	
Hooper (1553–1621)	1	
Humfrey (1647–74)	10	
Jewett (*c*.1603–75)	1	
Purcell (1659–95)	11	
Rogers (1614–98)	1	1
Tallis (1505–85)	2	1
Turner (1651–1740)	1	
Weldon (1676–1736)	2	
Wise (*c*.1648–87)	2	2
TOTALS	72	13

The most striking feature of this conjectured repertoire for 1700 is that there is virtually no overlap with the contents of *Anthems to be sung* or the Hosier MS. The only anthem from the word book which appears still to have been sung at the end of the century is Jewett's *I heard a voice from heaven*. The repertoire common with the Hosier MS consists entirely of five anthems by Pelham Humfrey, reflecting the continuing preference for Chapel Royal composers. It is hardly a coincidence that it is the newer compositions in the Hosier MS that had remained in the repertoire at St Patrick's. Certainly, more than eighty-five per cent of the music being performed by 1700 had been written within the previous forty years.

Another important manuscript which throws light on the repertoire in the late seventeenth and early eighteenth century is one which, like the Hosier MS, is no longer in Ireland: *GB-Ob*, Tenbury MS 1503. The copyist of this manuscript is John Phipps who became a vicar choral at St Patrick's in 1720.[43] The inclusion of

43 Lawlor, *Fasti*, pp 223, 245; Shaw, *Succession of organists*, pp 410, 419.

God is our hope and strength by Dublin-based Thomas Godfrey towards the end of Tenbury MS 1503 suggests that Phipps had the volume with him when he lived in Ireland.[44] Biographical details on Phipps are unclear but it may be that he had some connection with the Chapel Royal in London. Most of the anthems from Tenbury MS 1503 which have been positively identified are present in the conjectured repertoire at the Dublin cathedrals in 1700. The pre-Restoration anthems in Tenbury MS 1503 – Gibbons's *Behold, thou hast made my days* and *Sing unto the Lord* and Parsons's *Above the stars* – are not present in the eighteenth-century books at St Patrick's. This reflects a marked preference for a more up-to-date style of anthem at the time the part books were initially put together. It is significant that, although a source was available in Dublin in the form of Tenbury MS 1503, these anthems were not copied into the St Patrick's part books compiled in the 1730s.

The early eighteenth-century part books at the Dublin cathedrals contain an early symphony anthem by Henry Purcell which merits particular attention as it suggests probable transmission routes for music from London to Dublin in the late seventeenth century. *Praise the Lord, ye servants*, Z.N.68, is a setting of words from Psalm 113. Fragmentary sources for this anthem exist in two Chapel Royal bass part books: *GB-Lbl*, Add. Ms 50860 and *J-Tn*, N-5/10.[45] Both of these books are in the hand of William Tucker (d. 1679) but as John Blow is styled 'Mr Blow' in these books, the date of copying can be fixed reliably as before 10 December 1677, the date on which Blow's doctorate was conferred. Accordingly, *Praise the Lord, ye servants* is a very early example of Purcell's contribution to the symphony anthem repertoire. Indeed, the experimental and, at times, rather crude writing suggests that it may even be his first attempt at writing in this genre and could even date from his years as a chorister at the Chapel Royal.[46] The only other sources known to survive for this anthem are in fifteen part books in the Dublin cathedrals: six at St Patrick's[47] and nine at Christ Church.[48] This suggests that the anthem came to Ireland shortly after its composition and was copied into the early eighteenth-century manuscripts in Dublin from older sources. It seems that *Praise the Lord, ye servants* went out of circulation in England at an early stage. It may be that Purcell did not attach much importance to his youthful work.

The transmission route for *Praise the Lord, ye servants* coming to Dublin is likely to be the same as that for other Restoration Chapel Royal anthems found there. One likely purveyor of the anthem to Ireland is the above-mentioned Robert Hodge who had been a pupil of Purcell in the mid-1680s. As noted above, the payments for his copying activities recorded in the accounts of both

---

44 Godfrey was organist of St Patrick's from 1686 until 1688 or 1689 (Lawlor, *Fasti*, p. 249; Shaw, *Succession of organists*, p. 419). He was appointed organist of Christ Church in 1689 but seems to have died later in that year (Shaw, *Succession of organists*, p. 410; Boydell, *History of music*, pp 86, 96, 189).**45** For a full discussion of *Praise the Lord, ye servants* and its sources see Houston 'Music manuscripts', pp 84–101. See also Robert Shay & Robert Thompson, *Purcell manuscripts: the principal musical sources* (Cambridge, 2000), p. 144. **46** Purcell was a chorister at the Chapel Royal until his voice changed in 1673. **47** *IRL-Dpc*, MSS C.3.1–6. **48** *IRL-Drcb*, MSS C6.1.24.3.1–6, C6.1.24.4.3–4,

cathedrals certainly introduced new Chapel Royal repertoire, and this may have included *Praise the Lord, ye servants*. John Hawkins and others have claimed that the above-mentioned Daniel Roseingrave had been a chorister with Henry Purcell at the Chapel Royal in London but no documentary evidence to support this has survived. However, a copy of Roseingrave's anthem *Lord thou art become gracious* in Purcell's hand in *GB-Och*, MS Mus 1215 suggests that Roseingrave had close contact with Chapel Royal musicians before taking the posts of organist at Gloucester (1679–81), Winchester (1681–92) and Salisbury cathedrals (1692–8) and that he brought Chapel Royal repertoire with him when he came to Dublin in 1698.[49] Peter Holman suggests that when Roseingrave was organist of Winchester cathedral, he wrote to Purcell asking him to make a copy for him from a London source which is now lost. It is likely that Purcell would have travelled to Winchester when Charles II was considering establishing a court there and could have renewed his acquaintance with Roseingrave. These conjectures add weight to the possibility that music was exchanged between the two composers, and that Roseingrave may have brought Purcell's *Praise the Lord, ye servants* with him to Ireland. This hypothesis cannot be confirmed because, as mentioned above, no early music manuscripts have survived at Salisbury cathedral and the situation is similar at Winchester.[50]

A Peter Isaack was a chorister at the Chapel Royal in the late 1660s and it is likely that he is the Peter Isaack who was appointed a vicar choral at St Patrick's in 1672.[51] Isaack was organist of Salisbury cathedral from 1687 to 1692 when he returned to Dublin to become organist of both St Patrick's and Christ Church as well as a vicar choral at St Patrick's.[52] If this is the Chapel Royal Peter Isaack, he is another candidate for the transmission of *Praise the Lord, ye servants* and other Chapel Royal material to Dublin, as is Bartholomew Isaack (probably a younger brother of Peter). Bartholomew was a chorister in the Chapel Royal in the early 1670s and would have been in daily contact with Purcell at the probable time of the composition of *Praise the Lord, ye servants*. This is likely to be the same Bartholomew Isaack who was appointed a vicar choral at St Patrick's on 8 April 1685 (and removed for neglect of duty on 3 February 1687).[53]

Members of the Finell [Finall or Fynall] family are also possible routes of transmission for *Praise the Lord, ye servants* to Dublin. The Thomas Finell who held posts at both cathedrals from 1677 until his death in 1707 may be the same Thomas Finell who was a lay vicar at Westminster Abbey at the Restoration.[54] It is not clear if this is the 'Mr Thomas Finall' who is mentioned in royal payments on 22 October 1667: 'to wait in the room of Robert Strong, musician in ordinary to his Majesty for the violin.'[55] This is followed by frequent payments to 'Finall', 'Fynell' and 'Finell' as a violinist with sums paid almost every year until 1676,

C6.1.24.4.3–7. **49** Shaw, *Succession of organists*, pp 121–2, 264, 299. **50** There are numerous references to Roseingrave as copyist in both cathedrals' accounts until his death in 1727. **51** Lawlor, *Fasti*, pp 215, 222. **52** Ibid., pp 237, 245, 250; Shaw, *Succession of organists*, pp 264, 411, 419–20. **53** Lawlor, *Fasti*, p. 239. **54** Shaw, *Succession of organists*, p. 411 **55** *RECM*, i, p. 67.

the year before Thomas Finell took a position in St Patrick's cathedral. A John Finell was appointed half vicar choral of St Patrick's cathedral in 1711, and died in office two years later.[56] A Peter Finell held several posts at both Dublin cathedrals between 1700 until his death in 1728.[57] It is likely that Thomas and Peter (and possibly John) were brothers. Connections between the Finells and the Chapel Royal are suggested by 'A pastoral elegy on the much lamented death of the reverend and celebrated Mr Peter Finall' published in Dublin in March 1728.[58] This elegy opens 'Weep every eye, and every tongue deplore, our Purcell's dead, and Finall is no more.'

In addition to the Isaacks, Hodge, Daniel Roseingrave and the Finnels, John Phipps must be mentioned as a possible courier of Purcell's anthem. He was the copyist of *GB-Ob*, Tenbury MS 1503 noted above as the unique source for Purcell's *O Lord, grant the king a long life*.[59] Phipps was appointed a vicar choral at St Patrick's in 1720, and remained in the cathedral choir until his death in 1758 or 1759.[60] He may have been related to the Benjamin Phipps who was prebendary of Kilmactalway at St Patrick's from 1666 until his death in 1682, and simultaneously dean of Ferns from 1670 and chancellor of Christ Church cathedral from 1673.[61]

In conclusion, with the exception of the Hosier MS, the earliest surviving part books and organ books from the Dublin cathedrals date from the early years of the eighteenth century. It is however possible to deduce repertoire in earlier periods from *Anthems, to be sung* (1662); the Hosier MS; *GB-Ob*, Tenbury MS 1503; and from references in administrative records. Although the results of this research are necessarily somewhat speculative, some important patterns emerge which continued into the later eighteenth century when more documentary evidence survives.

First, the repertoire at the Dublin cathedrals was almost entirely dependent on English music which was imported by the many musicians who came to Dublin to take up lucrative posts at the cathedrals. Secondly, there was a strong preference for composers who had connections with the Chapel Royal in London, more than fifty per cent of the repertoire in the period from 1660 to 1730 reflecting such connections. At some periods it seems likely that as much as two thirds of the repertoire in Dublin was derived from Chapel Royal composers. Thirdly, there is very little music that was composed in Dublin: that which was, was mainly penned by English composers living there rather than by Irish composers.

Despite its geographical separation from England, the repertoire at the Dublin cathedrals proves to have been very up to date with its English counterparts, and the Dublin sources turn out to be important links in the transmission of material.

56 Lawlor, *Fasti,* p. 240.   **57** Ibid., pp 204, 218, 228; Boydell, *History of music*, p. 87 n. 109.   **58** Printed by George Faulkner and James Hoey (Dublin).   **59** Shay & Thompson, *Purcell manuscripts*, pp 157–8.
60 Lawlor, *Fasti,* pp 223, 245. Phipps was also attached to Christ Church cathedral: see Boydell, *History of music*, passim.   **61** Lawlor, *Fasti,* p. 121.

Much has survived there which perished at such high-ranking English cathedrals as Salisbury and Winchester. The repertoire was undergoing constant renewal in Dublin and displays a strong preference for 'modern' compositions. Many of the pieces which were introduced in the immediate post-Restoration period were quickly replaced by the latest compositions and pre-Commonwealth material soon fell out of use. Indeed, this pattern of renewal would continue to be a feature throughout the eighteenth century.[62]

---

62 See Houston 'Music manuscripts'.

Seventeenth-century Irish parish church music

DENISE NEARY

The study of church music in the seventeenth century has principally focused on the music of the cathedrals. However, parish churches have also undeniably contributed to the heritage of Irish sacred music. It is this contribution which is examined here within the context of the seventeenth century. The subjugation of the Catholic church and the acts of the Protestant ascendancy during this time and subsequently means that the extant historical evidence refers predominantly to the established church. Indeed, by the end of the century all the old churches, monasteries, cathedrals and church temporalities of Ireland that had escaped destruction were the property of the established church. Thus the study of parish church music of this period is, necessarily, overwhelmingly dominated by the music and tradition of the Church of Ireland. The records of Dublin city parishes survive largely complete and provide the principal sources for studying the music of worship. The relative absence of records relating to specific details about music in churches outside of Dublin inevitably results in the picture being skewed towards the capital. However, writers such as Edward Wetenhall,[1] who had experience both in parish churches and cathedrals throughout the country, provide valuable information about the musical practices of the day and offer some balance to this capital-based view. In addition, other seventeenth-century commentators on church music shed light on contemporary attitudes to the role of music in worship. Bringing together all these sources allows us to build up a fuller and richer picture of music in Irish parish churches in the seventeenth century.

Two traditions of Irish church music have developed since the sixteenth century but, as Harry White points out,

> the impoverished condition of Roman Catholics in Ireland between 1500 and 1800 excluded the possibility of a high culture of sacred music. The consequences of this exclusion for the development of church music after emancipation were ruinous: a vast population without any cultural base consonant with the prevailing aesthetic of church music as high art.[2]

Thus a study of Irish church music requires a distinction to be made 'between Roman Catholic and Protestant, between native and ascendancy, between the Pale and the provinces.'[3]

1 Edward Wetenhall (1636–1713) was master of the Dublin Blue Coat School and curate of St Werburgh's church, Dublin (1672–9), bishop of Cork and Ross (1679–99) and bishop of Kilmore and Ardagh (1699–1713). He was also prebendary of Castleknock (1675–9) and precentor of Christ Church cathedral, Dublin (1675–9). **2** Harry White, 'Church music and musicology in Ireland: an afterword', *IMS* 2, p. 333. **3** Ibid.

The Irish church was an extension of the English church on which it was originally modelled. On 13 June 1541 Henry VIII was declared 'king of Ireland' and on the following Sunday he was publicly proclaimed as such at St Patrick's cathedral, Dublin. When the Irish parliament of 1536 made Henry 'the only supreme head on earth of the whole Church of Ireland' it justified its action by the statement that 'this land of Ireland is depending and belonging justly and rightfully to the imperial crown of England.'[4] However, despite attempts to make Ireland Protestant by legislation, the reformed religion was associated with an alien government and the reformation was slow to take effect in Ireland. At first it was noticeable only in the towns and in the pale. However, in the early seventeenth century there was a protestant majority in the Irish parliament despite the fact that the native Irish population as well as the Anglo-Norman 'Old English' aristocracy remained loyal to Roman Catholicism. Nevertheless, by the late 1630s Dublin was indeed a protestant town, not just in terms of property and civic control, but in actual household numbers, and Protestants remained in the majority for more than a hundred years.[5]

The reformation brought about dramatic changes in the use of music in worship. Liturgical music was becoming increasingly elaborate in pre-reformation times. This was especially the case in the great choral foundations for which the most ambitious music was written. Reformers in the sixteenth century wanted, to varying degrees, to make liturgical music more accessible to congregations. A significant change introduced by these reformers was an increase in congregational participation in the services. This led to the metrical singing of psalms that became popular in parish churches. A direct result of this was the emergence of two separate styles of church music after the reformation – the 'parish church tradition' and the 'cathedral tradition'. In England this division remained until the late eighteenth and early nineteenth centuries when the Victorians, who wanted parish churches to be like cathedrals, changed the architecture and furnishings accordingly, put the choir into surplices, and made them sing 'cathedral service', sometimes even in small villages.[6] However, in the seventeenth century the difference was extreme. Cathedral choirs chanted most of the liturgy (including the psalms) and sang the canticles and anthems in polyphonic settings with organ accompaniment. In contrast, the liturgy was spoken throughout in the parish churches and the only music heard was the unaccompanied metrical singing of psalms by the congregation. Nicholas Temperley writes that in the established church in England the normal occasions for singing metrical psalms in parish churches were before morning prayer, before ante-communion, before the sermon and before and after evening prayer.[7] Metrical psalms were sung with organ accompaniment in some cathedrals but

4 G.A. Hayes-McCoy, 'The Tudor conquest: 1534–1603' in T.W. Moody & F.X. Martin (eds), *The course of Irish history* (rev. ed. Dublin, 1994), p. 180. 5 David Dickson, 'Capital and country: 1600–1800' in Art Cosgrove (ed.), *Dublin through the ages* (Dublin, 1988), p. 63. 6 Nicholas Temperley, 'The old way of singing', *MT*, 120 (1979), 943–7 at 943. 7 Nicholas Temperley et al., 'Metrical psalms', *Grove Music Online* ed. L. Macy www.grovemusic.com, accessed 15 Feb. 2008.

this was a parochial function of the cathedral. The majority of the population attended Sunday morning prayer in their parish churches and then went to the cathedral to hear a sermon preached in the nave, preceded and followed by a metrical psalm with organ accompaniment if the organist was still at his post. In many cathedrals the organist was given an additional payment to provide this service.[8]

A major disruption to cathedral services occurred in the 1640s: when the Long Parliament met in England in November 1640 it used its unprecedented power to carry out drastic religious reforms. The Puritan parliamentary forces gained control and in January 1643 a bill was passed 'for the utter abolishing and taking away all archbishops, bishops ... deans and chapters ... and all vicars choral and choristers ... out of the Church of England'.[9] The form of the public services was laid down in the *Directory for the publique worship of God.*[10] For the first and only time in English history it gave metrical psalms a full place in legally-established worship in its statement that 'It is the duty of Christians to praise God publicly by singing of psalms together in the congregation, and also privately in the family.'[11] Cathedral services began to be suppressed from as early as 1642[12] and by 1647 they had been completely abolished.[13] In May 1644 two ordinances had been issued by Parliament

for the speedy demolishing of all organs, images and all matters of superstitious monuments in all cathedrals, and collegiate or parish-churches and chapels, throughout the Kingdom of England and the Dominion of Wales; the better to remove all offences and things illegal in the worship of God.[14]

Although only the 'Kingdom of England and the Dominion of Wales' were specified it is clear that the order also applied to Ireland. Civil war had broken out in Ireland in 1641 and was thought to mark the end of organ playing at Christ Church cathedral, Dublin. However, Barra Boydell has shown that musical activity continued at both Dublin cathedrals until 1647.[15]

Although cathedral music was completely abolished during the common-wealth the musical part of parish services was unaffected. The singing of metrical psalms had been a puritan innovation in the first place and there was nothing for the new authorities to object to in the existing practice. Although it may have existed earlier, the practice of 'lining out' may have been introduced at this time as it was stipulated for the first time in the *Directory for the publique worship of God*:

---

8 For example, in Ely Cathedral the organist was paid an additional stipend from at least the end of the seventeenth century until well into the nineteenth century for 'playing to the psalm before sermon'. *GB-EL*, EDC 3/1/4–8 (Audit books, 1677–1839). **9** Spink, *Restoration*, p. 3. **10** Anon., *A directory for the publique worship of God, throughout the three kingdoms of England, Scotland, and Ireland together with an ordinance of parliament for the taking away of the book of common-prayer* (London, 1644). **11** Ibid., p. 83. **12** Boydell, *History of music*, p. 61. **13** Peter le Huray, *Music and the Reformation in England 1549–1660* (2nd ed., Cambridge, 1978), pp 53–4. **14** Quoted in Kenneth R. Long, *The music of the English church* (London, 1972), p. 206. **15** Boydell, *History of music*, pp 61–2, 189.

That the whole congregation may join herein, every one that can read is to have a psalm book, and all others not disabled by age, or otherwise, are to be exhorted to learn to read. But for the present, where many in the congregation cannot read, it is convenient that the minister, or some other fit person appointed by him and the other ruling officers, do read the psalm, line by line, before the singing thereof.[16]

The practice continued after the Restoration and as parochial congregations were left without musical direction the tempo of the psalms became slower and slower and they lost their distinctive rhythms. The parish clerks and more adventurous members of the congregation began to fill in the period between one note and the next with various kinds of embellishment. Later descriptions of this kind of ornamentation call it the 'old way of singing' and it is generally associated with lining out.[17] The practice was frequently described disparagingly as, for example, by Elias Hall who wrote that in most Lancashire churches and chapels 'what was then called singing was less harmonical than reading'. He described it in verse beginning 'Then out the people yawl an hundred parts, / Some roar, some whine, some creak like wheels of carts' and ending 'Like untamed horses, tearing with their throats / One wretched stave into an hundred notes.'[18] However, others realized that this 'common way' filled an important role in the worship of the people and resisted the efforts of well-meaning reformers to get rid of it.[19]

Specific information about music in parish churches in Ireland at the end of the seventeenth century is gleaned from the writings of several churchmen. Edward Wetenhall wrote extensively on church music in his publication *Of gifts and offices in the publick worship of God* (1678), written while he was precentor of Christ Church cathedral in Dublin. He devoted a 369-page section of his three-part treatise to singing but only focused on parochial practice in the final few pages.[20] However, it does give us an enlightened picture of the practice in parish churches at the time. He recommended improving services by removing the power to choose or set the psalms to be sung from the parish clerk and rather give it to the minister.[21] It is clear that Sternhold and Hopkins's 'Old Version' was still in use in Irish parish churches as Wetenhall expressed a wish for a new version of the psalms to be brought into use. He wrote:

I confess we shall still, while J[ohn] H[opkins] and T[homas] S[ternhold] and the rest of that vein must hold the possession of that authority which no one can justify, be at a great loss, comparatively to what we should be, might a new translation of singing psalms be substituted for this faulty one of theirs.[22]

16 *Directory*, p. 84.   17 Temperley, 'Metrical psalms', accessed 15 Feb. 2008.   18 Sally Drage, 'Elias Hall, "the faithful chronicler" of Oldham psalmody', *EM*, 28 (2000), 621–36 at 623.   19 John Patrick, *A century of select psalms* (London, 1679); quoted in Temperley, 'Old way of singing', 943. 20 Wetenhall, *Of gifts and offices*. The three-part treatise dealt with prayer, singing, and preaching. 21 Ibid., p. 563.   22 Ibid., p. 564.

Wetenhall acknowledged that the introduction of prose psalms, while the ideal, could not be achieved by a radical change but recommended that ministers of the parishes should choose what was 'fittest for their peoples devotion'. He also suggested that the ministers could occasionally alter some of the words to 'polish the style, and advance the sense, and by this means, some small amendment of the singing-Psalms may be effected.'[23]

Wetenhall expressed a desire to 'tune the people's voices into some decorum, or tolerable harmony, that the praises of God may be sung so, as not to make a great number loath the performance'. To achieve this, Wetenhall recommended the use of an organ but appreciated that very few parish churches at the time had organs. In the absence of an organ he proposed that

such a person begin the tuning of the psalm, as has himself a tuneable and harmonious voice, which may a little set the people in: then let some others who will keep tune tolerably be placed at meet distances, whole voices may be a kind of guide and government to the rest. And if there are any (as in most congregations there are some) who squeak, or bawl, or otherwise by indecent voices, disturb the rest, let those people be privately admonished by the ministers, not so much quite to desist from singing (for their hearts may be good) as to sing softly, and little above a whispering tone, to be heard chiefly by God and themselves.[24]

He also encouraged mothers to teach the psalms to their children at home so they would grow up with 'the praises of God and Christ in their mouths'.[25] His ideal was that the congregation would sweetly join with hearts and voices in singing the divine praises in the solemn and dedicated places of worship.[26] He believed that the direction and management of the singing in worship should not be entrusted to a parish clerk, who was 'an ignorant laick', especially 'when all circumstances being considered, 'tis ten to one but he chooses unluckily.'[27]

Wetenhall lamented the 'old way' of singing using ornamentation in performance of the psalms, writing that 'Such fancies may do prettily elsewhere: quaint divisions, sporting shakes and trills have a meeter place. It has ever been accounted of most dangerous nature to sport in holy things.'[28] Wetenhall recommended that all sacred performances should express gravity, seriousness, and devotion: 'the contrary interrupts, disturbs, and, in a sort, profanes both our own and others devotion; besides, that it brings inevitable scandal on our selves, and on the very service we are employed in.'[29]

Further discussion on the place of music in worship in Ireland took place in the 1690s. In 1694 William King, bishop of Derry, described the situation in the Church of Ireland when he wrote that 'Our church praises God every day with five or six psalms, besides other hymns, of His own appointment, and in His own

---

23 Ibid., pp 566–7. 24 Ibid., pp 567–8. 25 Ibid., pp 568–9. 26 Ibid., pp 570–1. 27 Ibid., p. 571. 28 Ibid., p. 574. 29 Ibid., pp 574–5.

words and method'.[30] King's treatise sparked off a heated dispute concerning the place of music in worship and led to a series of publications by King and by Joseph Boyse, a Presbyterian minister in Dublin, and Robert Craghead, a Presbyterian minister in Derry.

King's original publication set out to 'examine and compare the worship of God, which is directed and warranted by scripture, as well with that which is prescribed and practised by our church, as with that which is practised by such as differ from us.'[31] He wrote that the scriptures require the use of the psalms to praise God and stressed that where people could sing,

> They are obliged to do it, in obedience to God's command. But where through any defect of nature or art, they cannot sing decently, they may be dispensed with saying. Only people ought not by this indulgence to be encouraged to neglect singing altogether, or to think that God doth not require it of them. When by a little pains or industry they may attain to the art of decently performing it in his service.[32]

King informed his readers that the psalms should be sung in prose because 'we have no certain scriptural warrant for the use of verse or metre in the praises of God.'[33] He wrote that the psalms should be offered by way of responses or answering because 'this way of praising God by answering one another, is the most ancient we find in scripture.'[34] William King represented the view of the established church in his desire for the singing of psalms in prose using responses. However, the singing of metrical psalms was by now firmly established in parish churches and congregations would no doubt have a number of tunes that they could sing without assistance. The 'old version' was still there at the back of the bible or prayer book. The illiterate knew some of the psalms by heart, and could sing the rest with the help of 'lining out'. That this was still the practice in Ireland at the end of the seventeenth century is attested to by William King who wrote that it was

> a great interruption to the music, and to the understanding of the psalm, by breaking the sense of it, and in that respect very inconvenient, and is likewise a late invention of our own, never used by any foreign church, either Popish or Reformed, for ought I can find, to this day; and has been taken up to supply the negligence and laziness of people, who will not now, as formerly be at pains to get psalms by heart, or so much as procure books, or learn to read them.[35]

---

30 William King, *A discourse concerning the inventions of men in the worship of God* (Dublin, 1694), p. 24. King (1650–1729) was born in Antrim in 1650, studied at TCD and took orders in 1674. He became provost of the cathedral church of Tuam (1676), chancellor of St Patrick's cathedral, Dublin and rector of St Werburgh's church (1679), dean of St Patrick's (1689), bishop of Derry (1691) and archbishop of Dublin (1703). **31** Ibid., p. 5. **32** Ibid., pp 7–8. **33** Ibid., p. 8. **34** Ibid., p. 12. **35** Ibid., p. 22.

This view was disputed by Joseph Boyse whose response in 1694 to King's essay stated that

> Since the New Testament requires our praising God publicly by singing psalms, hymns and spiritual songs, it does fully warrant us to adapt the psalms of David to that use by turning them into metre.[36]

He added that the whole congregation was required to join in the praises of God by singing psalms but this was only possible if the psalms were in metre because the majority of people were unable to sing them in prose. Furthermore he stated that 'The psalms translated into metre (provided the true sense of the inspired writer be delivered) are as truly the 'word of God', as the psalms translated into prose.'[37] He believed that it was 'highly probable that the Psalms of David were composed in metre, quite contrary to what the bishop [William King] so frequently suggests.'[38]

Robert Craghead also refuted King's statements on the singing of psalms. He wrote that

> God recommendeth to us the singing the Psalms of David, which at God's direction were in metre, and therefore should be translated into metre; that they should be fit for singing in our language, as they were sung by the people of God in the Hebrew, that being their language.[39]

With regard to the use of musical instruments in church there was yet again a strong difference of opinion between William King on the one hand and Joseph Boyse and Robert Craghead on the other. King wrote that

> The holy scriptures recommend to us the use of instruments in the praises of God; the psalmist frequently uses and recommends them, and the whole book of psalms is concluded with this advice, psalm 150:3, 'Praise him with timbrel, praise him with stringed instruments and organs.'[40]

He added that 'Our church permitteth the use of some grave musical instruments to regulate the voices of those that sing, and to stir up their affections, which are the natural effects of music.'[41] He believed that the dissenters' refusal to accept the use of instruments was against nature, a dangerous superstition and an encroachment on Christian liberty.[42]

It is not surprising that the Presbyterian ministers responded to these remarks and Joseph Boyse looked to the roots of the Christian services in the Jewish

---

36 Joseph Boyse, *Remarks on a late discourse of William lord bishop of Derry; concerning the inventions of men in the worship of God* (Dublin, 1694), p. 15.   37 Ibid.   38 Ibid.   39 Robert Craghead, *Answer to a late book, intituled, 'A discourse concerning the inventions of men in the worship of God', by William lord bishop of Derry* (Edinburgh, 1694), p. 7.   40 King, *Discourse*, p. 13.   41 Ibid., p. 16.   42 Ibid., p. 23.

church to support his views on the use of instrumental music in church. Robert Craghead questioned why, if the scripture passage from Psalm 150 quoted by King was to be the authority for organs, there should not be 'high sounding cymbals, trumpets, and dances, in worship as well as organs'.[43] He added that 'We have neither direction nor practice of them, in the whole New Testament, the use of instruments in the worship of God of old was a part of the ceremonial law, and therefore expired with it.'[44]

Joseph Boyse acknowledged that organs could be used in parish churches to direct the congregation in the singing of the psalms:

I confess if any use of organs be allowable, 'tis that in the parish church of directing the people into the tune of the psalms they sing ... But as this very use of them is certainly destitute of any scriptural precept or pattern obligatory to us Christians; so however others may entertain a more charitable opinion of them, yet the bishop [William King], if he will be consistent with himself, must condemn them as a human invention.[45]

However, despite the attempts of many clergymen to allow the use of organs in worship, metrical psalm singing continued to be almost entirely unaccompanied until late in the seventeenth century. Nicholas Temperley points out that very few parish churches in England had organs before or after the Commonwealth and even in London only about thirty per cent of the churches had organs by 1700.[46] The situation was very similar in Ireland. St Audoen's church in Dublin seems to be the first parish church in Ireland to have had an organ and musical establishment. However, this was not typical of parish churches but was directly due to the guild of St Anne, whose guild chapel was located in St Audoen's parish church.[47] Links between the guild and the parish were close. The guild had appointed chantry priests (also referred to as chaplains) until 1564; in the 1540s they were required to sing at all divine services, and there were also two clerks who sang and read daily in the choir, one of whom played the organ at all services, principal feasts and holy days.[48] Up until the end of the sixteenth century the sympathies of the guild lay with the recusants,[49] but by 1606 the guild had replaced the six chantry priests and two clerks at St Audoen's and was now employing six singing men and two choirboys. The singers were drawn from the choirs of both Christ Church and St Patrick's cathedrals and were paid four pounds each per annum with an additional £1 6*s*. 8*d*. being paid to the choirman who had responsibility for the boys. The two choristers received £2 13*s*. 4*d*. each per year. In addition, the organist of Christ Church was paid ten pounds for playing at St Audoen's.[50]

---

43 Craghead, *Answer*, p. 17. **44** Ibid. **45** Boyse, *Remarks*, pp 29–30. **46** Temperley, 'Old way of singing', 943. **47** Boydell, *History of music*, p. 49. **48** Ibid., pp 49–50. **49** As late as *c.*1597 high mass was celebrated at St Audoen's with musical accompaniment. E. Hogan, ed., *Ibernia Ignatiana* (Dublin 1880), p. 41 quoted in Boydell, *History of music*, p. 50. **50** *IRL-Da*, MS 12.D.1, fos. 25v, 29r, 32r. See also Boydell, *History of music*, pp 49–52.

By 1645 St Anne's guild had been severely affected by the troubles of the civil war. The account book records that George Tadpole was appointed singer with a salary of three pounds sterling per annum. This represented a reduction in stipend of one pound per year 'in regard of the poverty of the said guild and the distractions of these times'. In addition, Tadpole had to wait for payment until 'five months after a firm and settled peace' was established 'within this kingdom of Ireland'. However, Tadpole was given 'lodging rooms ... in St Audoen's church during the pleasure of the said guild'.[51] The guild of St Anne continued to appoint musicians during the troubles, on 26 July 1645 appointing four priests and John Hawkshaw as organist. Hawkshaw was given an annual salary of three pounds with the condition that 'when the organs of St Ann's chapel shall be repaired and set up in the church of St Audoen's as formerly it hath been, then the said John Hawkshaw shall receive from the said guild the ancient stipend of seven pounds ten shilling per annum and no more.'[52] There is no record of where the organ was moved to during the interregnum or of the reason for appointing an organist when there was no organ to play on, but a possible explanation occurs in the 1660s.

On 26 July 1648 John Hawkshaw resigned his place as organist at St Audoen's church and was admitted into a priest's place then vacant due to the death of John Haddock. Randall Jewett, who had previously been organist at St Audoen's from 1638 to 1645, was reappointed under the same terms as Hawkshaw's appointment three years previously.[53] Payments continued to be made to the choir members of St Anne's guild and St Audoen's until at least May 1652 when John Tadpole was paid the salary arrears due to him 'and his two boys'.[54]

The year 1660 marked the restoration not only of Charles II but also of the established church and its liturgy. While the Restoration saw the building of new organs in the cathedrals, it took a few more years before any of the parishes were able to install organs in their churches. St Werburgh's church in the city of Dublin appears to have been the first parish church to install an organ after the Restoration. S.C. Hughes stated in 1889 that the organ was bought in 1676 at a cost of about fifty pounds from John Hawkshaw, organist and vicar choral of Christ Church cathedral, and was apparently an old instrument. A witness to the contract was Edward Wetenhall, who was then junior curate.[55] Following the restoration of Anglican liturgical worship a small organ belonging to John Hawkshaw had been installed at Christ Church cathedral in 1661.[56] This was a temporary measure; in 1664 George Harris began work on building a new organ at Christ Church, which was finished, perhaps by Lancelot Pease, by Michaelmas

---

51 *IRL-Da*, MS 12.D.1, fo. 70r.   52 Ibid., fos. 70v–71r, fo. 74r. Possibly an organist at Christ Church cathedral, Dublin *c*.1646–7, Hawkshaw was appointed organist at both Christ Church and St Patrick's cathedrals after the Restoration in 1660.   53 Ibid., fo. 74r. Jewett also served as organist at Christ Church cathedral from 1630 to 1638, at St Patrick's from 1631 to 1643, and possibly at Christ Church from 1646 to 1647.   54 Ibid., fo. 92r.   55 S.C. Hughes, *The church of St Werburgh, Dublin* (Dublin, 1889), p. 17. Hughes does not name the source of his information and this statement remains unverified.   56 Boydell, *History of music*, p. 85.

1666. Pease added a chair organ to provide a full 'double' organ for the cathedral in 1667.[57] It is likely that the organ purchased from Hawkshaw for St Werburgh's church was the instrument that had been set up in Christ Church in 1661. In turn, it is possible that this was the organ that had formerly been in use at St Audoen's church before the civil war. Barra Boydell notes that it was small enough to be carried from church to church and therefore it seems likely that Hawkshaw may have kept it in his possession during the troubles.[58] Perhaps the reason that Hawkshaw was paid three pounds per annum by the guild of St Anne during the interregnum may have been to store and maintain the organ. It is not known why Hawkshaw did not return the organ to St Audoen's church after the Restoration, instead bringing it to Christ Church cathedral when he was appointed organist there in 1660. In the absence of records to verify Hughes's statement that the organ was bought by St Werburgh's in 1676, it is possible that the date is misprinted in his book and should have been 1666 or 1667. This organ remained in use at St Werburgh's throughout the rest of the seventeenth century until a new organ was built for the church in 1719 by Thomas Hollister, who became organist there in the same year.[59]

Other parish churches followed St Werburgh's example with St Catherine's church procuring an organ in 1678, St John's in 1684, St Peter's in 1686, and St Bride's sometime before 1686. The organ that was bought for St Catherine's church in 1678 was probably an old instrument judging by its cost and the amount of work that had to be carried out in the following years: thirty pounds was paid for the instrument and £5 6s. to Lancelot Pease for setting it up.[60] Six years later, in January 1684, the vestry agreed to purchase a new organ.[61] However, their agreement was not acted upon until twelve years later when, on 8 November 1696, the vestry decided to procure a new organ for the church at a cost of £200 to be collected from the parishioners. Renatus Harris was employed to build the organ and the work was completed by June 1697.[62]

There is no evidence to suggest that Renatus Harris ever visited Ireland in person. Organs attributed to him were probably constructed in England, then shipped to Ireland and assembled by local builders.[63] Harris's 1697 organ for Christ Church cathedral was probably installed by John Baptist Cuvillie who had come to Ireland as his assistant and who became the leading organ builder in Ireland in the early eighteenth century.[64] Cuvillie, as well as being in business on his own account, may have served as an Irish agent for the Harris firm, erecting, 'finishing' and maintaining their instruments in Ireland.[65] It seems unlikely from the vestry minutes of St Catherine's church that Renatus Harris installed the organ himself: the decision on 13 June 1697 to pay the sum of two hundred pounds to Mr Renatus Harris 'or his order' suggests that he may not have been in

57 Ibid. Pease came from England and settled in Dublin *c*.1663, becoming a stipendiary in the choir of Christ Church cathedral in 1667. **58** Ibid. **59** *IRL-Drcb*, MS P.326/5/1, p. 8. **60** *IRL-Drcb*, MS P.117/5/1, p. 189. **61** Ibid., p. 259. **62** *IRL-Drcb*, MS P.117/5/2, pp 52, 66. **63** Grindle, *Cathedral music*, p. 133. **64** Denise Neary, 'Cuvillie', *NG II*, vi, p.793. **65** Michael Callender et al., 'The organ of St Mary's, Dublin', *The Organ*, 58 (1980), 133–40 at 134.

Dublin to collect the payment in person. It is most likely that the organ was installed by Cuvillie. Unfortunately, details of the registration and size of the organ have not survived, but comparison with the cost of other organs built in Ireland around this time suggests that it was an instrument of reasonable size. At one end of the scale Lancelot Pease's organ for St Audoen's church built in 1681 cost £110.[66] John Baptiste Cuvillie built an organ at St Peter's church in 1713 at a cost of £150.[67] Cuvillie also built an organ for Cloyne cathedral in 1713 for the sum of £220.[68] Renatus Harris's two-manual organ for St Patrick's cathedral, Dublin, completed in 1697 cost £505, including the chair organ.[69] At the top end of the scale, a total of £800 was agreed in 1697 with Harris for the new organ in Christ Church cathedral, Dublin.[70] The organ at St Catherine's church remained in use for seventy-two years: a new organ was built in 1769 following the rebuilding of the church during the years 1760 to 1769.[71]

There was an organ in St John's church in Dublin by the end of the seventeenth century. The church was knocked down and rebuilt in the 1680s. On completion of the building work, it was ordered in 1684 that a gallery be built at the west and south sides of the church with space left in the gallery at the west end for 'placing a pair of organs'.[72] It is not clear when an organ was erected and no details survive relating to the organ. However, the instrument was certainly in place by 1686 when John Walter Beck was paid six pounds for half a year's salary as organist and Mr Godfrey was paid 3*s.* 11*d.* for tuning the organ.[73] St Peter's church in Dublin also had an organ in the late seventeenth century. The earliest reference to music in St Peter's occurs on the first page of the extant vestry minutes, which date from 1686. In a list of accounts for the church, a payment to the organist, Roger Quilter, is recorded.[74] There are no details of the organ that was in place in the church at that time. It can be assumed that it was erected in the church sometime after the Restoration in 1660. The organ remained in use until 1713 when a new instrument was built by John Baptiste Cuvillie who was a parishioner of St Peter's.[75] An organ existed in St Bride's church in Dublin by 1685: in April 1686 William Thatcher was appointed as organist with an annual salary of thirteen pounds, back dated to 3 September 1685.[76] Again, no details of this organ survive but it remained in use throughout the eighteenth century, despite reference in 1731 to 'the new organ that is intended to be put up'.[77]

The appointment of a new organist at St Catherine's church in 1697 sheds light on the responsibilities of the post in the late seventeenth century. John Sabliar was awarded an annual salary of twenty-two pounds, for which he was to attend the church three times every Sunday, twice on holy days, and every week day at 7.00 p.m.[78] This is significant as it is the first record of the responsibilities of an

66 John Holmes, 'The Trinity College organs in the seventeenth and eighteenth centuries', *Hermathena*, 113 (Dublin, 1972), 40–8, at 41.   **67** *IRL-Drcb*, MS P.45/6/1, p. 161.   **68** Grindle, *Cathedral music*, p. 157.   **69** Ibid., p. 134.   **70** Ibid., p. 140.   **71** *IRL-Drcb*, MS P.117/5/4, pp 46 ff.   **72** *IRL-Drcb*, MS P.378/5/2, p. 115.   **73** Ibid., p. 134. Thomas Godfrey was organist at St Patrick's cathedral, Dublin from 1685 to 1689 and of Christ Church from January to Michaelmas 1689.   **74** *IRL-Drcb*, MS P.45/6/1, p. 1. **75** Ibid., pp 157, 161.   **76** *IRL-Drcb*, MS P.327/3/1, fo. 118r.   **77** Ibid., fo. 270r.   **78** *IRL-Drcb*, MS

Irish parish organist. Unfortunately, it is not recorded what the organist was required to play. However, an early eighteenth-century contract between John Woffington and the authorities of St Michan's church in Dublin clearly outlines the duties of the organist. Woffington was required to attend the morning and evening services on Sundays and weekdays. He was required to play 'A grave solemn composition or voluntary immediately before the first lesson to hold four minutes on week days and eight minutes on Sundays and holy days, rarely exceeding or falling short.' After the third collect at morning and evening prayer a psalm tune was to be played 'with modest graces and short transitions from time to time'; furthermore, this was to be played 'upon such stops as shall be well suited to the number of the congregation so as the sound of the organ, and the voice of the people may be duly proportioned and equally mingled, that the instruments of music and singers may be as one'. At morning services on Sundays and holy days there was to be a 'solemn introit or doxology' lasting 'about two minutes' immediately after the prayer from Corinthians II, 13:14 (the grace). Before the sermon another psalm was to be played in the manner already described. At the end of the service there was to be a 'dismiss' which was to be 'no way savouring of, or tending to excite airiness or levity, but like the voluntary very solemn, and suited to the season or service of the day'.[79] Although this is the first detailed picture of the duties and responsibilities of a parish organist in Ireland, it is likely that, rather than instituting new arrangements, it continues a tradition that probably dates back to the seventeenth century. The appointment of John Sabliar at St Catherine's church in 1697 may have marked an increase in the commitment required by the organist as his salary of twenty-two pounds shows an increase of eighteen pounds per annum on the salaries of the previous organists at St Catherine's. However, it may have simply been recognition of the fact that the previous salary of four pounds was considerably less than average. From 1687 to 1693 Roger Quilter was receiving sixteen pounds per annum as organist at St Peter's church. His successor, Thomas Hollister, was appointed in 1693 at an annual salary of eight pounds but due to poor attendance this was reduced in 1694 to six pounds. Succeeding him was Nathan Ellison who was appointed in 1695 at ten pounds per annum, later increased in 1696 to fifteen and in 1697 to sixteen pounds per annum. At the church of St John the Evangelist John Walter Beck was employed as organist from an unknown date until 1688 at twelve pounds per annum. His successor, Robert Hollister, was employed from 1688 to 1715 at ten pounds per annum. At St Bride's church William Thatcher was appointed organist in 1686 at the annual salary of thirteen pounds, reduced in 1691 to twelve pounds. His successor George Orr was organist from an unknown date until 1697 at the salary of twelve pounds per annum.[80]

P.117/05/2, p. 67.   **79** Barra Boydell, 'St Michan's Church Dublin: The installation of the organ in 1725 and the duties of the organist', *DHR*, 46:2 (1993), 101–10 at 110. John Woffington had previously been organist at St Werburgh's Church from 1721 to 1724.   **80** *IRL-Drcb*, MS P.45/6/1, pp 23 ff; P.378/5/1, pp 134, 142; P.327/3/1, fos 118r ff.

Despite his high salary, John Sabliar did not remain long in his position of organist at St Catherine's church. When his successor, Thomas Hollister, was appointed a year later in 1698 the salary was reduced to seventeen pounds. The appointment also shows a slight reduction in the duties of the organist who was now expected to attend the church every Sunday and holy day in the morning and afternoon and every evening on weekdays.[81] It can be seen from the details of John Woffington's duties at St Michan's that the majority of his playing was solo organ music. He was also required to accompany the congregational singing of two psalms in each service – after the third collect and before the sermon. This marks a difference from those churches that did not have organs, where psalms were sung in the place of such solo organ music.

It is clear that music played an important role in worship in parish churches in the seventeenth century. Unfortunately, few parish church records from the seventeenth century survive outside of Dublin. Although there were organs in some Dublin parish churches in the late seventeenth century, it should be noted that the capital possessed a large proportion of the country's wealth and the use of organ accompaniment in worship there may not be typical. However, it seems likely that music in the vast majority of churches in the country consisted of the unaccompanied singing of metrical psalms led by the parish clerk. As we have seen, this was not the ideal Anglican position but, despite the wishes of Church of Ireland commentators like Wetenhall and King, the music used in worship in Irish parish churches did not change until the late eighteenth and early nineteenth centuries.

---

81 *IRL-Drcb*, MS P.117/05/2, p 82.

Purcell's 'curiously poor and perfunctory piece of work': critical reflections on Purcell via his music for the centenary of Trinity College Dublin

MARTIN ADAMS

The music of the ode was composed by no less a person than Henry Purcell, and would certainly have been repeated at our tercentenary had it been equal to his standard works. But it is a curiously poor and perfunctory piece of work.[1]

Thus Purcell's music for the centenary celebrations of Trinity College Dublin was dismissed by John Pentland Mahaffey (1839–1919), internationally renowned scholar of Greek, reforming academic, 'the least clerical of clerics',[2] and later provost of the college. No published opinion on *Great parent, hail* (Z327) has differed significantly from Mahaffey's, including that of this writer.[3] This chapter will contend that, although Purcell wrote works that are far more accomplished than *Great parent, hail*, the almost universally low opinion of it is flawed by unidentified presuppositions and faulty comparisons. Moreover, the larger part of the thought and ink that has been devoted to it has evaded questions that arise from its perceived quality, or lack of it, and instead has sought answers to the empirical questions that traditional English-speaking musicological enquiry is so well equipped to address.

For example, the poem (Illustration 11.1) was printed shortly before or just after the celebrations on 9 January 1694. There is no mention of music, of Purcell, or of where the first performance took place; and records of the day's celebrations are contradictory as to whether the ode was performed in Trinity College or in Christ Church cathedral (nobody has been able to improve on Mahaffey's assessment that the contradictions cannot be accounted for).[4] Until around thirty years ago, there was occasional speculation as to whether or not Purcell travelled to Ireland for the occasion (commitments in London meant that he could not have).[5] Also, there are tantalising comments by W.H. Grattan Flood (1857–1928), whose claim that Purcell was of Irish ancestry is perhaps the least

---

1 J.P. Mahaffey et al., *The book of Trinity College Dublin, 1591–1891* (Belfast, 1892), p. 50. 2 J.V. Luce, *Trinity College Dublin: the first 400 years* (Dublin, 1992), p. 120. 3 Martin Adams, *Henry Purcell: the origins and development of his musical style* (Cambridge, 1995), p. 265. 4 Mahaffey, *The book*, p. 51. 5 Franklin B. Zimmerman, *Henry Purcell, 1659–95: his life and times* (2nd rev. ed. Philadelphia, 1983), pp 223, 232–4.

fanciful of his many attempts to claim for Ireland some of England's most famous musicians of yore, and who also reported that correspondence between the college and the composer had been seen by Mahaffey.[6]

A much more interesting question is why *Great parent, hail* is the work that it is, rather than the one our presuppositions may make us wish it to be. One of the most fundamental presuppositional flaws is that this, and countless other works by Purcell and others, have been approached via the 'great work' concept that lies behind Mahaffey's comments and, implicitly, behind those of writers since. If only because Purcell has long and justly been regarded as one of England's most accomplished producers of great works, it is worth considering briefly the extent to which this essentially nineteenth-century concept has shaped our view of this composer. His case is especially telling because he is one of those musicians whose high reputation, among the general musical public and musicians alike, is based on familiarity with a very small proportion of his output.

Why should this reputation have such a narrow base? Does that tell us anything about the composer as a whole, and in particular about the almost universally unfamiliar *Great parent, hail*? One might start by wondering why the most widely familiar work of Purcell, by far, is *Dido and Aeneas*? Its popularity cannot be based mainly on the power of its famous lament, even though its audience always waits for what Westrup rightly describes as 'one of the great things in music.'[7] Nor can its popularity rest mainly on the facts that it can be staged with comparatively little expense and that its vocal parts are not especially demanding. If those points – at least one outstanding aria, plus ease of production and performance – were all that was required, there would be more seventeenth-century operatic candidates for equivalent popularity. Nor can language be the issue, for *Dido and Aeneas* is well-known and admired almost everywhere.

The popularity of *Dido* rests on its modernity. Like Monteverdi's *L'incoronazione di Poppea* and Mozart's *Don Giovanni*, it speaks out of its time about some of the deepest aspects of the human condition. As if that were not enough, *Dido*, more than any other of Purcell's stage works, rises above its historical and stylistic constraints to the extent that it has always fitted comfortably into concepts of what opera should be and could be, and not just because of its surface conformity (in the surviving music at least) as an all-sung operatic tragedy. As Ellen Harris remarks, 'Purcell's composition withstands comparison with operatic works from any period for its ability to express human passion in a perfect blend of words and music.'[8] So it does! And that seems to answer the question why so much thought and ink has been devoted to this one piece – more than to any other written by a composer working in England except Handel's *Messiah* and, perhaps, Elgar's *The dream of Gerontius*. Generations of

---

6 For ancestry see W.H. Grattan Flood, 'Irish ancestry of Garland, Dowland, Campion and Purcell', *ML*, 3:1 (1922), 59–65; for documents relating to *Great parent hail*, see ibid., 64n.   7 J.A. Westrup, *Purcell*, revised Nigel Fortune (London, 1980), p. 123.   8 Ellen T. Harris, *Henry Purcell's Dido and Aeneas* (New York, 1987), p. 3. For the incomplete state of the sources see Peter Holman, *Henry Purcell* (Oxford, 1994), p. 196.

musicians and the musical public have agreed with Harris' assessment, at least since the first (corrupt) publication in score in 1841 launched *Dido* on its modern career. However, while that can explain the enduring popularity of *Dido*, it does not explain why so much of the thought expressed about *Dido* over the last 30 years has a revisionist tone. Most of the writers have recognized that, unless a previously undiscovered source turns up (tantalizing, and always a possibility), substantial reassessment of the incomplete and imperfect score is improbable. What most writers have sought to do is change the way we *think*.

Revisionist thinkers about *Dido* include Curtis Price, John Buttrey and Ellen Harris, all of whom have striven to counter the tendency to look at it through the lens of later opera. They acknowledge its relationship to the English masque and to the general culture of the time, with Price and Buttrey in particular having much to say about allegorical meaning, as well as history, text and music, and with Harris engaging in a detailed musico-dramatic analysis that befits the scholar-performer she is.[9] Another detailed analysis of the relationship between music and drama, with an emphasis on discovering the relationship between processes musical and dramatic has been undertaken by this author.[10] More controversially, Bruce Wood and Andrew Pinnock have suggested that *Dido*'s origins and date are rather different from what has been claimed – that it was not composed for the 1689 performance in Josias Priest's school for young gentlewomen, but comes from several years earlier, perhaps as early as 1684.[11]

Both kinds of reassessment – those addressing the music's insides, and those addressing its externals – are appropriate and worthwhile. For example, awareness of the fact that Purcell draws on a universal baroque device for the ground in Dido's lament heightens one's wonder at his achievement, for this is one of the great laments in all music. Knowing that the witches' scene is in the key of F minor because this is the key for 'horrid music' can evoke a similar response; and it makes one long to hear the scene in a seventeenth-century, unequal temperament. But none of this can change the simple fact that the power, and hence the popularity, of *Dido and Aeneas* rests on its excellence as a specimen of musical drama. We might be more-informed listeners; but like the less-informed listeners of 100 years ago, we are held in thrall by the power of music – by something that seems bigger than we are and that touches something universal and shared by us all.

A large proportion of these attempts to change how we think about *Dido* elevates context as a necessity central to a fuller understanding of music. Here one must recognize that, over the last forty years or so, contextualism has

9 Curtis Price, *Henry Purcell and the London stage* (Cambridge, 1984). John Buttrey, 'The evolution of English opera between 1656 and 1695: a reinvestigation' (PhD, University of Cambridge, 1967). Harris, *Dido*.   **10** Adams, *Henry Purcell*, 276–86.   **11** Bruce Wood & Andrew Pinnock, '"Unscarr'ed by turning times"? The dating of Purcell's *Dido and Aeneas*', *EM*, 20 (1992), 372–90. See also the responses: John Buttrey, 'The dating of *Dido*', *EM*, 20 (1992), 703; Martin Adams, 'More on dating *Dido*', *EM*, 21 (1993), 510; Curtis Price, '*Dido and Aeneas*: questions of style and evidence', *EM*, 22 (1994), 115–25. Wood & Pinnock, '"Singin' in the rain": Yet more on dating *Dido*', *EM*, 22 (1994), 3657.

developed agendas and practices that are distinctively modern in expression and methodology. Behind the seemingly simple search for deeper understanding of the work concerned lie philosophical and hermeneutic concepts that cannot be the concern of this chapter. However, it is worth noting the unusually persuasive definition of contextualism in music promulgated by Giles Hooper.[12] His use of the term accords generally with the *Oxford English Dictionary*'s definitions as applied to philosophy and literary criticism: 'Any doctrine emphasizing the importance of the context of inquiry in solving problems or establishing the meaning of terms' and 'The policy or practice, in literary criticism, of setting a poem or other work in its cultural context.'

However, Hooper demonstrates that, when applied to music, these concepts become messy. In particular, he shows that those who apply contextualism as a tool of revisionist thinking almost always struggle with the fact that two concepts which it inherently attacks – music's autonomy and the great work concept – stubbornly refuse to be released from the argument. Therefore, it is no surprise that his definition of musical contextualism, 'music as a thoroughly and multiply mediated concrete or symbolic phenomenon', is a lot less tidy than those applied to philosophy or literary criticism. It is also worth pointing out that contextualism is seen as the 'appropriate counterpart to formalism'. This is a circle that cannot be squared; and the forthcoming application of contextualism to selected works by Purcell – and ultimately to *Great parent, hail* – will demonstrate why those concepts refuse to go away. As this author has argued elsewhere, knowing the original context can enrich our experience; but its relationship to the directly musical experience of twenty-first-century ears is another matter, especially if the contextualization has been concerned with such subtle issues as allegory.[13]

It is revealing both that the historical roots of contextualism lie in the romantic admiration of great works and that contextualism is especially associated with the early-music movement. For example, the choice of works on which the pioneers of the early-music movement focussed is significant. It is no accident that Mendelssohn's ground-breaking performance of Bach in Leipzig in 1829 was devoted not to Bach's 'Coffee Cantata', but to the *St Matthew passion*; or that in the 1886 Leeds Festival Arthur Sullivan chose the *Mass in B minor* as the subject of his grand experiment 'to secure a faithful realization of Bach's intentions', as the report in the *Times* on 15 October put it. The report continued:

The high trumpets employed by the master had been specially manufactured, and the *oboe d'amore*, also grown obsolete in our time, was duly prominent in the obbligato accompaniment of the contralto air *Qui sedes ad dextram Patris*.

Mendelssohn's alterations of orchestration, and of many other things, seem blithely uninterested in context; but there is no doubt that, nearly sixty years later,

---

12 Giles Hooper, *The discourse of musicology* (Aldershot, 2006), especially pp 30–4 and 73–90.
13 Adams, *Henry Purcell*, 296.

the performance by Sullivan carries something of the modernist, contextualizing spirit in his desire to do justice to 'the master' by reproducing things as they had been in his time. Sullivan's historicist thinking was a precursor to a more wide-ranging type of contextualism that, even as he was preparing his performance, was in its earliest stages and that, like the more recent work on *Dido*, has led to fundamental reassessments.

The late nineteenth-century progenitors of the early-music movement did not merely blow the cobwebs off old scores and parts. Even more successfully than recent studies of *Dido*, they changed the way we think. Such changes include Arnold Dolmetsch's re-discovery of the esoteric greatness of seventeenth-century English consort music, and the much more recent realisation (partly through disciples of Dolmetsch) that Marin Marais was one of the great composers of his time. Such reassessment can be seen as an attempt (often successful) to alter our perception of what qualifies as a great work; and when applied to composers such as Marais or Jenkins, it seems both successful and beneficial. However, some aspects of the reassessment industry are of far less obvious benefit. In particular, the attempt to invalidate the great work concept has shown an inexorable tendency to throw the baby out with the bathwater. One cannot get away from the fact that, even in the centuries before the enthronement of the great work concept, some works of music were regarded as better than others. As a dominant system of belief and practice, contextualism eats away at the heart that fed the great work concept; and pressed hard, it reduces everything to a purely localized significance. It casts doubt on the autonomy that for centuries has been attributed to music, and especially to instrumental music – from the rarified thinking of the sixteenth-century *In nomine*, through Bach's *Kunst der Fuge* and Beethoven's piano sonatas, to Arvo Pärt's *Spiegel im Spiegel*. It is an odd passion for music that finds value primarily in the music's function. A piece of music becomes an exhibit in a cabinet of curiosities – a cabinet in which there is no meaningful, present-day access to the expressive power of music, because that music can be understood only in the context of the time and place for which it was written. Instead of engagement, there is gazing from afar. By implication, only if we understand the time and place can we fully appreciate what the work is – and by implication, respond to it properly. No wonder contextualism is so prominent in the early-music industry: find some little-known music written for a special occasion, produce an edition, record the music (preferably in the original building), write a contexualising programme note – instant understanding for all!

One of the most fundamental problems with contextualism's levelling tendencies is that they evade the very thing that, almost certainly, was what drew us into music in the first place – its sensual power. We might not understand everything about the context of *Dido and Aeneas*; but even if we understood not a word of English, and had no idea of the original context, the purely musical power of Dido's Lament endures, as the wordless (and much commented-on) use of this music at the end of Oliver Hirschbiegel's 2004 film *Der Untergang*

(*Downfall*) testifies. The search for context can say as much about the searcher's need to contextualize as about the work being studied. Indeed, the modern impulse (for that is what it is) to contextualize is consistent with the depersonalizing tendencies of modernism and post-modernism; and as Richard Taruskin has argued persuasively, the early-music movement is one of the most striking musical manifestations of dehumanization of the last fifty years.[14] Contextualization is a search for the unreachable – a desire to find certainty via a knowledge that can never be known because we can share only in part of the context. The fraught nature of the exercise is neatly encapsulated by Hans Keller's observation that underlying so much of the search for authenticity is the mistaken belief that 'their authenticity is better than ours.'[15]

So, if the problem with excessive contextualization is its excess, it must also be recognized that contextualization, provided it is twinned with discrimination, may have a special benefit for the 'not-great work.' Its beneficial aspects are especially evident in considering *Great parent, hail*, for although that piece cannot sustain any claim that it is an underestimated masterpiece, it is also a paragon of the work whose reputation has suffered partly from comparisons that are false precisely because they fail to consider context. Because it is an ode, comparisons (published or not) have tended to gravitate towards the odes that Purcell, Blow and others wrote for important celebrations in London, be they odes for royal birthdays or the famous 1692 Caecilian ode *Hail, bright Cecilia*. Those works for London and for Dublin are for different kinds of occasion; and the differences become evident if we compare the texts and music of the Trinity College ode with those for its nearest functional equivalents in English celebrations. Mahaffey's comments reinforce the falseness of the comparisons via a revealing comparison of his own. One of the works performed in the 1694 celebrations had been Blow's anthem *I beheld, and lo, a great multitude*; and for the tercentenary it crossed the minds of the college authorities to perform both the Purcell ode and the Blow anthem – or maybe they already had decided to reject Purcell and accept Blow.

John Blow (1649–1708) is a striking example of the high-quality composer sidelined by Enlightenment and post-Enlightenment obsessions with the 'great composer'. He had been Purcell's teacher; and until recently, the work of his most illustrious pupil so dominated our perceptions of late seventeenth-century English music that, within the last twenty-five years or so, anyone of a certain age has had to come to terms with the fact that during Purcell's lifetime the reputations of the two men were similarly high.[16] So Mahaffey seems surprised to find that Purcell's ode is 'a curiously poor and perfunctory piece of work, whereas the anthem then

---

14 See, for example, many such references in Richard Taruskin, *Text and act* (Oxford, 1995).   **15** Hans Keller, 'Whose authenticity?', *EM*, 12:4 (1984), 517–19.   **16** For a strong defence of Blow's reputation see Bruce Wood, 'Only Purcell e're shall equal Blow', *Purcell Studies* ed. Curtis Price (Cambridge, 1995), pp 106–44; for the relationship between Blow and Purcell, see also Martin Adams, 'Purcell, Blow and the English court ode', ibid., pp 172–91.

recently composed by Blow "I beheld, and lo, a great multitude" still holds its place in our Chapel, and we gladly reproduce it in the present [1892] festival.'[17]
Unspoken questions lie behind these late nineteenth-century views on the relative merits of music by the great Purcell and by the lesser contemporary, whose memorial in Westminster Abbey proclaims him to have been 'Master to the famous Mr H. Purcell' and of whom Bruce Wood has justly declared that 'his true stature approaches that of Purcell himself more closely than has generally been acknowledged.'[18]

Familiarity with *I beheld, and lo, a great multitude* may have played a part in its acceptance for the tercentenary; and that familiarity might have been reinforced by the close links between the college chapel and the Dublin cathedrals of St Patrick and Christ Church. The same anthem appears in their eighteenth-century music books; and as studies of the music holdings have shown, eighteenth-century sources in these cathedrals can be traced back, with some certainty, to seventeenth-century sources that made their way to Dublin in the first thirty years or so after the Restoration in 1660.[19] Moreover, the choristers in the two cathedrals also sang in the college chapel – an arrangement that, for utility alone, would ensure a large measure of common repertoire.[20] Blow's anthem did not only 'still hold its place' in the chapel: its presence epitomised the very continuity that Mahaffey and others were celebrating.

The date of *I beheld, and lo, a great multitude* is unknown, though it seems likely to pre-date 1677.[21] Nor is it known if it was written for a specific occasion in the Chapel Royal, where Blow was one of several composers who produced new works fairly regularly. However, it is one of this composer's most sumptuously scored anthems, its scale matched or surpassed by only a handful of his grandest works, such as *God spake sometimes in visions* written for the coronation of James II in 1685. The combination of the text and Blow's music made it singularly apt for the college tercentenary: because the words express a vision of the future, they express eternal values, while the music's complexity and high-baroque elaboration capture something of the text's transcendence. Then there is the text's metaphorical aptness: the envisioned multitude depicted in the Revelation 7:9–15 was praising God and the Lamb; the nineteenth-century multitude was praising the institution that, for three centuries, had sustained its founding mission to promulgate true religion. Moreover, as Helga Robinson-Hammerstein has shown, two hundred years earlier, the text had an immediate relevance for a community whose very existence had been threatened by the brief rise of Jacobite power in the late 1680s: it conferred upon the recent experiences

17 Mahaffey, *The book*, 50. **18** Bruce Wood, 'Blow, John', *NG II*, iii, p. 722. **19** See especially Houston, 'Music manuscripts'; Boydell, *History of music,* especially pp 78–9, 106, 157 and ch. 9, above. **20** For members of the cathedral choirs singing in the college chapel, see Boydell, *History of music,* pp 106–7, 157. **21** Bruce Wood (ed.), 'John Blow. Anthems IV: anthems with instruments', *Musica Britannica,* 79 (London, 2002), p. xxvii.

of deprivation an aura of redeemed suffering which allowed these worshippers to approach the throne of the Almighty.[22]

* * *

If we examine the occasion-specific text of *Great parent, hail* in the light of Mahaffey's likely reasons for accepting Blow's anthem, his rejection of it becomes more understandable – and all the more so when we consider that the opportunity to celebrate the tercentenary was also the great opportunity for Dublin's resident 'great man' in music, Sir Robert Prescott Stewart, to flex his own compositional muscles, and to a text that was less concerned with events that, by then, were two hundred years past.

Of all musicians living and working in Ireland, Stewart (1825–94) was the most vigorous polymath. He held a number of positions in Dublin and in Belfast, where he was appointed conductor of the Belfast Harmonic Society in 1877. Since 1844 he had been organist of Christ Church cathedral and, from 1852 to 1861 a joint organist of St Patrick's cathedral with William Murphy (though he continued to play at St Patrick's after relinquishing the post of organist to become a vicar choral).[23] In 1861 he was appointed to the chair of music in Trinity College. By 1892 he had produced a number of odes, including an *Ode to Industry* for the Cork Exhibition in 1852, and an *Ode to Shakespeare* for the 1870 Birmingham Festival.[24] All reports of the time suggest that, in his home country at least, Stewart was revered as a musician and loved as warm and generous man – qualities enshrined in the fine portrait commissioned by the University of Dublin Choral Society.[25] Indeed, for all-round musical ability he seems to have had no serious rival on the island. Nor, however, is there evidence to suggest that his most famous pupil, Charles Villiers Stanford (1852–1924), was essentially wrong when he declared that

> It was hard, even for one so gifted with so brilliant a brain, to live in a circle of half-baked musicians without being affected by their standard, and still harder to occupy a position in which he had no rival to excel or learn from.[26]

It must therefore have been with some trepidation that the authorities at Trinity, not least Stewart himself, had to consider what to do about the fact that no lesser

---

22 Helga Robinson-Hammerstein, '"With great solemnity": celebrating the first centenary of the foundation of Trinity College, Dublin, 9 January 1694', *Long Room*, 37 (1992), 30.   23 Shaw, *Succession of organists*, pp 413, 424.   24 Information on works as in W.H. Husk/Joseph J. Ryan, 'Stewart, Sir Robert (Prescott)', *NG II*, xxiv, 382. For a valuable summary biography, including some fascinating vignettes of Stewart's abilities as a musician, see Jeremy Dibble, *Charles Villiers Stanford* (Oxford, 2002), pp 22–4. See also Lisa Parker, 'For the purpose of public music education: the lectures of Robert Prescott Stewart' in *IMS* 9, pp 187–210; Lisa Parker, 'Robert Prescott Stewart (1825–1894): a Victorian musician in Dublin' (PhD, NUIM, 2009).   25 The portrait currently hangs in the music department, TCD.

person than Henry Purcell had written the centenary ode. And it must have been with some relief that they discovered supportable reasons for rejecting it. Perhaps they found some of those in the work itself; but if not, they certainly found them in comments made one hundred years earlier by the highly esteemed provost (from 1774 to 1794) John Hely-Hutchinson (1724–94). His dismissive view of the centenary ode is reflected in the later histories of the college by Constantia Maxwell and H.L. Murphy, and on whose wording Mahaffey's comment is based.[27]

Therefore, one must consider whether Stewart or anyone else actually saw Purcell's music; and if they did, in what source? It seems that the autograph copy has been lost; and although a number of manuscript sources have survived in London libraries, no early source has been found in Dublin.[28] If the music had been examined by Stewart, it probably would have been via the ode's publication in the second volume of Goodison's edition, *Purcell: odes and choral songs* (London, 1790?).

Whatever the reasons for the rejection, it must be admitted that, against the backdrop of late nineteenth-century understanding of Purcell, the rejection has validity; and all the more so when one considers the expectations that would have been aroused by the few Purcell odes Stewart was likely to have known from complete publications. *Great parent, hail* is not in the manner of *The Yorkshire feast song* from 1690, and which in 1878 had been the first work to be published in the Purcell Society's complete edition of the composer's music. Nor does it bear comparison with *Hail, bright Cecilia*, which had been published in 1847, or even with the much more intimate first Caecilian ode, *Welcome to all the pleasures*, which was published in 1684, a few months after its first performance. To Stewart, and to anyone else expecting something similar to the works for London, *Great parent hail* was certain to disappoint in its scale of expression, both in text and music. We may doubt whether, two hundred years from now, the ode Stewart produced for the tercentenary will command the attention we now afford to Purcell's; but as the press cuttings of the day show, the room made for him via the rejection of *Great parent hail* proved worthwhile. His new composition made its mark, and was honoured via publication in Novello's octavo series of choral music.

With the distance engendered by a further one hundred years we are perhaps in a position to ask some questions that, to Stewart and Mahaffey, might not have seemed relevant. First, why was Tate chosen to write the words and Purcell the music? Secondly, what type of celebration, and therefore what type of words and music, was appropriate for the celebration of a college centenary? Thirdly, what might have been expected of a poet and a composer based in London who was asked to celebrate an event in Ireland? For Trinity College, Tate and Purcell were natural choices, the first representing Ireland, the second the England on which

---

26 As in Dibble, *Stanford*, p. 43. **27** Robinson-Hammerstein, 'With great solemnity', 38n. 40. **28** Purcell: *Miscellaneous odes and cantatas*, Purcell Society, 27 (London, 1957), pp xvi–xvii.

the college depended for its foundation and present existence. In 1693, when the plans for the celebrations were underway, there were other options for the choice of poet and composer, but none of them matched the prestige of this combination.[29]

Nahum Tate (1652–1715) had been born in Ireland, almost certainly in Dublin. His father and grandfather were clergymen. He received his BA from Trinity College in 1672 and then moved to London, where he worked as a poet and playwright. In 1692 he was appointed Poet Laureate in succession to Thomas Shadwell (1642?–92).[30] As far as the present age is concerned, Tate's most famous poem by far is the Christmas hymn *While shepherds watched*, which first appeared in the 1702 edition of the enormously influential Anglican psalter that he and Nicholas Brady (1659–1726) had first produced in 1696.[31] In the world of literature he is best known (or infamous) for his adaptations of Shakespeare, especially of *King Lear*. For musicians, his reputation rests in his work as the librettist for Purcell's *Dido and Aeneas* (1689) and for several other texts that Purcell set, including the elaborate 1693 ode for Queen Mary's birthday *Celebrate this festival* (Z231), the dazzling 1694 ode *Come, ye sons of art* (Z323), and the sacred song *The blessed virgin's expostulation* (*Tell me, some pitying angel*, Z196) which was published in 1693.

The likely sequence of events was that the college approached Tate – or that he volunteered the poem as acknowledgement of his formative years in the college and in Dublin. Tate might have suggested Purcell, or have approached him independently. Whatever the mechanism that led to Purcell's involvement, he too was a natural choice, and not just because of Tate's record of work with him. His settings of odes for the court and other venues had made a considerable impact; and his name was by far the most prestigious in the London theatres.

It is worth remembering that the ode is a literary form and that all references to it until the nineteenth century give pride of place to the poet (note the titles above the published text in Illustration 11.1). Any modern reassessment must begin with the words, as the composer did. It is revealing to compare Tate's text with that of Thomas D'Urfey (1653–1723) which Purcell had set some four years earlier. *The Yorkshire feast song* (*Of old, when heroes thought it base*) had been performed in March 1690 to celebrate the Glorious Revolution of 1688 and to offer the gentry of Yorkshire the opportunity, in their annual London feast, to demonstrate both the continuity of their county's traditions and glorious deeds and their loyalty to the new regime. For what was by all accounts a magnificent celebration D'Urfey neatly adapted the methods of the court and Caecilian odes that were by then an established part of London's artistic life.

29 For the college's plans, see Robinson-Hammerstein, 'With great solemnity', 28.   30 For details of Tate's life see Christopher Spencer, *Nahum Tate*, Twayne's English Authors series, 126 (New York, 1972); Samuel A. Golden: 'Nahum Tate' (PhD, TCD, 1954).   31 N. Tate & N. Brady, *A new version of the psalms of David, fitted to the tunes used in churches* (London, 1696). The first appearance of *While shepherds watched their flocks* was in N. Tate & N. Brady, *A supplement to the new version of the psalms ... with additional hymns for the holy sacrament, festivals, &c.* (London, 1702).

AN ODE

Upon the Ninth of JANUARY 169$\frac{3}{4}$

THE FIRST

SECULAR DAY

SINCE THE

UNIVERSITY

OF

DUBLIN'S FOUNDATION

BY

QUEEN ELIZABETH.

By Mr. TATE.

Great Parent Hail! all Hail to Thee,
Who haft from laft Diftrefs furviv'd,
To fee this joyful Year arriv'd;
Thy Mufes Second JUBILEE.

Another Century commencing
No Decay in Thee can trace;
Time with his own Laws difpencing,
Adds new Charms to ev'ry Grace,
That adorn'd thy Youthful Face.

After War's, Alarms repeated,
And a Circling Age compleated,
Vig'rous Offspring thou doft raife;
Such as to *JUVERNA*'s praife;
Shall *LIFFEE* make as proud a Name,
As that of *ISIS* or of *CAM*.

Awful Matron take thy Seat,
To Celebrate this Feftivall;
The Learn'd Affembly well to Treat
Bleft *ELIZA*'s Days recall.
The Wonders of HER Reign recount
In Songs that Mortal Streins furmount:
Songs for *PHÆBUS* to repeat.

SHE was the firft who did infpire,
And ftrung the mute *HIBERNIAN* Lyre;
Whofe deathlefs Memory
(The Soul of Harmony)
Still animates the Vocal Quire.

Succeeding Princes next recite:
With never dying Verfe require
Thofe Favours they did fhow'r;
'Tis that alone can do 'em right
To fave 'em from Oblivion's Night
Is only in the Mufes pow'r.

But chiefly Recommend to Fame,
MARIA and Great *WILLIAM*'s Name;
For furely no *HIBERNIAN* Mufe
(Whofe Ifle to Him, Her freedom owes)
Can Her Reftorer's Praife Refufe,
While *BOYN* or *SHANON* flows.

Thy Royal Patrons fung ; Repair
To Illuftrious *ORMOND*'s Tomb:
As, Living, He made Thee His Care,
Give Him, next thy *CÆSARS*, Room.

Then a Second *ORMOND*'s Story
Let aftonifht Fame recite;
But fhe'll wrong the Hero's Glory,
Till with equal Flame fhe write
To that which He difplays in Fight.

CHORUS.
With Themes like thefe ye Sons of Art
Treat this Aufpicious Day;
To Bribe the Minutes as they part,
Thofe Bleffings to bequeath, that may
Long, long rem, ain Your Kindnefs to repay.

DUBLIN: Printed by *Jofeph Ray,* on *College-Green,* 1694.

Illustration 11.1: Nahum Tate's text for *Great parent, hail*. Oxford, Bodleian Library.

The Yorkshire feast song consists of verses describing episodes in the past and present life of the county of York. In this respect it follows a pattern that can be identified in most of the odes written for musical setting during the last half of the seventeenth century. However, its text (and its music) represent a high point of the genre, whose hey-day was in the last twenty-five years of the century, and whose music by Purcell and Blow is the main reason why these works command our attention today.

The main English model for this type of verse was Abraham Cowley's *Pindarique odes* that were first published in 1656.[32] Cowley's purpose was to develop an English equivalent of the flamboyant style of Pindar's odes, and it is significant that he finds himself obliged to excuse his methods. The opening words of his preface are 'If a man should undertake to translate Pindar word for word, it would be thought that one mad man had translated another'.[33] That did not inhibit him from producing some of the most virtuoso demonstrations of English linguistic flamboyance in that flamboyant century. Most of those who followed him – certainly most of those who wrote odes for the public and court occasions for which Purcell and Blow wrote music – could not touch him. As Robert B. Hinman has said in a thoughtful and sympathetic reassessment of a poet who has aroused as much scorn as praise, Cowley finds 'the norm of great lyric art, the middle ground between wildness and formalism.'[34]

Cowley might have regarded Pindar as his primary debtor, but he also mentions Horace; and it is difficult to resist the conclusion that odes written by Cowley's successors for the court and other public celebrations were as indebted to Horace as to Pindar and Cowley. It is in Horace that one finds such themes as the divinity of the emperor, of the human saviour whose deeds are immortal – and these are the themes that dominate most court odes of the time.[35]

This brings us to what the ode for Trinity College (i.e. its text) is not, and what it never could be. First, it is not a celebration of monarchy, of heroes, or of loyalty. Above all other things, Tate's text salutes the college for what it has been and may be; it gives thanks for the college's survival and continuity; and it names the benefactors on whom all these things depended. While it includes homage to the new regime, it would have been inappropriate for Tate to take on board the imagery of royal praise. Nor would it have been appropriate, in an ode steeped in quasi-religious thanksgiving, to use the flamboyant imagery that D'Urfey used in *The Yorkshire feast song*. D'Urfey was writing immediately after the Glorious Revolution that had brought William and Mary to the throne; and given Yorkshire's long record of taking an independent line, including some notably bloody rebellions over the previous 170 years, he and his Yorkshire patrons had

32 *Poems written by A. Cowley* (London, 1656).   33 Ibid., preface to *Pindarique odes*. See also A.R. Waller (ed.), *The English writings of Abraham Cowley* (Cambridge, 1905. An edited reprint of *The works of Mr Abraham Cowley*, London, 1668).   34 Robert B. Hinman, *Abraham Cowley's world of order* (Cambridge, MA, 1960), p. 89.   35 See *Iam satis terris*, and especially the commentary on it by R.G.M. Nisbet & Margaret Hubbard in *A commentary on Horace: odes, book 1* (Oxford, 1970), pp 16–40.

a point to make. By contrast, Tate was writing some three years after the victory of Williamite forces, a victory that had been seen as an act of divine deliverance. The college did not need to demonstrate its loyalty, and one of the most prominent themes of the text is that, although destructive change had threatened when the college was occupied by the Jacobite forces in 1689–90, all was now well. As Tate puts it, the 'Great parent ... hast from last distress survived'.[36] Tate speaks of recent history. Unlike *The Yorkshire feast song*, there is no ancient history to recite and the first hero to whom they can look is Eliza – Queen Elizabeth I who in March 1592 had granted the foundation charter. 'Succeeding princes' are praised in one verse; but the main matter is to 'Chiefly recommend to Fame, / Maria and great William's name.' Also praised are the dukes of Ormond – the Butler family who had been stalwart supporters of the college throughout the larger part of its existence. 'Illustrious Ormonde' was James Butler, first duke of Ormonde (1610–88), who from the 1640s onwards sought to effect a compromise between the competing demands of Ireland's Catholic and Protestant peoples (as the college also had done), who played a role in the negotiations that led to the restoration of the monarchy in 1660, and who from 1645 to his death was the chancellor of Trinity College. The 'second Ormond' was his son, also James (1665–1745), and chancellor of the college from 1688 to 1715.

This emphasis on known and recent figures is consistent with the pattern and purposes of the day's celebrations which, as Helga Robinson-Hammerstein has pointed out, had an agenda that subtly intertwined history, learning, religion and the promise of change.[37] The college was mounting a public relations exercise that declared both continuity and progress. For example, the language of Provost Ashe's sermon, preached that morning during the service of thanksgiving held in the college chapel, was clearly related to the lessons read earlier in the service. Taken together, they announced that the college's restoration was also the beginning of a new approach to learning, one that respected ancient learning but that sought to develop the modern concepts of the natural sciences. While this new approach was building on the foundations laid over the previous century, it was recognised that, to succeed in the future, the college would need new benefactors. Liberally drawing on biblical quotations and precedents, Ashe declared that

'tis certain our church and religion can never be safer than amidst the consequences of a rational learned age, and all the various improvements of knowledge, since they aim not at the captivity but freedom of men's minds.[38]

This thoroughly modern mode of thought was implicitly comparing the freedom of individual conscience that Protestant thinking claimed for itself, against what Protestants saw as the controlling spirit of Catholicism.

---

36 Robinson-Hammerstein, 'With great solemnity', 27–8. For details of TCD's despoliation see Luce, *Trinity College*, pp 32–3. 37 Robinson-Hammerstein, 'With great solemnity', 29–34. 38 Ibid., 32.

Nevertheless, in Ireland, and above all in the institution that had been supported by Ormonde the conciliator, there was no room for triumphal statements about the defeat of the Catholic forces of James II. In Tate's text, triumphalism is notable by its absence; and in keeping with so much in the day's celebrations, he writes with a subtle mixture of joy at deliverance, but also with an air of contemplation and self-examination.[39] It makes a revealing comparison with *The Yorkshire feast song*, which includes a martial praise of William – 'when the renowned Nassau [William, of the house of Orange-Nassau] / Came to restore our liberty and law', and jubilation to hear 'the knell of falling Rome'.

So Trinity College's celebration sought to emphasise dignity rather than self-aggrandisement, thankfulness and humility rather than self-congratulation. After all, the college was an institution that depended for its existence on the grace of God and the generosity of its benefactors. Even the references to the power of music are more oblique than in several other odes that Purcell set, including *Hail, bright Cecilia* (1692) and the final birthday ode for Queen Mary, *Come, ye sons of art* (1694). The 'Awful matron' should inspire awe, as well as dignity; but this was not something to get worked up about – certainly not in the way *The Yorkshire feast song* ends with a loud communal hurrah in praise of 'the city and county of York.' The nearest Tate gets to that is in his final verse which refers to the same 'sons of art' as the 1694 birthday ode. But even this declaration acknowledges the college's dependence on its supporters. After all, this 'learned assembly' was dominated by clerics who, scarcely less than the college itself, depended on patrons and benefactors. No wonder so much of the music shows the kind of rhetorical restraint (though not necessarily the musical style) found in the verse anthem.

There were perhaps additional reasons for the restraint of Purcell's music. *Great parent, hail* is the only large work that Purcell wrote for musicians he did not know – or few of whom he knew. There is a definite sense in the vocal and the instrumental writing of playing a bit safe. One account of the centenary performance says that it was 'sung by the principal gentlemen [i.e. choirmen] of the kingdom.'[40] While there is no clear record suggesting the abilities of those singers, they might well have been comparable with the best that English cathedrals could draw on. Nevertheless, it seems unlikely that Purcell would have been writing with specific abilities in mind, as he did in London with Richard Leveridge and, above all, with John Gostling.[41] Nor is there any firm evidence of Dublin trumpeters who could have done for Purcell's music what players like the Shore family (and perhaps others) had done for composers working in London, including Giovanni Battista Draghi, Blow and Purcell himself.[42] The scoring itself might reflect this caution, or perhaps that the composer had been warned

---

39 Ibid., 27. **40** Ibid., 36. **41** Olive Baldwin & Thelma Wilson, 'Richard Leveridge, 1670–1758. 1: Purcell and the dramatic operas', *MT*, 111 (1970), 592–4; for Gostling and Purcell, see several references in Zimmerman, *Henry Purcell*. **42** See especially Peter Downey, 'On sounding the trumpet and beating the drum in 17th-century England', *EM*, 24 (1996), 263–77.

Example 11.1: Henry Purcell, *Great parent, hail.* Opening symphony (first section).

about comparatively limited resources – or both. Strings, continuo and recorders is a line-up far more economical than most of the odes written after 1687. However, it is worth observing that the first violin line of the opening symphony, in C, includes no pitches that are not played on trumpets in the previous year's sumptuously scored birthday ode, *Celebrate this festival*, which is in the same key. Could this perhaps reflect a calculated flexibility on Purcell's part, so that the symphony could have included trumpet at the musicians' discretion? There is no evidence either way, and comparable flexibility cannot be certainly identified anywhere else in Purcell's larger works. However, the 'trumpetness' of the writing does reinforce something fundamental about Purcell's methods of responding to Tate's text.

If we consider the music from the perspective of rhetorical representation, its restraint acquires a distinctive and entirely appropriate function. There is a celebratory aspect to this expression of thanksgiving. Purcell communicates this not by forceful demonstration, but by using representational techniques to shadow precisely the grandiloquent expression epitomised in *The Yorkshire feast song* and many other odes from the 1690s. It was necessary only to write in the trumpet style to make the point. Neither the numbers of instruments, nor their tone colours, nor their weight of sound, is as important as the idea (Example 11.1). Such writing was a commonplace of the time (and before and since), and can be seen in string writing by composers as varied as Biber (1644–1704), G.B. Vitali (1632–92) and Blow, as well as in other works by Purcell himself, such as the celebratory verse anthem *O sing unto the Lord*. The cleverly concentrated imitation is a Purcellian characteristic designed to appeal to the cognoscenti without mystifying the general public. Equally pointed is the material for the symphony's second section (Example 11.2) – firmly in the terse canzona style

Vn1

Example 11.2: Henry Purcell, *Great parent, hail.* Opening symphony (second section).

that Purcell deployed so effectively (and generally with trumpets) in several of his later odes and stage works.[43]

In many of the subsequent movements we see the same principles followed in ways that are never less than resourceful, and the music's representative qualities often work in subtle alliances with the text. One example is Purcell's setting of the opening words. The salutations are dealt with in essentially the same way as Purcell had done just over a year earlier in *Hail, bright Cecilia.* In that work, the massive forces and the intense contrasts between verse, chorus and instruments are deployed to create a startlingly extrovert, communal acclamation. Here the same techniques, including the off-beat repetitions of 'Hail', are condensed into more restricted time and forces (Example 11.3); and the same condensation is seen in the choral amplification of the verse opening.

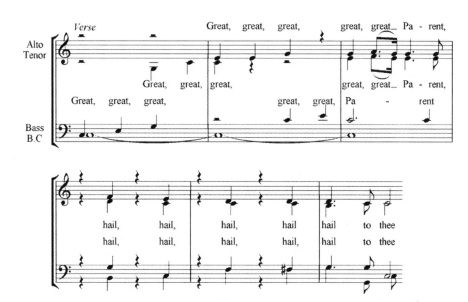

Example 11.3: Henry Purcell, *Great parent, hail.* Opening verse.

43 Adams, *Henry Purcell*, pp 160–3 and elsewhere.

A particularly subtle specimen of universal rhetoric comes after the chorus's amplification of the opening salutations. A central idea of Tate's first verse is encapsulated in the line 'Who hast thro' last distress survived.' Throughout the seventeenth century chromatically rising lines had been a standard device for expressing pain, from Gesualdo to Lully and beyond. Purcell himself had used it memorably in his funeral sentences to represent 'the bitter pains' (of eternal death); and here he uses it to represent the pain of the distress, without explicit mention of the pain itself. (Example.11.4)

However, there is another even more subtle issue involved. With striking insight Helga Robinson-Hammerstein writes that this music's task is 'to lay the ghost in the manner of exorcism'.[44] What an apt analogy! The rising chromaticism is expunged in the close onto the dominant at the end of the example – a highly intensified version of the standard Phrygian close, with the passage's accumulating density of texture culminating in pungent dissonance between the two upper lines, which emphasises the relief of the concluding consonance. Also, the key of this passage, F minor, is the one that Purcell often used for theatre scenes involving ghosts or witches – Act II of *Dido and Aeneas*, and the 'Symphony for flat trumpets' (later reworked as the funeral march for Queen Mary) that accompanies the appearance of ghostly apparitions in Shadwell's *The Libertine*. Both in the musical process and in this passage's rhetorical associations, the ghosts that had threatened Trinity College are indeed exorcised.

Finally we might refer to one of Tate's most striking verses, where the mother of learning is invited to 'take thy seat.' Purcell's music follows the common pattern for theatrical representations of priestly ceremonies, from 'Hark, behold the heavenly quire' in his first important work for the stage, *Theodosius* (1680), to Ismeron's incantation 'Ye twice ten hundred deities' from *The Indian queen* (1695), Purcell's last substantial contribution to the London theatre. With a measured solemnity that all would have recognised as processional – scalic movement epitomises the steps of progression musical and physical – instruments set the scene for a priestly bass solo (Example 11.5). Although the vocal line is in phrases separated by rests, the instrumental patterns overlap with them and produce a continuity of motion that brings the matron forward in musical ascent. As the master of ceremonies bids her take her seat, the music returns to the pitches of its starting point so that she settles with a dignified plonk. The music for this ode is full of such gestures economical and direct, gestures whose meaning in an age of common rhetorical language would have been recognised by all. The power of music heightens the power of words, but with a constraint that fits the quasi-ecclesiastical nature of the body corporate, and with the solemn thankfulness that befits the occasion.

If we are disappointed by *Great parent, hail* because it fails to live up to the communal hurrahs of *The Yorkshire feast song* or because it lacks the self-

---

44 Robinson-Hammerstein, 'With great solemnity', 36.

Example 11.4: Henry Purcell, *Great parent, hail.* 'Who hast thro' last distress survived'.

Example 11.4: Henry Purcell, *Great parent, hail*. 'Who hast thro' last distress survived'.

conscious musical bravura of *Hail, bright Cecilia*, that says at least as much about our expectations as it does about Purcell's music. That misguided expectation also opens the possibility that, if we are willing to think differently, contextualism can teach us a great deal – provided it is melded with critical thought. Purcell's peerless ability to capture the inner meaning of a text is as evident in *Great parent, hail* as it is in *Dido and Aeneas*. However, Tate's operatic text deals with a subject whose emblematic aspects are embedded in the history of western culture and in the views of human nature that sprang from that culture. It is the combination of that universal subject and Purcell's music that makes *Dido* speak across the ages. Equivalent points can be made about the higher acclaim given to *The Yorkshire feast song* and *Hail, bright Cecilia*. Although both were designed for a specific place and occasion, the underlying subjects are sufficiently universal to have modern equivalents; and with little or no stretch of the modern imagination the sheer extrovert flair of the music projects them vividly into our own time.

By contrast, in *Great parent, hail* Tate was writing for and rooted in a time, place and purpose so restricted that the language and concepts are inevitably remote. Although Purcell's music is a bridge between historical remoteness and the present, it cannot turn the subject into something it is not. The work's lower musical quality has little to do with that inevitable limitation; and the quality of

Example 11.5: Henry Purcell, *Great parent, hail.* 'Awful matron, take thy seat'

text is irrelevant, for the history of music is replete with fine music that sets poor texts. This work will never command widespread popularity. Nor will a large proportion of this composer's music. Purcell's fame rests on a small number of works precisely because so much of what he did operated in a context far removed from our own and, as we shall see, because of a musical language that, from the early eighteenth century onwards, is often unsuited to public discourse. Many works considerably better than *Great parent, hail* are at least as obscure and likely to remain so. Such works would include: the symphony song *See where she sits* (Z508); the superb third setting of *If music be the food of love* (Z379C) – a much more profound penetration of the text than the more popular version, of which there are two variants (Z379A & B);[45] the Latin laments on the death of Queen Mary, *Incassum lesbia* (Z383) and *O dive custos* (Z504); and,

---

45 For a detailed discussion see Adams, *Henry Purcell*, pp 218–21.

among the late works for theatre, sets of instrumental pieces such as those for *The double dealer* (Z592), *The married beau* (Z603) and *Abdelazer* (Z570).

The continuing obscurity of these fine works, let alone *Great parent, hail*, is underlined by the hopes held by some during the years surrounding the Purcell tercentenary commemorations, but that now seem to be disappointed. The recording and publishing industries had a field day and many commentators seemed to be anticipating the long-hoped-for Purcell revival. Presumably this would be a revival in which professional musicians and the general musical public alike would come to appreciate, in all its breadth and its depth, the full output of the man of whom Roger North said 'A greater musical genius England never had'.[46]

It has not happened, and nor does it seem likely that it ever will. Purcell remains a composer universally acknowledged by name, but by experience only through a tiny proportion of his output. Andrew Pinnock, one of the few commentators to have adopted a thoughtful and critical approach to this matter, has rightly observed that 'perhaps Purcell is the first example in English musical history of a phenomenon very familiar now, though difficult to object to in his case, considering the quality of the product ... a public figure.'[47] The recognition, in his lifetime and immediately afterwards, that he was an icon of musical Englishness has meant that subsequent generations have had to struggle with challenges of critical assessment; and Pinnock is surely correct when he observes that his modern value 'is founded upon eighteenth-century judgements.'[48]

One of the greatest barriers to a wide acclaim for Purcell's music is the very nature of his compositional thought and practice. For musicians there might be a natural appeal in his very-English predilection for elaboration, and perhaps in the high-baroque nature of the dramatic operas for which he wrote much of his theatre music. Devotees of early music will always be there to listen to concerts and buy recordings, on all of which musicians depend for their living; but they will always be a comparatively small number within the ranks of serious music lovers.

As Andrew Pinnock has said, Purcell has been fêted in his lifetime, enshrined immediately after his death, and praised ever since.[49] But the journey of his music into later centuries and the failure of early attempts at complete publication all suggest that the larger part of his music was altogether too high-baroque. Westrup's instinct was surely right when he conjectured that 'the breezy straightforwardness of some of Purcell's most popular songs and choruses was not the outcome of a natural talent for simplicity but the product of the hard labour of refinement.'[50]

In his 1710 publication *The life of Thomas Betterton* Charles Gildon (1665–1724) had this to say about Purcell's superiority as a composer for the stage, over the Italianate taste that by then was prevailing in London:

46 John Wilson, *Roger North on music* (London, 1959), p. 307.   **47** Andrew Pinnock, 'The Purcell phenomenon', *The Purcell companion*, ed. Michael Burden (London, 1995), p. 5.   **48** Ibid., p. 10.   **49** Ibid., p. 5.   **50** Westrup, *Purcell*, p. 173.

To this I answer, that I find the best judges of music, those who are masters of the composition, as well as performance, prefer what he has done to all the operas we have had, on our stage at least. I would therefore fain know how our taste is mended? Do the promiscuous audience know more of the art of harmony and music? No – not one in a thousand understands one single note.[51]

We must acknowledge that Gildon was not noted for his critical acumen in music. Nevertheless, his claim that musicians understand Purcell while the general public does not is concordant with the published claims of many professional and amateur musicians. These include: his contemporary and former fellow-chorister in the Chapel Royal, Thomas Tudway (c.1650–1726); an anonymous but well-informed contributor to the *Universal Journal* in 1724; the anonymous (almost certainly J.S. Shedlock, 1843–1919) editor of *The Monthly Musical Record* in 1895; Donald Francis Tovey (1875–1940), who interestingly couples to Purcell's name another ignored, great composer known only through a handful of works, Heinrich Schütz (1585–1672); and the great biographer-critic of Purcell, Jack Westrup (1904–75), who in the tercentenary of the composer's birth declared that 'Purcell's music has always been admired by discerning musicians, but has not always been well known.'[52] If we take seriously an anecdote of Roger North (1653–1734), Purcell himself was aware of the dichotomy between his own concepts of public appeal and musical excellence:

The noble Purcell, lately stole[n] from us into another world … used to mark what did not take for the best musick, it being his constant observation that what took least, was really best.[53]

By no considered measures of judgement can *Great parent, hail* be regarded as Purcell at his best. And although J.V. Luce's claim that 'words and music alike lacked inspiration' might rouse the ire of some for their anachronistic appeal to concepts of artistic inspiration, it is singularly difficult to find evidence that effectively counters his assessment.[54] Nevertheless, it is impossible to deny *Great parent, hail*'s mastery of rhetorical and technical panoply, its thoughtful expression of Tate's poem, and its deployment of orchestral and vocal forces. Purcell, no more or less than Tate, was doing what artists have always done and always will do: producing a work designed precisely to fit a specific purpose. He was doing his job.

---

51 Charles Gildon, *The life of Thomas Betterton* (London, 1710), quoted in Michael Burden, ed. *Purcell remembered* (London, 1995), p. 107. 52 All as in Burden, *Purcell remembered*, pp 135–51. 53 As in Burden, *Purcell remembered*, p. 42. 54 Luce, *Trinity College*, p. 37.

Index